Reconstructing Psychological Subject

Bodies, Practices and Technologies

edited by

Betty M. Bayer and John Shotter

SAGE Publications

London · Thousand Oaks · New Delhi

First published 1998

SAGE Publications Ltd
6 Bonhill Street
London EC2A 4PU

SAGE Publications Inc
2455 Teller Road
Thousand Oaks, California 91320

SAGE Publications India Pvt Ltd
32, M-Block Market
Greater Kailash - I
New Delhi 110 048

British Library Cataloguing in Publication data

A catalogue record for this book is available from the British
Library

ISBN 0 8039 7613 5
ISBN 0 8039 7614 3 (pbk)

Library of Congress catalog card number 97–068908

Typeset by Type Study, Scarborough
Printed in Great Britain by The Cromwell Press Ltd, Broughton Gifford, Melksham, Wiltshire

Contents

Contributors' Notes

Betty M. Bayer is Assistant Professor of Social Psychology and teaches in women's studies at Hobart and William Smith Colleges, Geneva, New York, USA. She has published papers on feminist theory and questions of the body in psychology, and is engaged in research on the history of gender constructions in small group research and on the human–technology remakings of the scientist and scientific practices in twentieth-century psychology.

Michael Billig is Professor of Social Sciences at Loughborough University, UK. His early work was in the field of experimental social psychology, investigating intergroup relations. Subsequently, he has conducted research into the psychology of prejudice, extreme right-wing ideology and nationalism. Together with fellow members of the Discourse and Rhetoric Group at Loughborough, he has been interested in developing new ways of approaching psychology, based on the study of language and rhetoric. His recent books include *Arguing and Thinking*, *Ideology and Beliefs*, *Talking of the Royal Family*, and *Banal Nationalism*.

Ben Bradley works as Reader in Psychology at James Cook University of North Queensland, Australia, and in private practice. His interests are focused on strengthening traditions which link psychology with political action. His current research funding is for projects on depression during pregnancy, changes in infants' blood-circulation during *en face* social interaction with adults, the letters of William James, and indigenous understandings of development among Australian aborigines and islanders of the Torres Strait. His publications include *Visions of Infancy: A Critical Introduction to Child Psychology* (1989), and a Special Edition of *Theory & Psychology* called "The Future of Developmental Theory" which he edited with William Kessen (1993).

Kenneth Gergen is the Mustin Professor of Psychology at Swarthmore College, Pennsylvania, USA, where he also coordinates an interdisciplinary program in Interpretation Theory. He is a co-founder of the Taos Institute, a non-profit organization dedicated to the realization of social constructionist ideas in societal practices, and an Associate Editor of *Theory & Psychology*. Gergen is the author of *Toward Transformation in Social Knowledge*, *The Saturated Self*, and *Realities and Relationships*.

Susan E. Hawes is a faculty member and Director of Research at the Clinical Psychology Department of Antioch New England Graduate School, New Hampshire, USA. She is responsible for the doctoral level research curriculum in this "practitioner-scholar" program, and also teaches courses in the historical and social contexts of psychology, qualitative research methods, and postmodern feminist theories. She is currently exploring the following areas: woman-to-woman clinical supervision, and popular discourses on adolescent girls. A practicing clinical psychologist, she maintains a part-time clinical practice in Amherst, Massachusetts.

Ian Lubek, Professor of Psychology, University of Guelph, Ontario, Canada, and visiting researcher at the GEDISST/IRESCO/CNRS, Paris, France, follows research interests in theory, metatheory and epistemology; violence; history of social psychology; and gender and mentoring issues in the social psychology of science. He has previously written with H.J. Stam (1995), on "ludicro-experimentation", co-edited two books on theoretical issues in psychology (1995, 1996) and two special journal issues on the history of social psychology (1992, 1993), and is the author or co-author of numerous book chapters, journal articles, and after-dinner ephemera.

Kareen Ror Malone is Associate Professor of Psychology and on the Women's Studies faculty at State University of West Georgia, Georgia, USA. She has published in the areas of feminist studies, depth psychology, Lacanian psychoanalysis, and social construction. She has recently developed psychological performance pieces that address issues of representation, subjectivity, and body.

Jill Morawski is a Professor of Psychology at Wesleyan University, Connecticut, USA, whose research includes work in the psychology of gender and the history of psychology. She is author of *Practicing Feminisms, Reconstructing Psychology: Notes on a Liminal Science* (1994) and editor of *The Rise of Experimentation in American Psychology* (1988). She currently is working on a study of reproductive technologies and a history of the experimenter and experimental practices in twentieth-century psychology.

H. Lorraine Radtke is Associate Professor of Psychology at the University of Calgary, Alberta, Canada. Her current research involves the use of a discursive approach in the study of gender and social psychology. She is co-editor of *Power/Gender: Social Relations in Theory and Practice* (1994).

Edward E. Sampson is Professor of Psychology at California State University in Northridge, California, USA. In addition to teaching four undergraduate courses each semester, he has somehow found time to write a dozen books and numerous articles, including *Celebrating the Other, Justice and the Critique of Pure Psychology*, and, forthcoming, *Dealing with Differences: An Introduction to the Social Psychology of Prejudice*. During the last 25 years, most of his work has contributed to the development of a critical and transformative rather than a traditional psychology.

John Shotter is Professor of Interpersonal Relations in the Department of Communication, University of New Hampshire, USA. He is the author of *Social Accountability and Selfhood* (1984), *Cultural Politics of Everyday Life: Social Constructionism, Rhetoric, and Knowing of the Third Kind* (1993), and *Conversational Realities: Constructing of Life through Language* (1993). Currently, he is an Overseas Fellow at Churchill College, University of Cambridge, and Visiting Professor at the Swedish Institute for Work Life Research in Stockholm.

Henderikus J. Stam is Professor of Psychology at the University of Calgary, Alberta, Canada. He is the founding and current editor of *Theory & Psychology* and writes on the history of the body in psychology.

Acknowledgments

For the many ways contributors' chapters pushed the bounds of the initial conception of this volume, and for their patience and kindness of spirit throughout its evolution, our thanks. We also extend our gratitude to our editor Ziyad Marar for his encouraging support and critical insights into changing directions on psychology's disciplinary compass.

As the first editor of this volume, I thank my co-editor John Shotter for his guidance and assistance, many thought-inspiring conversations, and enlivening contributions to the introductory chapter. I am also deeply indebted to Susan Henking whose sparkling intellect and mindful suggestions invigorated both the introduction and my own chapter. My gratitude also goes to Lee Quinby for her helpful comments on the introduction, as well as for her warm and enthusiastic support. Warmest thanks also to Elena Ciletti for her generous gift of art for the book cover. For his reassurances all along the way, and for giving hope to "the good" in academic life, I thank Jeffrey Greenspon. To Jill Morawski, my appreciation for making this project conceivable. And, lastly, I want to recognize Lloyd Strickland for being a constant source of ideas and discussion on social psychology, reminding me that sometimes tangents are the most direct route, and showing me time and again how to meet critical challenges with grace and intellectual courage.

Introduction: Reenchanting Constructionist Inquiries

Betty M. Bayer

> Extricating ourselves from the debilitating pessimism accompanying the failure of modernist straight-line trajectories seems to involve some creative wandering. Not deterministically going forward or panglossianly staying behind means reenchanting, redoing, and reenlightening the fields of inquiry we have inherited from the past.
>
> (Barbara Maria Stafford, *Good Looking: Essays on the Virtue of Images*)

By many reads of popular culture, everyday discourse and intellectual debate, social construction seems to have come of age. From those experimenting with body morphing and simulated communities in virtual worlds of the internet through to our cultural fascination with resculpting not just the face but also the body such that "something other than flesh is being altered" (Siebert, 1996: 20), talk about subjectivity as fixed, immobile, determined, essential, or integral seems at odds with the very pulses of late-twentieth-century life – psychological, social, and cultural. Emerging all around us is a discourse on subjectivities, selves, and bodies that places its accent on the *hows* of transforming or remaking our selves, bodies, and relations, and so on fluidity, multiplicity, and partiality. Leaving in their wake the modern subject, such discourses, often called postmodernist, prompt "creative wandering" afield of disciplinary bounds for rethinkings on and remakings of psychological subjects and subjectivities.

Although many regard social construction as having arrived, it would be rash to suggest either that social construction is a finished disciplinary composition, or that it goes unmet by resistance or wanton rejection. There are certainly struggles and contests over meanings and meaning making amongst social constructionists, not to mention between constructionists and nonconstructionists. For alongside such discursive transformations there beats an oppositional heart of nostalgia for the social, cultural, and psychological comforts of an imagined age of innocence – in everyday life and the profession of psychology. While feminist gains are everywhere evidenced, they are encircled by anti-feminist rhetoric and political counteraction. Whereas cyberspace reconfigures time, space, mind–body relations, and embodiment, it also often works to reinstate and even intensify conventional configurations of gender, race, class, and sexuality. Running parallel to the pro-feminist men's movement there exist reentrenchments of traditional versions of masculinity, such as those found in the Iron John movement or the Promise Keepers (Quinby, 1997). Such tensions between the "lore" of yore and changing tides of cultural and psychological life are what make discussion of subjects and subjectivities so politically charged, so vital at this time of transition, for what is in the cultural air is most surely rippling through the very individual, social, cultural, and professional ground on which we live out our lives. And this is precisely why it is important for psychology to be engaged in the changing discourses and politics of our times. Quite simply, it is about who we are as psychological subjects and what we are about, our subjectivities. This book is a timely venture into changing discourses on and constructive transformations in selves and bodies webbed together – objects/subjects in relation, to each other, to technologies, and to the socio-politics of everyday life.

*Re*Viewing Constructionism

Having stated and restated how psychology's history is revealing of its place and part in the cultural–political swings of sensibilities and subjectivities, we might well ask what looms on the horizon for social construction in psychology. Just as social constructionists claim to have supplied one and another transformation in our understanding of psychology's disciplinary practices, so the question arises as to the transformation of constructionism itself, its disciplinarity and its practices. Is social construction above or beyond the very entanglements of culture, history, technology, or politics that it so astutely unravels in psychology's theories of the subject, its epistemology or disciplinarity? Is social construction sufficiently reflexive to supply a critique of its own workings and to move from these to transformation?

Querying the interchange between cultural moments and social constructionist formulations means thinking through their mutually constitutive relations rather than positioning social construction as a way to see (from above or outside) the social and cultural terms of psychological life. Such queries might look something like the following. If *fin de siècle* Vienna worries and anxieties about splits, fragmentations, and multiplicity were part of the stirrings helping to call out Freudian splits in consciousness (Showalter, 1990), then what might our own century's end-time discourse of fragmentation and multiplicity translate into for social constructionists? If the soil of industrial America, including the early twentieth century's "wave of industrial unrest," helped to ready the way for behaviorism and to shift psychology to the prediction and control of behavior (Collier et al., 1991; Samelson, 1981), then what social constructionist spaces are being opened by the closing of the mechanical age and the dawn of what many deem the age of electronics or virtual reality? If Maslow's humanist self-actualization "rested self-consciously on the type of environment that the postwar United States allegedly offered: a society of abundance" (Herman, 1995: 279), then what seeds of constructionist transformation are sown by our late-twentieth-century emphasis on flexible and adaptable bodies, psyches, workers, economy, work–home sites, and the world wide web

(Lifton, 1993; Martin, 1994)? And, if the cyberworld in disrupting mind–body dualisms and transforming the body and embodiment suggests the obsolescence of the "psychoanalytic narrative of gendered subjectivity" (i.e., where "castration anxiety is replaced by the possibility of a systems crash;" Foster, 1996: 281), then how might cyberspace discourses revamp social construction's constituting forces of subjects and subjectivity?

The point here is that in revealing the historicized "nature" of shifting and changing subjectivities of twentieth-century psychology, and in trying to restore to psychology's subject – that "anaemic and lopsided creature, an asocial and ahistoric monad" (Staeuble, 1991: 420) – cultural flesh and blood (materiality) commingled with cultural signs (discourse), social construction cannot claim any special residency outside of culture, history, movements, technology, or politics. Indeed, as a force of critical resistance to psychology's mandate of a positivist paradigm, social constructionism gained an initial foothold, however precarious, amidst 1960s American counter-cultures of second-wave feminism and the civil rights movement. As Herman writes, "For feminists, who understood keenly the danger of reducing women's social status to the psyche, the challenge was to link the dots between self and society, between the personal and the political, without making either appear to be a by-product of the other" (1995: 303). For social constructionists, the connecting links between self and society became pre-eminent too, albeit via different outlets, such as sociology of knowledge, symbolic interactionism, and Wittgensteinian philosophy. Different theoretical and philosophical approaches brought within a constructionist purview how the life of a word carries the life of culture, linguistic practices the transport of social relations, and theory the vehicle of prevailing worldviews. Inherently interdisciplinary, social constructionism displaced psychology's penchant for a generic subject with the promise of a more interesting and lively psychological subject, one who would be construed as more fully in and of the world, and given the amenabilities of discourse, one who could presumably issue in new possibilities for self and social life, personal and political emancipation.

Despite the fact that social construction has made inroads into innumerable areas of psychology, there remain stubborn core-psychology-minded types who seek beyond any *reasonable* doubt a universal subject who, like one of Darwin's butterflies, can be snatched from its habitat, pinned to a stable (monochrome) backing, and placed on eternal display. That social constructionism has never positioned itself as a core psychology has been and most likely continues to be one of its strengths. Just as social constructionists argue that we make the worlds and relations in which we live, so its argument circles back to the discipline as one of many cultural actors creating the terms of psychological life. This view contrasts itself with traditional psychology's penchant for seeing the world as "out there" waiting to be discovered, and, moreover, that psychology's prevailing positivist paradigm supplies the much sought-after decoder ring to translate into psychological terms the meanings of our everyday world. Contrary to the aims of "pinning" down subjects and subjectivities, social construction has

largely kept with its initial impetus to *participate* in meaning making and to
see meaning making as a participatory process from which emerge psychological subjects and subjectivities. As social construction's emphasis is
placed on the ways we negotiate the meanings of our lives, so its practices
have for the most part stressed language as history's and culture's agent in
fashioning psychological subjects. In furnishing this alternative approach to
think through and to contest psychology's reigning paradigm, social construction's psychological subject is always at once one that is open to the
cultural and historical terms of negotiation and one that throws asunder traditional psychology's preference for an unchanging generic subject.

From Gergen's (1973) early call to see psychology as primarily an historical endeavor, social construction brought within its scope language,
history, and social context. This linguistic or discursive turn, as it has recently
come to be called, has been multiply-influenced (e.g., feminism, poststructuralism) and encompasses an ever-expansible assortment of practices.
Feminists, having been "on to" the personal as political and having devised
ways to show how language, social practices, and institutions "naturalized"
gender, race, class, and sexual inequalities, assembled methods to reveal the
craft of sociosymbolic systems and relations of power in the making of subjects (Bordo, 1993; Canning, 1994). Their approach, while not synonymous
with Foucault's, shares much in common with his appreciation of discursive
practices as covering that gamut of "words and things," of material and non-
material practices, which are themselves shot through with productive
relations of power and knowledge. Seeing knowledge–power relations as
working "from below" and as productive of subjects and subjectivities
carries over into those ways in which disciplines are themselves constitutive
agents in the making of subjects and subjectivities. For psychology, the
implications of this discursive turn have been such that Levine was to write:
"Language, and history and social context in fact become psychology, and
psychology . . . becomes language and history" (1992: 2).

Changing Debates, Remaking Psychology

Of late, questions have arisen concerning the scope of this linguistic or discursive turn *as ushered in* by many social constructionists. The questions fan
out from here to a number of different critical dimensions. For some, concern
centers on what might be construed as an overemphasis on particular kinds
of discursive practices, mainly linguistic, conversational, and literary devices.
Questions about this truncation of discursive practices address whether the
ribbons of words weaving the social and cultural tapestry between psychological subjects and subjectivity and the particular contexts and relations of
our lives might, in some way, return us to a notion of correspondence
between psychological subjects and the "word" as the world, a mechanistic-
sounding position social constructionists set out to disavow. Furthermore, in
staying with talk and language, social construction, however inadvertently,

may have served to reinscribe dualisms, such as that of mind and body, that it purportedly aimed to undo. Indeed, we might well ask where the body is in social construction. Entering a related criticism of social constructionism's stress on our worlds being in the grip of language or interpretation, Rouse points out how often this reliance on language allows for a "semantic realism" to slip back in – "that is, that there is an already determinate fact of the matter about what our theories, conceptual schemes, or forms of life 'say' about the world" (1992: 17). For Rouse, social constructionism could usefully draw on cultural studies of science to widen its discursive compass. This transformation in social construction would allow for a "stronger reflexive sense of . . . cultural and political engagement," of the two-way traffic between science and culture, and of the tangle of material and discursive practices and "alignments and counteralignments shaping an epistemic situation" (1992: 21).

Critical queries have also been aimed at the seemingly endless circling around in Derridian-type textual "beyonds," or to what Quinby refers to as a mainstreaming of Foucauldian theory such that "the subject" is discussed "as if it embodied a single entity" (Quinby, 1994: 59). Foucauldian-influenced analyses have also been questioned for their use of notions of power–knowledge relations in such a way that the micro-level details of practices and disciplinarity are overshadowed by a more macro- or master narrative on subjects and subjectivities. Whether or not this problem arises as well from a mainstreamed rendition of Foucauldian theory, it remains the case that a master narrative is principally what social construction's attention to currents and crosscurrents of discursive practices was supposed to supplant (Burkitt, 1994). From another critical tack, Weir (1996) asks whether there is a way out of the poststructuralist or postmodernist conundrum of selves and identity only and always emerging from repression or domination. Without renouncing the importance and strength of attending to how material–social-symbolic relations of power constitute subjects and social life, Weir is interested in moving to an intersubjectivity and social relations of practice that do not rely solely on what she calls a "logic of sacrifice." Such a logic, she argues, reduces identity to "an instance of the repression or negation of 'the other' (and 'the other' can refer variously to other selves, to the unconscious, to the body, to nature, and to otherness as an abstract category)" (1996: 7). Yet another question arises from those who see a move away from discursive practices of the Foucauldian type and towards the "symbiotic relationships between flesh and technology" (Macauley and Gordo-Lopez, 1995: 434). Leveling a somewhat different critique of social constructionism, Staeuble (1991) takes up social construction's vagueness about concepts such as society or culture, positing that links with critical social theory may invigorate constructionist rethinking of a historicized subjectivity. In this move towards a historicized subject, Danziger argues further that "for psychology there is a particularly intimate connection between the historicity of the subject-matter and the history of conceptions about that subject matter. . . . between subject-matter and disciplinary practices" (1994: 479–80).

My aim in delineating these criticisms is twofold. They first highlight issues facing critical theorists, from matters of the subject, subjectivity, and the body through to those of discursive practices and the particularities of culture and history. Second, they situate the chapters of this volume within that larger stream of interdisciplinary discussion on transforming epistemology, subjectivity, and disciplinarity. Such questions and challenges thereby foreground critical issues attended to by authors as we seek to open up the critical terrain of psychological subjects and subjectivity. As part of this course of constructive transformations, various chapters bring a renewed attention to the body, to discursive practices of embodiment and disembodiment, and to body–technology coordinations. Their concern resides as much with the matter of corporeality itself as it does with the kinds of tools and techniques to rethink the intricacies of bodies as objects *and* subjects, as sites of cultural inscription and emancipation, and as entities of pleasure and pain, desire and repugnance, adoration and repudiation. As opposed to incorporating the body into social construction, for these authors the body enables transformations of social construction, and, by extension, subjects and subjectivities. With this change of course comes another concerned with the constructive spaces of intersubjectivity. Further displacing rigid boundaries drawn around "the individual," the authors move towards the dynamic flow of historicized and enculturated bodies and selves *in relation* to one another and to time, place, and circumstance.

In the realm of psychology's experimental research, such rethinkings have readjusted social construction's lens to zero-in on not only the "less thans" of experimental research (i.e., as contextless, ahistorical, asocial, and so on) but also on the "more thans." This refocusing has entailed finding another angle of entry into the laboratory as a venue of social relations and practices, investigative gambits and technologies. It builds on important work showing how changing constellations of social–political life re-patterned questions, concepts, and theories of psychological research more than data themselves (e.g., Samelson, 1978). It also entails a reworking of psychology's scientific apparatuses and instruments as more than simply neutral or passive tools used to sort, classify and categorize interests, abilities, and the like. Psychology's investigative technologies are shown instead to function as agents of social control and devices constituting subjects as particular kinds of workers, lovers, parents, children, friends, and so on (e.g., Rose, 1990). Representing a return of a different kind to the laboratory, this revisiting of laboratory practices combines sleuthing techniques from anthropology and archaeology with those of sign reading and cultural studies. These kinds of studies approach science as culture and the laboratory as a place where investigative technologies, from measuring instruments, statistics, laboratory arrangements, divisions of labor, and apparatuses through to written reports, bring all manner of objects into being, acculturate them, and then set them in motion through the hearts, minds, and bodies of subjects. Influenced in large part by cultural studies of science (e.g., Haraway, Latour, Woolgar, Pickering), instruments, scientists, and a host of other laboratory practices and technologies are regarded as agents networked in the production of all kinds of social and cultural actors. To quote Latour: "Humans for a few million of years now have extended their social relations to other actants with which, with whom, they have swapped many properties, and with which, with whom, they form a *collective*" (1994: 793). But, as Haraway (1996) qualifies "human/nonhuman mingling," because some collective worlds matter more than others, alliances and formations of object- and subject-making practices in knowledge production are also always about the politics of location.

Whether putting before social construction the call of the body, intersubjectivity, social relations, investigative practices or technology, or the bid to historicize any one of these facets, each proposed move in one or another way brings us fully around once more to matters of epistemology, subjects, and subjectivity. The contributors to this volume are thus concerned with doing more than simply evidencing the social constructionist nature of current forms of psychological knowledge, to do more than churn out yet another cluster of compelling analyses of how contemporary disciplinary practices and technologies function to produce knowledge, or to reproduce hierarchy and domination. Engaging the "what next" of social constructionism, in the sense of critical rethinking rather than sequences or stages of development, the authors bring out into the open tensions and opposing viewpoints at work in the construction of subjects, subjectivities, and subject matters. While holding onto the main tenet of social construction that subjects, subject matters, and subjectivities are things made or fashioned, the authors extend this social constructionist reach through perspectives afforded by feminism, dialogics (Bakhtin and Volosinov), logics of practice (Bourdieu and Heidegger), poststructuralism (Foucault), hermeneutics (Gadamer), Lacanian psychoanalysis, and cultural or social studies of science (Haraway, Latour, Rouse). The authors thereby shift us away from the foreclosures of psychology to reconstructive alternatives. And they do not stop here, for the authors also bring into their consideration different matters of the subject such as those of the body, human–machine coordinations, desires, intersubjective spaces, and lives lived in relation to one another. Issuing from their critical intercourse with social construction are new ways to think about subjects and subject matters, as well as an enlargement upon alternative disciplinary practices. In this spirit of remaking psychology, we find the points of convergence among chapters along the three critical dimensions of the body, situated knowledges, and social relations and practices.

Critical Dimensions for Critical Subjects

The Call upon the Body

If, as some claim, late-twentieth-century life has that feel of things being up in the air, then one might suspect that the recent fix on the body symbolizes some deep-rooted desire for a foundational base amidst the flux. Not so. Or, at least, not as the body has been entered into a critical rethinking of reason, knowledge, objects, and subjects. Nor can we so easily claim that this return to the body reflects a simple shift in critical excavation sites from one to the "other" side of a Cartesian mind–body dualist divide. For, as feminists have pointed out, there has always been a certain kind of fascination with and vigilance exercised over the body. From the Cartesian legacy of mind–body dualism, this heedfulness was tied in with a privileging of mind over body. Because the mind (consciousness) was held to be the superior route to knowledge, and because the body's needs and desires could fuel tempests of the mind, philosophical methods were devised as means to transcend the body's limiting or contaminating conditions. The knower in this epistemological scheme had to be disencumbered of the body; in short, to be dis-embodied. Furthermore, the gender associations of mind with men (and masculinity) and body with women (and femininity) served to exclude women from the realm of knowers, or producers of knowledge, and to align women with nature and, by extension, with that which was to be controlled (Alcoff, 1995). Indeed, the meanings of "woman" have for so long been tied to the "body" and its regulation, it is difficult to imagine any simple return to the body (Bayer and Malone, 1996).

The complexities of this heritage of dualisms and the ways in which they have filtered into the order and arrangement of individual and social life from macro- through to micro-levels means that the "body" has to be thought through on many levels and with some specificity (Grosz, 1995; Probyn, 1992). To quote Bordo:

> [M]ind/body dualism is no mere philosophical position to be defended or dispensed with by clever argument. Rather, it is a practical metaphysics that has been deployed and socially embedded in medicine, law, literary and artistic representations, the psychological construction of self, interpersonal relations, popular culture, and advertisements. (1993: 13–14)

Thus, resolutions to the legacy of privileging mind over body are not to be found in hasty assertions that ours is the century of the body, for the body has long captured attention and imagination. As Stafford (1991) so convincingly demonstrates in her examination of Enlightenment science, appeals to the body or the appeal of bodies were themselves caught up in enlightenment projects where the body was pivotal to dialectical tensions between inner and outer, visible and invisible, surface and depth. Probing what the body concealed, measuring, sorting, classifying, and mapping bodies and body parts, simulating the body and body functions were all efforts to turn the body inside out, to make the hidden interiors visible. Bodies, body maps and bodily functions served at one and the same time as sites of the impress of and resistance to historical forms and functions of social life. In Stafford's words, the body is a "complexly bordered zone" (1991: 16).

Whether focusing on outer adornment of the body (clothes, tattoos, painting, piercings), the nude body, or the laying bare of the body's interior, the body has been configured and reconfigured by art, science, medicine, and psychology. Encouraged by the twinned yet complementary desires to manage the seemingly unmanageable and to obtain the unobtainable body (perfectibility), constructions of, for example, automated figures, wax figurines, and medical atlases revealed and transformed the body without closing off its meaning (Jordanova, 1995; Stafford, 1991). The painter's tools, much like those of the photographer, the sculptor, the poet, or the scientist were technologies of metamorphoses of the corporeal, and of relations between material and metaphysical worlds, all of which became intertwined with the economic, cultural, and political inclinations of different historical moments. Yet such technologies were neither unidirectional in their effects nor totalizing in their practices. They did not solely write the story of various mainstays or upheavals of culture or social life into representations of the body, they brought different kinds of bodies into being. Eighteenth-century anatomical wax figures as that century's waxwork of Sleeping Beauty, whose rhythmical breathing was simulated first by a clockwork mechanism and then an electric one, no less than up-to-date computer and virtual reality technologies, change the conditions of the body and embodiment.

Shape-shiftings in the body, from a clockwork mechanism to an electric smooth-running machine and thence to an informational field of programs, copies, and virtual images, arrange and rearrange relations between body and mind, public and private (Stafford, 1991; Warner, 1995). Recent visualizing technologies such as fetal sonograms, function, says Lisa Cartwright, "as an artifact of the natural, anatomically complete body, a relic used in the management of cultural anxieties about shifting and disintegrating familial, sexual, and corporeal models" (1995: 224). What Cartwright says of the technology of fetal sonograms as "wreaking havoc with conventional developmental theories" and as hinging visual images to subjecthood, has counterparts in psychology's history of yoking the psyche or character types to facial features (e.g., Galton's pictorial statistics), bumps on the head (e.g., phrenology), body types (e.g., Sheldon's somatypes), or more recently, the fastening of women's images of their bodies to an assortment of psychological problems. Alternatively, the body has never been entirely a passive surface for inscription or reflection, as evidenced by women and members of other oppressed social groups who have used their bodies to interrupt or resist cultural scripts or representations, to image bodies and use body-imaging technologies differently.

All of this is by way of saying that given the body is a "complexly bordered zone," there are many avenues of interchange to trace in *thinking* through the body. Counter-repudiations of the body in late-twentieth-century debate thus invite exploration of how bodies "unsettle" traditional epistemic schemes, in conjunction with those problematics that bodies set in motion for psychology and for subjects and subjectivity. Recognition of this means that theorizing the body in psychology spans moves towards an historicized embodied subjectivity (see Chapter 1, by Sampson), an appreciation of bodies as an embodied social poetics (Chapter 2, by Shotter), and bodies as having desires of their own (Chapter 3, by Malone). Taking up the body also means looking at those technologies, from writing and rhetoric through to the assemblage of investigative practices (experimental procedures, statistics) that hook the inner psyche to corporeality through particular kinds of embodiments and, relatedly, disembodiments (Chapter 6, by Gergen, and Chapter 7, by Billig). Psychology's investigative technologies of rhetoric, tools, and apparatuses also configure and reconfigure body–machine coordinations, thereby constructing particular kinds of laboring bodies for science (Chapter 8, by Stam, Lubek, and Radtke) and coordinations of technoscience in the masculinization of scientific identity (Chapter 9, by Bayer). It follows that rethinking the body prompts reconstructing epistemology, and reevaluations of knowledges inspire reworkings of subjectivity. Turns to the body thus carry implications for rethinking feminism, social constructionism, cultural studies of science and the like.

Views from Somewhere

Set over against the conventional positivist doctrine of the knower and knowledge as above and beyond time and space contingencies are social constructionist and feminist ventures into the politics of location, embodied objectivity, and social epistemologies that turn on what Donna Haraway refers to as "views from somewhere," that is, "situated knowledges" (1991: 196). Advancing situated knowledges as "politics and epistemologies of location, positioning, and situating," Haraway unseats traditional assumptions of objectivity as a "view from above, from nowhere, from simplicity" (1991: 195; also see Bordo, 1990). That the knower is specified or located within knowledge production in particular ways has been central to those critiques articulating how axes of differentiation, such as gender, race, class, ethnicity, and sexuality, are structured into the relations between subjects and objects of knowledge. The countervailing forces of a view from somewhere, or from below, are about a thorough transformation in the production of knowledge. This transformation comes with the hard work entailed in revisioning the knowing subject as a critical position that foregrounds reflexive relations, situated ("noninnocent") conversations (Haraway), objectivity as particular and specific embodiments, and the body as an "engaging being." As Haraway puts it, "[w]e need the power of modern critical theories of how meanings and bodies get made, not in order to deny meaning and bodies, but in order to live in meanings and bodies that have a chance for a future" (1991: 187).

Changing our epistemological frameworks is thus as much about an oppositional politics to dominating and exclusionary knowledge practices as it is about constructive transformations in the way we live out our lives. The projects are intimately intertwined with one another, and require rethinking on many levels of the production of knowledge. In addition to grappling with those ways in which the knowing subject, or knower, is not without perspective, there are the matters of investigative practices or technologies as neither neutral nor detached from the objects of study, and of objects of knowledge as not independent of the processes of knowledge production. Knowledges need to be understood as having *internal* to them historicity, materiality, and relations of power (Foucault, 1977; Grosz, 1993). Knowledge needs also to be regarded as an activity, "a *practice* and not a contemplative reflection" (Grosz, 1993: 203). With respect to scientific knowledge, as Keller (1992) argues, science does not simply *represent* the world, its representations also *intervene* in that world – science changes the world. Far from a one-sided affair in which science leads and the world follows, science itself, its structure, content and practices, is bound up with language, culture, and the socio-politics of the world. The world then also *intervenes* in science. A kind of reciprocity or reflexivity thereby obtains, one in which science and the world enter into a set of relations of exchange as agents mutually involved in the constitution of psychological, cultural, and social life.

Furthermore, if, as Grosz argues, inquiries into the subject of knowledge have revealed a "blind spot" in knowledge production, one that can be understood as reason's inability to "know the knower," then a "discipline whose object is *man* is necessarily incomplete unless it can include its own production as a discipline within the knowledges it produces" (1993: 192–3). This reflexive and constitutive property of science has proved to be a pernicious problem for psychology where the subject and object of knowledge are inescapably similar, and where subjects of knowledge interact with both human and nonhuman subjects/objects (Keller, 1992). Thus along with the recognition of reflexive relations between subjects and objects of knowledge, and between these subjects/objects and the cross-cuttings of local and global conditions of historical and material relations, comes that of knowers and knowledges as constitutive agents who are situated and partial.

So, rethinking epistemology as historical specificities of epistemic situations proves as crucial to remaking the psychological subject as does the critical positioning of subjects of knowledge and working out the links amongst language, meanings, and bodies. Such critical linkages become evident throughout the chapters collected here despite the authors' disparate points of theoretical departure. Re-positionings of knowing subjects, whether clinical supervisors, researchers, or teachers, into the political webs of a dialogic reflexivity are as likely to bear on remaking knowledge–power relations, subjects, and subject matters (see Chapter 5, by Hawes) as is a transformative move beginning with living in the body or the body as *voice* of social codes and cultural practices (Chapter 1). Similarly, just as pedagogy and theatre of the oppressed breaks the hold of the desire for the sublime in knowers (Chapter 4, by Bradley), so bringing the subject of desire into social construction and feminism counteracts closures on subjects as either rational, cognitive beings or irrational (Chapter 3). Likewise, an embodied social poetics that foregrounds the usually taken-for-granted background work of relating and relational selves exerts its own forces against the strictures of objectivity in ways that are as transformative as those examining psychology's writing technologies to reveal the gaps and fissures of standard conventions of objectivity (Chapters 2, 6, and 7). Looking at the apparatuses of bodily productions in psychological research is equally pertinent, as these arrangements of bodies and technologies are correspondingly about objective practices and ways of life, social orders, and arrangements (Chapters 8 and 9). While dovetailing in the aims of this critical project, the authors' differing points of critical entry, their differing perspectives and problematics around changing epistemologies and subjects evidence well the multiple and multi-faceted kinds of efforts called for by critical projects to remake psychology (Chapter 10, by Morawski).

Social Relations and Practices

Throughout this discussion reference has been made to social relations and practices. Central to a focus on social relations and practices is the creation of what might be called "deconstructive moments," moments in which singular new possibilities can be sensed that might otherwise be obscured.[1] In such moments, our task is not at all to "find" or "discover" already-existing things or events, hidden behind appearances – not to grasp what such supposed things or events are, their actual nature – but something quite different. Each of the chapters seeks instead to grasp something new, as yet unseen on the surface of things, in the emerging articulation of appearances. Such emerging articulations are to be found in the interweaving of talk and writing with other actions and activities. As Foucault puts the matter:

> [Our task] consists of not – of no longer – treating discourses as groups of signs (signifying elements referring to contents or representations) but as practices that systematically form the objects of which they speak. Of course, discourses are composed of signs; but what they do is more than use these signs to designate things. It is this *more* that renders them irreducible to language (*langue*) and to speech. It is this "more" that we must reveal and describe. (1972: 49)

Discourses, texts, writing, and investigative technologies, then, bring forth subjects, subjectivities, and psychological intelligibilities. More than sense-making devices or tools of representations, discourses and technologies are constitutive agents that organize and arrange meanings of everyday and social life. Studies of disciplinary practices require attention to what these practices make visible or seeable in particular ways and to what they silence or render invisible. Similarly, a focus on practices serves to reveal moments of choice and decision, struggle and negotiation, and to open spaces for interventions towards change. Practices are thus mechanisms to be examined critically and ones to be reworked and redeployed towards change and transformation.

Having conceived of knowledge as a practice and practices as productive of critical positionings and of subjects and subjectivities, there remains the question of how to engage a "practice of practices." Importantly, the authors by their varied perspectives on and uses of practices give full play to their complexities and multiplicities. For some, "investigative practices" are "social practices" in the sense of that complex of social relations in research of investigators and participants and in that of the larger "social matrix" of norms of research communities, knowledge interests of different historical moments, and social contexts (see Danziger, 1990: 4–5). For others, practices encompass humans and nonhumans as actors and actants who are networked together through exchanges of competencies, skills, attributes, and so on. Such crossovers between humans and nonhumans are not "swapped haphazardly," nor do humans' and nonhumans' attributes and capacities simply collapse into one another. Rather, as Latour shows, that conglomerate of actor– network practices and relations needs to be studied for "what has been learned from the nonhumans and reimported back onto the social link, what has been rehearsed in the social realm and exported to the nonhumans" (1994: 806). For still others, there is "more" to the Foucauldian "mores" of inscriptions of knowledge–power relations being exercised on, through, and in the body. This "more" resides with bodily skills and practices, such that the body "knows," "remembers," or "understands," and with those ways in which the body and bodily practices (ways of standing, walking, sitting, gesturing, or the attitude of the body) produce and reproduce cultural specificities of subjects of differing races, classes, or genders. Whether construed through Pierre Bourdieu's logic of practice, Ludwig Wittgenstein's language games, Bruno Latour's actor–actant network theory, Jacques Lacan's subjects of desire or *jouissance*, Donna Haraway's cyborgs and technologies of bodily production, or Judith Butler's performative practices, the authors address the conjunction of bodily practices and embodied subjects. As Katherine Hayles puts the case of exchanges between apparatuses of bodily production and embodiment:

> [E]mbodiment is contextual, enwebbed within the specifics of places, time, physiology and culture that together comprise enactment. Embodiment never coincides exactly with "the body," however that normalized concept is understood.... [E]mbodiment is the specific instantiation generated from the noise of difference, ... at once excessive and deficient in its infinite variations, particularities, and abnormalities. (1992: 154–5)

Furthermore, these bodily and embodying practices are situated in relational space and time. For it is in the spaces between bodies, humans and machines, and so on that we open up relational interlinkings, critical positionings and interchanges of skills, abilities, and the like. So, situated knowledges are social relations of practices where the traditional view of knowing subjects, be they theorists, researchers, analysts, teachers, or clinicians, is transformed into critical positionings. Science, politics, and culture are thus repositioned within these webs of knowledge as practice. Using these three critical dimensions as the meeting place of the chapters in this volume brings them together in their emphasis on the importance and necessity for doing psychology differently, for remaking the psychological subject. Diverse in their desiderata of constructive transformations, varied in their approaches and areas of consideration, the chapters are critical nodes networked through situated knowledges for social change.

Overview of Chapters

In Chapter 1, Edward Sampson thinks *through* the body to push the boundaries of social construction as we have known it. He begins his thinking through the body with a reflexive meditation on the disorientation he experienced when visiting Yad Vashem, the Holocaust memorial in Jerusalem. Using this critically reflexive subject-position, Sampson's call upon the body is one for social construction to press "beyond verbocentrism," "beyond representation," and "beyond the immediate." Sampson's "three beyonds" shift social construction from a politics of disembodiment to a politics of embodiment, from a distanced or spectator view of the world to one in which we are situated within the production of knowledge as we are in the world, in a "deeply bodily practical way." Sampson's chapter thus opens up a number of dimensions of embodied subjectivity, from the temporal and spatial through to the unspoken, the felt, the experienced, the spoken, and the movements, gestures, and practices of cultural and social life.

With Sampson's chapter serving to usher the body into social construction, other chapters expand on the matter of bodies and embodiments to challenge traditional psychology's view of the body as housing biological instincts, emotions, thought and the like. Supplanting such body-as-container views with one of the body as agent and matter, as in relation with other bodies, coordinated with machines, and as that which registers protest, desire, and misrepresentations, the complexities of bringing the body into rethinking subjectivity begin to emerge. In Chapter 2, John Shotter reexamines Oliver Sacks's well-known account of Dr P in the book *The Man Who Mistook his Wife for a Hat* to advance a social poetics of embodied relational practices. For Shotter, Dr P's bodily relation to routine life reveals bodily movements as rhythms of bodily practices of knowing and remembering. In these ways, Dr P's "music" of the body orchestrates his ability to orient himself to those around him, to the routines of everyday life, and to past memories. Neither strictly cognitive nor conversational, the relational practices bridging the gaps of intelligibilities between Sacks and Dr P thus confront the limitations of traditional "official" clinical assessment as much as they foreground the practices of an embodied social poetics.

Positioning feminism and psychoanalysis as central allies to social construction, and using the sex war debate as her illustrative case, Kareen Ror Malone (Chapter 3) places the body front and center of any analysis of subjectivity. By tracing the route of embodied subjectivity through the analytic trajectory of feminism and psychoanalysis, Malone dislodges the hold of the (rational) cognitive subject delivered by some social constructionist work. Through her critical analytic border crossings, Malone inquires into bodies that not only matter, but that also move to a beat of their own – *jouissance*. The body is not wholly the nodal point through which text and context, word and being, social construction and subjectivity write their stories or produce their effects. Rather, the body asserts its own signifying wager in subjecthood and subjectivity.

While, for each one of these authors, the body is deeply intertwined with cultural–historical significations, power and desires, their different theoretical approaches do not deliver the body as either a single or fixed entity. There is not one body, but bodies; there is not one all-encompassing view of the body, but many. Bodily relations and embodiment are themselves never completed through sociosymbolic systems for there is always something "more" to the body. There is thus another productive sense to the body's unruliness, one that revels in the disruptive or unsettling effects of the body for rethinking knowledges, subjects, and subjectivities. As both a site of cultural inscriptions and an agent or scribe of cultural transactions, the body – or bodies – pushes us to rethink relations between the inside and outside, between surface and depth, between power and desire.

To examine these relations, Grosz (1994) employs the model of the Mobius Strip ("the inverted three-dimensional figure eight") which allows us to imagine a drift of mind into body and body into mind as well as the "torsion" of the corporeal exterior with the psychic interior. This model also helps to revision surface–depth relations, not by reinscribing boundaries between them but by inquiring into how surface inscriptions become depth and conversely (deep) interiors surface inscriptions. In addition, this model usefully construes relations between theories of the body, especially in their movements from the inside out or the outside in. Insofar as Sampson emphasizes how subjects and subjectivities become embodied through the "noncognitive, prediscursive world of human activity, performance and practice," the embodiment he envisions might be likened to the twists and enfoldings of the body and the world such that the body also "enwords" culture, politics, and history. Shotter's dialogics of bodily relations brings into view those previously unacknowledged or ignored functions of the body in memory and in bearings on relational realities. And, inverting movements between life from the inside out and the outside in is Malone's feminist psychoanalytic view where "unconscious thought comes first to the body" and where "desiring libidinal bodies" project their bodily form into the psyche and intersubjective spaces.

Extending this line of reworking subject positions and subjectivity are the next two chapters. Ben Bradley, in Chapter 4, trains his critical eye on the dominant hold in developmental psychology of what philosophers call the "genetic fallacy," anchoring present life in past individual histories, in what has transpired rather than what might come to be. Commensurate with this epistemological framework is the subject position of the sublime, or the cult of the expert. But, as Bradley makes clear, this legacy of Darwinian thought has resulted in few developmental psychology assurances other than the virtual effacing of subjects from the currents of time, space, culture, and politics. To counter this predilection for the past and for a sublime subject-position, Bradley draws on radical pedagogy to reenvision a critical subject-position as a "view from below," one situated in the relational dynamics and temporal pulses of cultural and social political life.

Pursuing further this question of critical subject-positions, Susan Hawes, in Chapter 5, proposes a "dialogics" of reflexivity in feminist clinical supervision. Bringing the authority of the supervisor into a critically reflexive subject-position is one facet of this process. Added to it are the particularities of any supervisory relationship, the institutional context, the social implications of therapeutic and psychological practice, and the ways all of this extends to clients. Power then becomes an explicitly attended-to "object" of dialogic analysis. Only by entering into a dialogic reflexivity, first with the private thoughts of participants, and, second in dialogic practices between participants, are ways found to empower previously marginalized discourses, and to bring critical points of resistance to bear on hierarchical systems.

Further elaboration of knowledge production as complex sites of social relations, practices, culture, history, and politics follow in subsequent chapters. Kenneth Gergen (Chapter 6) presses on to those discursive practices of texts that function to create forms of psychological intelligibilities while constraining other ones. Uses of literary devices, such as metonyms, metaphors, and rhetoric, create psychological intelligibilities, thereby helping scientists to bring into being novel ontologies, to fashion anew persons and social-cultural life. Through these investigative technologies, culture is injected with a host of conceptions of the mind, emotions, reason, intention, and so on, and countless categories of psychological problems, inadequacies, or pathologies. Gergen thus calls for critical reflection on psychology's emphasis of certain kinds of subjectivity to the exclusion of others.

Whereas Gergen attends to literary mechanisms producing certain albeit limited versions of psychological subjects, Michael Billig (Chapter 7) looks at psychology's writing technologies, its rhetorical practices, for how they produce a psychology "stripped of . . . ordinary individuality." By this he means the ordinary individuality Foucault referred to as "the everyday individuality of everybody." It is Billig's position that psychology's writing technologies, while producing the objects they claim to discover, nevertheless "depopulate" psychology by turning persons with history, culture, and all manner of interpersonal relations into unnamed, unknown, and standardized characters of "E," the experimenter, and "S," the subjects. Issuing an invitation to repopulate social psychology's texts with speaking subjects, Billig advances ways to remake psychology's literary and investigative practices such that selves of investigators and those whose lives are studied become integral to theorizing and to connecting the dots between social-cultural history and the everyday of everybody.

Pursuing Billig's line of the rhetorical practices transposing embodied subjects into "disembodied fictions," Henderikus Stam, Ian Lubek, and Lorraine Radtke (Chapter 8) revisit Milgram's obedience studies where the coordination of bodies and machines yield a particular kind of "disembodied," docile subject. Such docile technobodies eventuate from psychology's experimental machinery's flattening the body into "one object among many." So flattened, the body is made more amenable to scientific management as a laboring body in the laboratory industry, a data-producing body. And, as part of this Taylorized version of body-machine productions, the bodily struggle between obedience and resistance to authority is given over to a reproduction of domination, eclipsing attention to victims, harm, violences committed against subordinated subjects, and to resistance, social change, and practices of freedom.

While Stam et al. focus on Milgram's shock machine, the history of psychology's laboratories stands as a vast warehouse of instruments, apparatuses, and machines. Indeed, scientific psychology, much like American culture, has had an enduring romance with machines and changing technologies. Seeing this romance as a coupling of machinic and spectral desires, Betty Bayer (Chapter 9) explores the cross talk of bodies and machines in psychology's relatively unexamined history of apparatuses and apparitions (technologies of deception) through the symbolic vehicle of phantoms of the laboratory. From their otherworldly place, phantoms lead into study of psychology's historical struggle with the meanings of life and death, the dreams of techno-salvation and the fears of techno-destruction, and the hopes of attaining divine truth and the fear of meaninglessness. Whether phantoms as the ghostly double of scientists, as apparitional practices (phantasmagoria), or as phantomizations inspiriting apparatuses with phantasmic powers of objectivity, "phantom" helps to make visible anxieties around the coordinations of technoscience with technoman, and the uncertainty of human bodies in a technologically oriented future.

Just as each one of the authors herein offers a constructive transformation in conceiving of the psychological subject and subjectivity as partial, multiple, in flux, and more fluid or protean-like than traditional psychology would have it, so the final chapter by Jill Morawski is in keeping with this broader effort. Forging lines of alliance between realist and relativist positions, Morawski proposes that we broaden research practices to encompass collaborative ventures where everyone participates, to incorporate routinely reflexivity "as acts of self-consciousness," and to include both the disharmony and harmony of relations. Through these means, Morawski outlines a reconstruction of subjects and subjectivity as dynamic, multiple positioned beings who are themselves engaged in making and remaking social, psychological, and moral life.

Raising the curtain on changing social constructionist practices, the authors reveal how acts of remaking the psychological subject are in play with reformulating the practices of psychology. Without foreclosing on the matter of psychological subjects or the modes and manner of psychological study, this volume illuminates relational spaces of bodies, practices, and technologies as complex sites of subjectivities-in-the-making that are always located somewhere. In pursuing these inquiries into disciplinary practices, subjects, and subjectivities, the chapters are intertwined with cultural impulses marking the coming end of the twentieth century. Often wrought through the discourse of "endism" – of authors, history, science, and even telephones – this century's ending is said to have some cyclical reverberations with the nine-teenth century's *fin de siècle* anxieties around identity, subjectivity, and the body. Then, as now, questions of limits and boundaries moved into the fore-ground as upheavals around gender, feminism, sexuality, and the family carried within them the contradictory signs of chaos and loss, possibilities and emancipation (Showalter, 1990). And, then, as now, social-cultural anxieties reinvigorated attention to the subject and subjectivity, the body and embodi-ment, humans and machines. Any temptation to run the conceptual wilds between our own century's end and that of *fin de siècle* Vienna, however, risks slipping into tarantella-like spins of presentism, of seeing life pass before us as a blur of what has already transpired, and thus of missing in all of these goings-on "the embryonic stirrings of a new order" (Showalter, 1990: 18).

Compelling as the semblance of similarities between these two end-time sensibilities may be, they serve more as telling reminders about how selves, bodies, and subjects are located in time, place, and circumstance, inflected by broader and more specific cultural histories, social struggles, and the poli-tics of subjects and subjectivities. Focused on recent disciplinary stirrings, inside psychology and elsewhere, this book navigates between the shoals of the old and the new in rethinking subjects and subjectivities along the criti-cal dimensions of the body, epistemic situations, social relations and prac-tices, as we acknowledge that our constructions of cultural life are our practices of freedom. As such, the authors intervene into the preference of psychology's scientific conventions for "[l]ife in its hard shell safe from the waters above and the waters below" (Winterson, 1994: 31). This volume, then, ends on a note of beginnings, of constructive transformations such that psychological subjects and subjectivities located outside of the dynamic flow of history, culture, and politics will indeed be unimaginable.

Note

1 My thanks to John Shotter for his input on this discussion of practices, especially for his idea of "putting a new, extra practice (not a theory) into an already existing practice" – a "prac-tice of practices."

References

Alcoff, L. (1995) "Feminist theory and the problem of experience," The Ann Palmeri Lecture, Hobart and William Smith Colleges, Geneva, NY.
Bayer, B.M. and Malone, K.R. (1996) "Feminism, psychology, and matters of the body," *Theory & Psychology*, 6: 667–92.
Bordo, S. (1990) "Feminism, postmodernism, and gender – scepticism," in L.J. Nicholson (ed.), *Feminism/Postmodernism*. New York: Routledge. pp. 133–56.
Bordo, S. (1993) *Unbearable Weight: Feminism, Western Culture, and the Body*. Berkeley, CA: University of California Press.
Burkitt, I. (1994) "The shifting concept of self," *History of the Human Sciences*, 7: 7–28.
Canning, K. (1994) "Feminist history after the linguistic turn: historicizing discourse and experience," *Signs*, 19: 368–404.

Cartwright, L. (1995) "Gender artifacts: technologies of bodily display in medical culture," in L. Cooke and P. Wollen (eds), *Visual Display: Culture Beyond Appearances*. Seattle, WA: Bay Press. pp. 218–35.

Collier, G., Minton, H. and Reynolds, G. (1991) *Currents of Thought in American Social Psychology*. New York: Oxford University Press.

Danziger, K. (1990) *Constructing the Subject: Historical Origins of Psychological Research*. Cambridge: Cambridge University Press.

Danziger, K. (1994) "Does the history of psychology have a future?," *Theory & Psychology*, 4: 467–84.

Foster, T. (1996) "'The sex appeal of the inorganic': posthuman narratives and the construction of desire," in R. Newman (ed.), *Centuries' Ends, Narrative Means*. Stanford, CA: Stanford University Press. pp. 276–301.

Foucault, M. (1972) *The Archaeology of Knowledge*. New York: Pantheon Books.

Foucault, M. (1977) *Discipline and Punish: The Birth of the Prison*. New York: Vintage Books.

Gergen, K. (1973) "Social psychology as history," *Journal of Personality and Social Psychology*, 26: 309–20.

Grosz, E. (1993) "Bodies and knowledges: feminism and the crisis of reason," in L. Alcoff and E. Potter (eds), *Feminist Epistemologies*. New York: Routledge. pp. 187–215.

Grosz, E. (1994) *Volatile Bodies: Toward a Corporeal Feminism*. Bloomington, IN: Indiana University Press.

Grosz, E. (1995) *Space, Time and Perversion: Essays on the Politics of Bodies*. New York: Routledge.

Haraway, D.J. (1991) "Situated knowledges: the science question in feminism and the privilege of partial perspective," in D.J. Haraway, *Simians, Cyborgs, and Women: The Reinvention of Nature*. New York: Routledge. pp. 183–202.

Haraway, D.J. (1996) "Modest witness: feminist diffractions in science studies," in P. Galison and D.J. Stump (eds), *The Disunity of Science: Boundaries, Contexts, and Power*. Stanford, CA: Stanford University Press. pp. 428–41.

Hayles, K. (1992) "The materiality of informatics," *Configurations*, 1: 147–70.

Herman, E. (1995) *The Romance of American Psychology: Political Culture in the Age of Experts*. Berkeley, CA: University of California Press.

Jordanova, L. (1995) "Medicine and genres of display," in L. Cooke and P. Wollen (eds), *Visual Display: Culture Beyond Appearances*. Seattle, WA: Bay Press. pp. 202–17.

Keller, E.F. (1992) *Secrets of Life, Secrets of Death*. New York: Routledge.

Latour, B. (1994) "Pragmatogonies: a mythical account of how humans and nonhumans swap properties," *American Behavioral Scientist*, 37: 791–808.

Levine, G. (1992) "Introduction: constructivism and the reemergent self," in G. Levine (ed.), *Constructions of the Self*. New Brunswick, NJ: Rutgers University Press. pp. 1–13.

Lifton, R.J. (1993) *The Protean Self: Human Resilience in an Age of Fragmentation*. New York: Basic Books.

Macauley, W.R. and Gordo-Lopez, A. (1995) "From cognitive psychologies to mythologies: Advancing cyborg textualities for a narrative of resistance," in C.H. Gray (ed.), *The Cyborg Handbook*. New York: Routledge. pp. 433–44.

Martin, E. (1994) *Flexible Bodies: Tracking Immunity in American Culture from the Days of Polio to the Age of AIDS*. Boston: Beacon Press.

Probyn, E. (1992) "Theorizing through the body," in L.F. Rakow (ed.), *Women Making Meaning: New Feminist Directions in Communication*. New York: Routledge. pp. 83–99.

Quinby, L. (1994) *Anti-apocalypse: Exercises in Genealogical Criticism*. Minneapolis, MN: University of Minnesota Press.

Quinby, L. (1997) "Apocalyptic masculinity," in C. Strozier and M. Flynn (eds), *The Year 2000*. New York: New York University Press. pp. 154–65.

Rose, N. (1990) *Governing the Soul: The Shaping of the Private Self*. London: Routledge.

Rouse, J. (1992) "What are cultural studies of scientific knowledge?," *Configurations*, 1: 1–22.

Samelson, F. (1978) "From 'race psychology' to 'studies in prejudice:' Some observations on the thematic reversal in social psychology," *Journal of the History of the Behavioral Sciences*, 14: 265–78.

Samelson, F. (1981) "Struggle for scientific authority: The reception of Watson's behaviorism, 1913–1920," *Journal of the History of the Behavioral Sciences*, 17: 399–425.

Showalter, E. (1990) *Sexual Anarchy: Gender and Culture at the Fin de Siècle*. New York: Penguin.

Siebert, C. (1996) "The cuts that go deeper," *The New York Times Magazine*, 7 July: 20–6.

Staeuble, I. (1991) "'Psychological man' and human subjectivity in historical perspective," *History of the Human Sciences*, 4: 417–32.

Stafford, B.M. (1991) *Body Criticism: Imaging the Unseen in Enlightenment Art and Medicine*. Cambridge, MA: MIT Press.

Stafford, B.M. (1996) *Good Looking: Essays on the Virtue of Images*. Cambridge, MA: MIT Press.

Warner, M. (1995) "Waxworks and wonderlands," in L. Cooke and P. Wollen (eds), *Visual Display: Culture Beyond Appearances*. Seattle, WA: Bay Press. pp. 178–201.

Weir, A. (1996) *Sacrificial Logics: Feminist Theory and the Critique of Identity*. New York: Routledge.

Winterson, J. (1994) *Art and Lies*. London: Jonathan Cape.

1

Life as an Embodied Art: The Second Stage – Beyond Constructionism

Edward E. Sampson

A few years ago, my wife and I visited Yad Vashem, the memorial to the Holocaust in Jerusalem. After some aimless wandering, we decided to look at the children's memorial commemorating the 1.5 million Jewish children who had perished. Most of the museum is underground with an almost tunnel-like entry at the end of a sloping paved ramp. As we walked slowly down the ramp we listened to the sounds of moaning voices while viewing the faces of little children that had been carved into the entry wall.

We pushed open the door and found ourselves suddenly enclosed in nearly total darkness. Candlelight, kaleidoscopically reflecting from the wall of mirrors, provided the only illumination. Clinging to the railing thankfully provided along one wall, we moved tentatively forward. The voices grew louder. We could now clearly hear what they were saying as they rhythmically recited the names of children who had been killed in the camps: "Yoshe, aged 12 from Poland; Miriam, age 7 from. . . ."

Although our eyes soon accommodated to the darkness, we could not see anything clearly. The mirrored walls, reflecting the candles' light, made the entire experience thoroughly disorienting.

All I could think of was getting out of there and returning to a more familiar surround. I resented the entire experience and worked hard to keep both my anger and emerging panic at bay. We finally made it through the museum, pushed open the exit door, and found ourselves flooded with the bright sunlight of the June day. It was then I began to complain, railing loudly against the designers who had created such a poor display: "Much too confusing to really see anything clearly: too dark; too disorienting."

Months later, in describing this experience to a friend, and still complaining, I finally understood. The friend said: "But your confusion, your disorientation, your panic and eagerness to escape and return to a more familiar place – that was the whole point!" And, the friend was correct.

The Lesson

The eye that saw in Yad Vashem on that June day reveals the depths to which the spectator's approach to the world had become my approach to my world. My training in social psychology and my years as a university professor had directed me to approach life in the manner of a visitor to a museum who was there to observe the exhibits and to assume that only things that I could see, and see clearly at that, were important. My eyes, it seems, had automatically and rather skillfully directed my gaze, leading me to deny that my confusion, disorientation, and panic were a valid part of my experience. I treated these as annoying interferences that ruined what might have otherwise been an illuminating encounter.

I have not presented this little story, however, in order to reveal just how much a fool I was, but rather to illustrate a point. Traditionally, most of us have been taught to approach understanding in the same way as I had approached Yad Vashem: as a spectacle to be viewed from some safe place far removed from the action; to approach life as though it could be grasped in its entirety from a distant place of vision and contemplation. Dewey (see Handy and Harwood, 1973) has described this as the spectators' theory of knowledge: only spectators can see things objectively and as they really are without being affected by what they see; only spectators, with their distancing and dualistic approach (i.e., a subject confronting a separate object) have privileged access to real knowledge. To be disoriented and confused because I could not see clearly, and to be at the edge of panic because I could not escape quickly – aspects of my fully embodied contact with this exhibit – were experienced as disruptive to valid knowledge, not as elements intrinsic to that very knowledge.

I had been a victim of the very things I had opposed. Previously, I had written in a praiseworthy manner about the feminist critique of the male gaze (e.g., Sampson, 1993a) and of what Catherine MacKinnon (1989) had called a point-of-viewlessness that was anything but that. As MacKinnon noted, the claim of being without a standpoint reflects a definite position that has historically been associated with the masculinist project of knowing in order to master and control. How apt a description of me at Yad Vashem.

Of course, in my constructionist best, I knew all of this. And yet, at the moment of truth in Yad Vashem, these lessons had been cast aside as I returned to my automated ways of being in the world: as a distant subject gazing out upon a world of separate objects and objecting loudly when that controlling gaze was compromised by the exhibit's "poor" construction. Advocates of the constructionist approach, emphasizing the role of discourse and rhetoric in the construction of reality, have taken strong exception to the spectator's approach to knowledge (e.g., Gergen, 1994; Shotter, 1993a, 1993b). Constructionism has taken great pains to reveal the various rhetorical devices that spectators use to construct a world that has the appearance of being independent of those very rhetorical devices, or as Edwards (1991) states it, how we use talk to construct the impression of a talk-independent world.

Although both feminism and constructionism and me as part of both movements agree in challenging the spectators approach, the events in Yad Vashem had forced me to contend with the degree to which I had reverted to my old habits. I could not spend the rest of my life, however, punishing myself for those well-honed habits. It seemed that my task was to go beyond that informative experience. Increasingly, I also came to believe that I would have to move even beyond constructionism, since it had failed to inoculate me from the spectator's affliction. And so, my purpose in this chapter is to examine the failure of constructionism so that I and we can move beyond it.

Verbocentrism

One of the prime markers of nearly every current constructionist account is the importance attached to language and discourse. The reference, however, is not to language as a neutral system of signs that expresses something that exists independently of language, but language as a system by which reality is actively and collectively constructed. Strong versions of this argument insist that everything we know is discursively constituted, that conversations are the fundamental human reality (e.g., Harré, 1992; Shotter, 1992) in and through which our everyday world is constructed, sustained, or transformed.

This is a very powerful insight that has been employed, effectively, to challenge the seeming naturalness of all the categories by which our everyday world is known and taken for granted. For example, the naturalness of dividing the world into males and females is seen to be an outcome of cultural choices based on systems of domination that are carried in and through these socially constructed dualistic categories. A similar analysis has been rendered for the seemingly natural categories of race and ethnic group membership. In each case, the insight that the constructionist account provides argues against treating as natural what are not only socially constructed categories, but categories usually erected to serve the interests of power.

My purpose does not involve dismissing this important insight. I do not wish to undermine constructionism, therefore, but rather to move beyond it so that we avoid the kinds of problem I encountered at Yad Vashem. It is my contention that the constructionist model is so verbocentric that it fails to address the embodied nature of discourse itself. In this way, constructionism encourages us to sustain the kind of spectator-like connection to the world that led me astray. To be more specific, constructionism's current failure and thus my motivation to move beyond it, is its failure to recognize that talk is inherently embodied.

Embodied Discourse

I find it useful to distinguish between talk that is *about* something and talk that is accomplished *with* something. The distinction is important.

Constructionism emphasizes how it is that talk about the world is in fact not about something that exists independently of that very talk but rather is constituted in and through that talk. Thus, for example, talk about the dualistic division of the world into men and women is not about two objects whose existence is independent of the very dualistic distinctions that the talk generates.

So far so good. But, so far, in this case, is not good enough. What is missing in this account is any awareness that *talk about* is simultaneously *talk with*. That is, constructionism's emphasis on the about-aspect of talk entirely misses the point that the one who talks about objects is also talking with a particularly important object, namely the human body. To phrase this somewhat differently, when I talk about the body, I must use that very body in this talk. In other words, talk, conversation and discourse are embodied activities, not merely disembodied linguistic recitations.

As long as we engage in talk about things in our world, we confront that world, ourselves included, only as a kind of ocularcentric (e.g., Jay, 1993; Levin, 1985, 1993) object of our inquiry and not as an aspect of the very process by which any inquiry must take place. Discourse is not disembodied; we cannot stand outside the body when we engage in discourse, for we are always within the body in and through which we are able to talk. To do otherwise is like trying to talk about breathing without breathing while we talk.

My problem at Yad Vashem, therefore, was in remaining trapped in the *about-aspect* while failing to experience the *with-aspect*. I approached the entire situation as a disembodied spectator and so missed the point. What I missed, of course, was the fact that I was a fully embodied being, and that this embodied feature cannot be avoided, as mightily as we may try, in great measure because even those mighty efforts to avoid the embodied quality of our discourse are in-themselves embodied.

By introducing the idea of embodied discourse, I am doing unto constructionism's basic thesis about the world what it has done to those objectivist (i.e., nonconstructionist or conventional) accounts that it challenges. Even as constructionism argues that there is no way to encounter the world free from the hold of that world – we are inherently situated beings – I am arguing that there is no way to talk about the world that is disembodied: we are inherently embodied beings as well.

Constructionism takes its opponents to task for their failure to address the discursively constructed character of the human experience. And I am taking constructionism to task for its failure to address the inherently embodied nature of discourse itself.

Examples of Embodied Discourse

It might be helpful at this point to provide a few illustrations of what I mean when I refer to discourses as being embodied. Even as we stand with another to converse together, the distance we choose to stand and the postures we employ are embodied aspects of the conversation in which we engage. The intimate conversation is differently embodied than the formal conversation. Angry words are conducted "in your face." Not only have we been socialized to use particular words but also to employ our bodies in particular ways. Even the most mundane of our actions, including how our mouths, lips, lungs, vocal cords, and breath patterns are all socialized to form the words we speak, tell us clearly of the embodiment of discourse.

Historical examples are also instructive. We read, for example, about a second-century treatise on physiognomy (e.g., see Gleason, 1990) outlining how a proper male and female body should be socialized to conform to the desired adult manner of bodily comportment. Bourdieu's more current work adds to this early picture as he comments on how male–female differences are based on "a durable way of standing, speaking, walking, and thereby of feeling and thinking . . . in posture, in the gestures and movements of the body" (1980: 70). And, anyone who had read Engels's (1987) work on the impacts of social class on the person's carriage and demeanor or is familiar with the detailed advice on essential bodily preparations given to Buddhists preparing for meditation (e.g., Levi, 1989), is aware of the wide sweep of embodiment in human affairs.

Bourdieu and Habitus

Of all current theorists, it is primarily Pierre Bourdieu (1977, 1980; also Bourdieu and Wacquant, 1992) who offers us some of the most relevant examples of embodied discourse in explicating his central concept, *habitus*: "a set of historical relations 'deposited' within individual bodies in the form of mental and corporeal schemata of perception, appreciation and action" (Bourdieu and Wacquant, 1992: 16). Habitus calls our attention to the embodied nature of discourse. As Bourdieu notes, habitus is very much a bodily matter; it is a kind of kinetic or somatic knowledge or a feel for the game that both reflects a person's specific position in a social field while simultaneously generating the very set of relations and practices that gave it birth in the first place.

The concept of habitus appears to have originated in the writings of Mauss (1950), for whom bodily techniques, socialized early into each individual within a culture, played an important role in that person's cultural stock of knowledge. Bourdieu has adapted these embodied practices and given them centrality in his writings. As is true of my idea of embodied discourse, habitus likewise is not outside culture; it is as deeply embedded in cultural practices as is language itself. However, unlike our usual understanding of many cultural concepts, habitus refers to that aspect of our cultural learning that is deeply carved within our bodies, so deeply in fact, that it generates a kind of "feel for the game" that describes a practical rather than a purely theoretical kind of knowledge.

Two key points are being made: (1) Habitus/embodied-discourse does not describe a transcendent entity outside either culture or history. Our bodies are rather fully socialized. And so, when I refer to embodied discourse, I am referring to learnings and knowledges placed into our bodies by virtue of where and when we dwell. (2) Habitus/embodied-discourse, however, differs from abstract or theoretical knowledge about our world. Embodied knowledge is usually deeply engrained within each of us, affecting how we stand, move, talk, and understand as a skilled performer rather than as an outside observer. For this reason, Bourdieu (and I concur) insists that our practical, habitus and embodied, knowledge follows a logic that is

> reasonable without being the product of a reasoned design, still less of rational calculation; informed by a kind of objective finality without being consciously organized in relation to an explicitly constituted end; intelligible and coherent without springing from an intention of coherence and a deliberate decision; adjusted to the future without being the product of a project or a plan. (Bourdieu, 1980: 50–1)

Bourdieu's point and mine is not to separate the world into one more dualism: in this case, the discursive and the prediscursive. Rather, we are encouraged to recognize how the discursive contains aspects beyond mere words: it is fully embodied. Embodied-discourse/habitus challenge the dualisms that have animated and continue to animate much of the Western world's system of inquiry, encompassing both the dominant traditions and the constructionist challenger. The idea of embodied discourse or habitus introduces us to the ways in which we are always socialized into a jointly functioning language and embodied community. We are thereby not only in the world through language or through the body, but because language is in-itself embodied even as the body is in-itself enworded; we are in the world in both ways, deeply intertwined.

Constructionism's Disembodied Ocularcentrism

At this point it should be apparent that my effort to move beyond constructionism involves a move beyond the disembodied *talking about* by recognizing that there is no way to talk about the world that is not also a necessarily embodied *talking with*. My problem at Yad Vashem, I believe, was rooted in a deeply engraved cultural predilection to follow what some have termed the ocularcentric bias of the Western world (e.g., Jay, 1993; Levin, 1985, 1993), which Bourdieu (e.g., Bourdieu and Wacquant, 1992) has described as the intellectualist bias or the scholarly gaze.

Jay (1993) and Levin (1985, 1993) have provided a rather thorough and highly instructive analysis of the privileging of vision and visual metaphors within the language and practices of the West since at least the Greek era. Along with Synott (1993), they argue that some of the most notable philosophers whose works serve as the foundation of the Western paradigm, Plato and Aristotle for example, extol the nobility of vision, while that keynoter of modernism, Descartes, has employed a visual metaphor as central to his entire project. Jay describes Descartes as "a quintessentially visual philosopher" (1993: 69) who, while sharing Plato's distrust of the senses, including sight, nevertheless has built his entire edifice upon the mind's eye whose clear and distinct vision would establish at long last a secure basis for all human knowledge and for truth itself.

This ocularcentric approach is nowhere more evident than in our scientific conceptions. Not only do we demand observations of phenomena in order to understand their workings, but we also insist that these observations be carried out as a spectator, a third-person observer, who must remain at a distance from what is being observed.

The scholarly gaze or intellectualist bias of which Bourdieu has spoken fits in perfectly with this ocularcentric scenario. In listing the various types of bias that beset the typical social science investigator, Bourdieu comments on the by now familiar listing, including, for example, the bias that derives from our class or social position. The scholarly gaze or intellectualist bias, however, runs far deeper and is much more difficult to eliminate as it involves

> the invisible determinations inherent in the intellectual posture itself, in the scholarly gaze that he or she casts upon the social world. As soon as we observe . . . the social world, we introduce in our perception of it a bias due to the fact that, to study it, to describe it, to talk about it, we must retire from it more or less completely. This . . . bias consists in forgetting to inscribe into the theory we build of the social world the fact that it is the product of a theoretical gaze, a "contemplative eye." (Bourdieu and Wacquant, 1992: 69)

It is my contention that constructionism has not avoided the snares of ocularcentrism and intellectualism and that only by moving beyond constructionism towards embodied discourse can we hope to repair the damage.

Butler's Ocularcentrism

Judith Butler (1990, 1993) offers an excellent example of the ocularcentric problem with a disembodied constructionism, made even more apt given that her entire focus is on the social construction of the sexed body. Butler argues that the dominant discourses, which she terms *objectivist*, assume a world of neutral objects and natural meanings on which culture writes its particular message – in the case of interest to her, the message of sex and gender. In this objectivist account, with which Butler disagrees, sex differences are assumed to be real in that each culture and epoch writes its particular message on a pregiven natural division of the world into a male and a female body and so establishes its own accent on an object that exists independently in the world: that is, culture writes on a pregiven noncultural object.

The constructionist position that Butler adopts argues that there is no independently real body, hence no sexed male or female outside culture. Thus, culture cannot write on an already existing object that is sexed, but rather creates the sexed objects which then appear to be naturally occurring objects in the world. Butler tells us that "the body is not sexed in any significant sense prior to its determination within a discourse through which it becomes invested with an 'idea' of natural or essential sex" (Butler, 1990: 92).

According to Butler and others who have adopted a similar argument (e.g., Connell, 1987; Kitzinger, 1987; Lacqueur, 1990; Riley, 1988; Synott, 1993), power differentials are built into the founding cultural definitions of male and female. Because of this, in order to transform the current power hierarchy, those very definitions must be challenged. She argues that if a *precultural* body existed, it would serve as an invitation to house those power differentials that are by now so familiar to us: for example, that men are by nature dominant, etc. And so, by challenging the naturalness of bodies, Butler, along with these others, hopes to challenge those theories of difference that are grounded in nature rather than in culture.

On its face, there would seem to be no more extreme separation than that which distinguishes the objectivist from the constructionist accounts. Yet, I believe that both positions, as different as they appear to be and in many respects are, are nevertheless married to the ocularcentric bias that lives so deeply in the Western tradition that even those who challenge that tradition seem unable to disengage from its hold.

Both objectivism and constructionism share an interest in the external world in which we live. They differ primarily in their understanding of how that world has come into being. For the objectivist account, the world pre-exists individuals, culture, and history, and the task of mind is to recover the main features of that world by means of clear mental representations. For constructionism, by contrast, the world does not preexist culture and history, but rather is constituted on the basis of socially generated discourses. Whereas objectivism is concerned with the fit between representation and reality, constructionism is concerned with how what is taken to be real is socially constructed and appears to be independent of the very human endeavors that made it possible. In this, both lead us away from the sense of embodied discourse that I believe is central.

Once again, Butler proves helpful to my case. She, of course, questions the objectivist view in which any social construction "happens to a ready-made object, a pregiven thing" (1993: 11). Her argument here hinges on the notion that in order to refer to any extra-discursive object there must inevitably be a prior and hence discursive delimitation of what is to be taken as an object in the first place. And, therefore, she maintains, insofar "as the extra discursive is delimited, it is formed by the very discourse from which it seeks to free itself" (Butler, 1993: 11). In other words, says Butler, there must be an initial discursive act that sets forth the boundaries of whatever will become an object in the first place. In order to have an object on which a culture can write, there must first be a discursive (i.e., cultural and historical) act that discriminates what is to be taken as an object. This inevitably provides a constructionist basis for all theories that would otherwise adopt the objectivist stance and deal with a world of so-called natural objects.

Although Butler's arguments are persuasive as far as they have gone, what they exclude is the very embodied nature of discourse itself that I suggest is requisite to our understanding of construction. I believe that her critique of objectivism is impressive in noting how discourse constitutes the initial act by which objects are delineated in the first place and thereby undermining the objectivist claims. Yet, her emphasis is on a kind of disembodied discourse about the body rather than recognizing that those discourses are themselves not pure in the sense of being carried by disembodied words but that embodiment pervades all human endeavor, all human practices, including all discursive practices. While it is indeed reasonable to join with Butler and others in insisting that words construct the body, it is also reasonable to insist that those words are themselves embodied. In short, discourses that construct the body are not simply *about* the body; they are also discourses carried on *with* the body.

Conclusion

I would like to end as I began, at Yad Vashem. I have puzzled over why this one experience has been so troubling to me. Why did I care so much that I had missed the point? I suspected that it was far more significant than simple embarrassment. My foolish error would not even have been publicly known had I not revealed it. I believe that what was really at stake at Yad Vashem, and indeed in this move towards embodiment, cuts deeply into the very values that I hold. In brief, the issue is political and not merely embarrassment or a minor intellectual oversight. And so I would like to conclude by spending a little time exploring the political dimension as I currently understand it.

The Politics of Disembodiment

It is now obvious to me that the disembodied framework that had driven me to error at Yad Vashem and that I have claimed lies at the core of both the dominant Western tradition of inquiry and its constructionist challenger involves the political domination that disembodiment accomplishes. Constructionism has made a compelling case on behalf of the politics of objectivism, while failing to deal adequately with the politics that resides not only in objectivist accounts but in disembodied accounts as well, constructionism included.

I was annoyed with myself because by employing a way of knowing that I had spent so much of my professional life opposing, I had unwittingly engaged in a political act at Yad Vashem. To have been captured by the ocularcentric spectators' disembodied approach was not simply an intellectual error in judgment, but to have employed the very device by which the powerful dominate others. And for me, a Jew, to have done this at Yad Vashem, the memorial depicting the hideous results of such domination, was severely disturbing. Yet, it was somehow also quite appropriate to be awakened in this manner and in this place.

The Annoying Particularity   The body has had a rather long and somewhat distressful history within the Western tradition. Although it has not invariably been denied, for the most part, the body has been seen as a disturbing element, more often to be denigrated than cherished. Many reasons have been put forward to explain this Western treatment of the body, including for example, its apparent impermanence: bodies decay and cease to exist and so seem to make a shaky foundation for stability and certitude. I am impressed, however, with the arguments developed by the Hebrew scholar Daniel Boyarin (1994), as I believe they give us an even better focus on the politics of disembodiment.

In his analysis of Paul's letter to the Galatians, Boyarin suggests that the body represented the very particularities that Paul sought to transcend in his efforts to shape a universal religion – that is, a religion that would encompass everyone. According to Boyarin, the key to Paul's political effort to wrest control from the rabbinic Jews in favor of what would eventually emerge as Christianity, was his universalistic appeal contained in that letter: "There is neither Jew nor Greek, there is neither slave nor free, there is no male and female, for ye are all one in Christ Jesus." In other words, the sweet-sounding erasure of the signs of embodiment's particularities was requisite to establish something spiritual and hence universal that could bind all together. This called for erasing the differences that both rabbinic Jews and females represented, in both cases carried in great measure (though not entirely) by the unique configurations of their bodies.

Rabbinic Judaism sought to maintain its particularities of both body (e.g., male circumcision) and religious practice (e.g., eating requirements) and so was to be cast aside because of its refusal to abandon these particularities and accept the encompassing One Paul sought for all. In turn, women were acceptable, but only insofar as they left their bodies behind and became celibate, spiritualized beings. To put it bluntly, as Boyarin does, the enshrinement of spirit and the requisite undoing of embodiment were political acts done to garner control and domination of a newly emerging sect of worshipers. And as we now know, Paul's success had repercussions with which we are still dealing.

Philosophers who both preceded and followed Paul, similarly challenged the body's annoying particularities in their pursuit of something universal. The ocularcentric bias and spectator theories of knowledge to which I have previously referred still carry this message. And so, when I missed the point at Yad Vashem I was not in error but simply conducting myself as a member in good standing of a rather long and well-honored tradition in the Western culture in which I dwelt. But as I had to reflect on my actions, it struck me that in fitting into this tradition at this very special place, I was advocating a position that not only contradicted those values expressed in many of my writings (e.g., Sampson, 1977, 1993a, 1993b), but those values represented in the memorial itself. After all, it had been their refusal to erase their differences that had brought my people to this place. I could not countenance myself applauding a view that brought this about.

The Politics of Embodiment

To call for an embodied discourse, then, is not simply a call for yet one more intellectualist stance; it is rather a call for a movement and a political commitment directed towards challenging a history in which the denial of embodied differences has been employed more often to destroy than to nurture humanity. In recognizing that our words are embodied even as our bodies are enworded and that in light of this we cannot stand outside our world but must be invested participants within, I am adopting a political position in support of sustaining collectively established, identity-serving human differences rather than seeking their meltdown on behalf of some universalistic appeal for oneness that in itself must of necessity be built upon a preliminary duality and hierarchy (i.e., of mind or spirit over body).

Yad Vashem, a memorial to a time that many believe must never be erased from our memories lest in forgetting we repeat its tragedy. Yad Vashem, a place where I encountered another potential tragedy in the making. For me the two are linked forever. The Holocaust is a time in which Paul's letter came to fruition; a time in which, in order to establish a purified oneness, millions were exterminated. There is a politics to our works. I am pleased to have again encountered mine, even if it required a foolishness I thought I had long ago eliminated.

Note

This chapter is a blending of two papers delivered at two separate conferences at two separate points in time. Parts were presented at the Social Constructionism Conference held in June 1993 at The University of New Hampshire; other parts are based on a presentation at a conference held at The University of Huddersfield in England, in July 1995.

References

Bourdieu, P. (1977) *Outline of a Theory of Practice*. Cambridge: Cambridge University Press.

Bourdieu, P. (1980) *The Logic of Practice*. Stanford, CA: Stanford University Press.

Bourdieu, P. and Wacquant, L.J.D. (1992) *An Introduction to Reflexive Sociology*. Chicago: University of Chicago Press.

Boyarin, D. (1994) *A Radical Jew: Paul and the Politics of Identity*. Berkeley, CA: University of California Press.

Butler, J. (1990) *Gender Trouble: Feminism and the Subversion of Identity*. New York: Routledge.

Butler, J. (1993) *Bodies that Matter: On the Discursive Limits of "Sex."* New York: Routledge.

Connell, R.W. (1987) *Gender and Power: Society, the Person and Sexual Politics*. Stanford, CA: Stanford University Press.

Edwards, D. (1991) "Categories are for talking: on the cognitive and discursive bases of categorization," *Theory & Psychology*, 1: 515–42.

Engels, F. (1987) *The Condition of the Working Class in England.* London: Penguin. (Original work published 1845.)

Gergen, K.J. (1994) *Realities and Relationships: Soundings in Social Construction.* Cambridge, MA: Harvard University Press.

Gleason, M.W. (1990) "The semiotics of gender: physiognomy and self-fashioning in the second century C.E.," in D.M. Halperin, J.J. Winkler and F.I. Zeitlin, (eds), *Before Sexuality: The Construction of Erotic Experience in the Ancient Greek World.* Princeton, NJ: Princeton University Press. pp. 389–415.

Handy, R. and Harwood, E.C. (eds) (1973) *Useful Procedures of Inquiry.* Great Barrington, MA: Behavioral Research Council.

Harré, R. (1992) "What is real in psychology: a plea for persons," *Theory & Psychology,* 2: 153–8.

Jay, M. (1993) *Downcast Eyes: The Denigration of Vision in Twentieth Century French Thought.* Berkeley, CA: University of California Press.

Kitzinger, C. (1987) *The Social Construction of Lesbianism.* London: Sage.

Lacqueur, T. (1990) *Making Sex: Body and Gender from the Greeks to Freud.* Cambridge, MA: Harvard University Press.

Levi, J. (1989) "The body: the Daoists' coat of arms," in M. Feher, R. Naddaff and N. Tazi (eds), *Fragments for a History of the Human Body.* New York: Zone Books. pp. 105–26.

Levin, D.M. (1985) *The Body's Recollection of Being: Phenomenological Psychology and the Deconstruction of Nihilism.* London: Routledge and Kegan Paul.

Levin, D.M. (ed.) (1993) *Modernity and the Hegemony of Vision.* Berkeley, CA: University of California Press.

MacKinnon, C.A. (1989) *Toward a Feminist Theory of the State.* Cambridge, MA: Harvard University Press.

Mauss, M. (1950) "The notion of body techniques," in *Sociology and Psychology: Essays.* London: Routledge and Kegan Paul. pp. 97–119.

Riley, D. (1988) *"Am I that Name?" Feminism and the Category of "Women" in History.* Minneapolis, MN: University of Minnesota Press.

Sampson, E.E. (1977) "Psychology and the American ideal," *Journal of Personality and Social Psychology,* 35: 767–82.

Sampson, E.E. (1993a) *Celebrating the Other: a Dialogic Account of Human Nature.* Boulder, CO: Westview.

Sampson, E.E. (1993b) "Identity politics: challenges to psychology's understanding," *American Psychologist,* 48: 1219–30.

Shotter, J. (1992) "Social constructionism and realism: adequacy or accuracy?" *Theory & Psychology,* 2: 175–82.

Shotter, J. (1993a) *Conversational Realities: Constructing Life Through Language.* London: Sage.

Shotter, J. (1993b) *Cultural Politics of Everyday Life: Social Constructionism, Rhetoric and Knowing of the Third Kind.* Toronto: University of Toronto Press.

Synott, A. (1993) *The Body Social: Symbolism, Self and Society.* London: Routledge.

2

Social Construction as Social Poetics: Oliver Sacks and the Case of Dr P

John Shotter

> ... philosophy ought only to be written as a *poetic composition*. (Wittgenstein, 1980b: 24)

> ... experience exists even for the person undergoing it only in the material of signs. (Volosinov, 1986: 28)

> Any organic activity or process: breathing, blood circulation, movements of the body, articulation, inner speech, mimetic motions, reaction to external stimuli (e.g., light stimuli) and so forth. In short, anything and everything within the organism can become the material of experience, since everything can acquire semiotic significance, can become expressive. (Volosinov, 1986: 28–9)

> Actually I should like to say that ... the *words* you utter or what you think as you utter them are not what matters, so much as the difference they make at various points in your life. .... *Practice* gives words their significance. (Wittgenstein, 1980b: 85)

Unlike computers and other machines, as living, embodied beings, we cannot be indifferent to the world around us. Without having "to work it out," we continuously react and respond to it spontaneously, in a direct and immediate way, whether we like it or not. And, in so doing, in one way or another, we necessarily connect and relate ourselves to our surroundings. Certain sounds, smells, movements, physical shapes, etc., occurring around us, "move" us; they "call out" from us vague, but not wholly undifferentiated responses; we find "movements" of this or that kind, originating from the others or an otherness outside of ourselves at work within us. Sometimes, we react with surprise or bewilderment to such events; occasionally, we fail to react at all. As a result, we are always in one or another kind of living, bodily relation to our circumstances, and such relations constitute the source of all our later, more deliberate activities. Indeed, we can follow Wittgenstein when he says that: "The origin and the primitive form of the language game is a reaction; only from this can more complicated forms develop. Language – I want to say – is refinement, 'in the beginning was the deed' " (1980b: 31).[1] In other words, what we do later, individually, deliberately, and cognitively, originates in what we do earlier, responsively, unthinkingly, and bodily. Yet somehow, in all our current disciplinary practices in the human and behavioral sciences, the way in which our immediate, bodily reactions *necessarily relate* us to our surroundings, has remained *rationally invisible* to us.

As professionals, we have (mostly) ignored our embodied embeddedness in this routine flow of spontaneous, living, responsive activity.[2] Not only have we let it remain unnoticed in the background to everything that we do but we have also ignored its importance *as* a sustaining and resourceful setting that is always present in our attempts to make sense of and in our lives. Especially, we have failed to notice the occurrence within it of those special but in fact everyday events, those departures from the routine, which enable us to gain access, not only to the "inner worlds" of certain kinds of social groups – the "worlds" of mathematics, music, medicine, and literature, etc. – but also to the unique "inner worlds" of the other individuals around us, including, sometimes, the bizarre worlds of those living in strange relations to their circumstances, utterly unfamiliar to the rest of us.

What I want to explore below, then, is the part played by those special spontaneous embodied reactions we "invite" or "call out" from each other, in our gaining access to each other's "inner lives" or "inner worlds." And further, unlike our other studies in the social sciences, I want to suggest that it is only in terms of what is unrepeatable, novel, playful, and poetic – the unique, first-person expressions in which people express themselves – that such responsive activity can be understood. Indeed, aspects of this previously ignored, everyday background flow of activity can be brought to our attention, and characterized – from within the activity itself – by the use of some special "poetic" methods (to be outlined below) whose importance has yet to be "officially" recognized as a proper part of our professional practices.[3] They are exemplified, for instance, in Oliver Sacks's (1985) own account of Dr P – the man who mistook his wife for a hat – and, later, I shall outline their nature by reference to that case. Here, I shall just add that I call these methods "poetic," as they are to do with novelty, with processes of creation (Gr. *poiesis* = creation), with "first time" makings and with "first time" understandings – with, as Bakhtin (1993: 1) calls them, only "once-occurrent" events. Through such events, Sacks not only gains access to the all-but-unimaginable world of Dr P, but gives us an access to it also.

How is this possible? If, as professionals, we are to understand what it is that makes it possible for people to make their own, unique, unrepeatable "inner worlds" known to each other (and to us), we do not straightaway need, I suggest, another new *theory*. Something else altogether is needed. We must first ask ourselves why the crucial, responsive, embodied phenomena have remained so long unnoticed and unacknowledged, and what is involved in our all coming to attend to them in the same way. For without a shared ability to "see" the phenomena in question, directly and unproblematically, we cannot discuss them between ourselves or formulate agreed ways of studying them. Thus, initially at least, the kind of transformation involved is not to do with new ideas, with anything cognitive in us as individuals, with seeing something differently, but with seeing something we have not seen before, for the first time. It is to do with our whole way of relating ourselves to our surroundings, our relational way of being in the world. To "get" a grasp of the kinds of connections and relations between things required in a social constructionist approach, we need to embody a *new relational practice*, to change what we notice and are sensitive to (as well as what we care about, and feel are the appropriate goals at which to aim). In other words, we need to change ourselves, our *sensibilities*, the "background" practices we have embodied that make us the kind of professionals we are. It is to a study of their nature that I first turn.

The Invisibility of Our Embodied Being and Social Embedding in Our Disciplinary Practices

It is now a social constructionist commonplace to accept the socially constructed, relational character of people's subjectivities, their selves, their identities, their "structures of consciousness" . . . at least, in theory it is. In practice, however, particularly if we take our training in one or another academic discipline seriously, its meaning for us as disciplinary (or disciplined) professionals is less clear. What is it that we have been trained to do in practice that we must now, so to speak, "undo"? To grasp what is involved here, we can turn to Foucault, for very briefly, as he reminds us, it is not that a discipline " 'makes' individuals . . ." (1979: 170), rather it "produces subjected and practised bodies, 'docile' bodies" (1979: 138), i.e., bodies which function in certain ways unthinkingly. And in particular, the modern academic disciplines – in which the central technique of disciplinary power is administered through the *examination* and the *review* (see Foucault, 1979: 187–92) – "make" the quintessential modern, professional academic. To pass our exams, etc., we must come to *embody* unthinkingly all the background techniques, shared sensitivities and discriminations, all the desires and aversions, shared exemplars, and so on, as well as "the will to truth" (Foucault, 1972), that are all a part of what Kuhn (1970: 181–7) calls a discipline's "disciplinary matrix." Instead of matrix, I shall call it a discipline's "evaluative stance" or "evaluative sensibility."

A crucial part of this stance is, as Foucault (1973, 1979: 187–92) calls it, a discipline's "gaze:" that is, a way of intently looking at its subject matter that is interwoven into its methods and procedures for gaining knowledge. In proving ourselves worthy of inclusion in the discipline of psychology as a science, we had to learn to see "objectively," to see its "subjects" as "objects," as entities "caused" or "forced" to behave solely in accord with the limited influences allowed visibility in their circumstances. And in this way of "gazing" at both others and ourselves, it is precisely our *embodied agency* and the special nature of our *social embedding* that have been rendered rationally invisible to us. Indeed, as Foucault points out, while a discipline imposes upon those it studies a "principle of compulsory visibility," modern disciplinary power itself "is exercised through its invisibility . . ." (1979: 187).

In other words, to be "licensed" to operate in such a discipline as modern psychology, one must come to embody within oneself a tendency to ignore, not only one's own embodied academic and social skills, but also one's own professional circumstances – the economic institutions and power arrangements in which one lives, as well as the procedure-entwined-sensibilities making the exercise of one's disciplines possible. Indeed, one is sanctioned if one fails to do so! But if it is the case that disciplines have their origins in the disorderly, the playful, the passionate, feelingful, powerful, and the poetic, in short, in the unique and unrepeatable – as I shall claim below that they do – then it is these unrepeatable *background* events that are excluded. They are in fact rendered invisible by "rules of *exclusion*" (Foucault, 1972: 216) that are *internal* to discourse itself, "rules concerned with principles of classification, ordering and distribution" (Foucault, 1972: 220).[4] These are the usually unnoticed, background phenomena to which I want especially to draw our attention. Thus, in what follows below, while wanting to draw attention to the special discursive and dialogical nature of our socially embedded, embodied agency, I want also to draw attention to how, *due to our embodiment*, those around us – in their unique, novel, and unrepeatable, first-person activities – can "call out" responses from us, spontaneously. And to suggest that it is in the functioning of the poetic and playful, the singular and disorderly, in the only-once-occurrent event, that we can originate utterly new forms of life between us.

In so doing, I want to explore what strange new and unique changes are involved in our coming, not simply to *talk*, but to *live*, as social constructionists. For, as I see it, it is entirely possible to talk academically and knowledgeably "about" a whole set of social constructionist concepts, in theory, while still embodying in our academic practices, the mainstream, essentially individualistic, separatist, Cartesian subjectivity or sensibility into which we have been trained, unchanged. For us, it still both represents how we are, and, how things are, for us! As a result, it is only too easy for us to talk and to think of ourselves as still seeking understandings in terms of inner, mental representations – in terms, that is, of theories – when new practices, new talk-entwined ways of relating ourselves bodily to each other and our surroundings, should be our goal.

For instance, we often still catch ourselves thinking that when we talk of such "things" as people's "selves" or "identities," their "language," "thought," "speech," or "discourse," of "perspectives," or "frameworks," of "power," "knowledge," "discourse," etc., we are all talking in the knowledge of what such "things" are. Indeed, in seeking "theories" to explain their workings, we act as if such "objects" are already in existence "out there" in some complete, finalized form, and that the way to change the world is by (often evidence-based) arguments between us in seminar rooms or conference halls "about" their proper description or interpretation . . . hence the vehemence of our talk in such places, for more than just our theories is at stake. But this way of proceeding – by our "picturing" our circumstances to ourselves, because the real things of interest to us are in some way "hidden" from us, and require discovery by research – "stands in the way of us seeing the use of [our talk] as it is" (Wittgenstein, 1953, no. 305). Beguiled by the tendency of our disciplinary discourses to "form the objects of which they speak" (Foucault, 1972: 49), we find it difficult to find our own, spontaneous, academic talk problematic. The self-induced invisibility of our own disciplinary procedures prevents us from noticing that our embodied sense of them, as being applied to certain "objects," has been "developed" not by such "objects" imposing themselves on us but by our creating a "sense of their objective reality" within our own disciplinary discourses. Hence, we talk "about" *those* others we study as being, somehow, distinct and quite separate from ourselves, utterly unrelated in fact.

Monological and Dialogical Stances

In Bakhtin's terms, this professional stance toward the others around us is a one-sided, or one-way, *monological* stance: that is, it is a stance in which we are, simply, bodily unresponsive to the activities of the others around us. While we may "observe" their "movements," we ignore any (evaluative) "responses" that they, as other living, embodied beings, spontaneously "call out" from us (or we from them): e.g., pity at their suffering, or joy at their successes. As Bakhtin puts it:

> With a monologic approach (in its extreme or pure form) *another person* remains wholly and merely an *object* of consciousness, and not another consciousness. No response is expected from it and could change anything in the world of my consciousness. Monologue is finalized and deaf to the other's response, does not expect it and does not acknowledge in it any *decisive* force. Monologue manages without the other. . . . (1984: 292–3)

In other words, from within this (traditionally "scientific") stance, we are uninterested in interacting with the people themselves, and unconcerned with their concrete circumstances; we are only interested in collecting what they say "about" themselves, their self-talk, as "data." We can then say that, for us, it is indicative of the nature of their inner states, or inner mental representations.

We could call this a *retrospective-objective* stance toward those we study, for we are concerned not with responding to what people are actually doing or saying now, but with looking back on what they did or said as a now completed process. And, instead of seeing their self-talk as playing a part in their living out their lives, we see it as separated from its surrounding context, and as conveying this or that kind of information about certain supposed objects or events hidden within their heads somewhere. Indeed, here, we would be testing our own "explanatory theories" as to the meaning of their utterances, and writing "about" our findings from within what we can call a *disciplinary-representational* genre. Where our "cool," intellect-only form of response to them is all of a part with the Cartesian sensibility into which, as modern, professional academics, we have been trained.[5]

If, however, we are to live as social constructionists, then, instead of a dialogically unresponsive, Cartesian, monological stance, we must acknowledge and become sensitive to a whole new range of not-before-noticed dialogical and relational phenomena in our speech-intertwined relations with others. Indeed, we must go on to develop both with our colleagues, and with our "studied ones" alike, new shared forms of life, new practices, along with all the new kinds of wants, urges, impulses, and desires that such new practices might entail. And in particular, among the new practices that we must develop, I shall argue, is a whole new way of intertwining certain non- or pre-disciplinary,[6] "poetic" forms of talk in with our ways of interacting with those we study. For it is only talk of this kind that will allow us to get a grasp of their unique "world," their unique "inner life," as the individuals they are (in relation to us), in a way that does justice to the "scenarios" it creates (cf. Volosinov, 1976: 109).

In responding to people's self-talk in this way, we could be said to be taking a *prospective-relational* stance toward it, seeing it as providing, not information, but different possible relational openings or opportunities of a "poetic" kind. In it, we would be writing and talking "with" them, rather than "about" them. It would constitute a *nondisciplinary-dialogical* genre, i.e., a genre from which their ordinary ways of uniquely expressing themselves – in saying "I feel this," "I think that," as well as their expressions of, say, joy and anger, and so on – are not excluded. It is this *relational* focus on people's immediate, embodied, first-person, responsive reactions to each other's words that is central to the "social poetics" approach that I want to outline here (also, see Katz and Shotter, 1996). For, it is in the way that people's responsive utterances connect, link, or relate them with their (not always immediate) surroundings, that they "point" or "gesture" beyond themselves, toward their "world." For people "show" what their "world" is for them, in their fleeting reactions to, and understandings of, what is occurring around them, in practice. And, in being irresistibly "moved" or "arrested" by their reactions, in finding ourselves spontaneously responding to their responses, we are dialogically provided with an initial, crucial grasp of their unique world.

The trouble with a one-way, bodily unresponsive, monological stance is that, from within it, we are denied (or we deny ourselves) access to these two-way, dialogical and relational phenomena. Dialogically, due to our embodiment, besides sensing a responsive reaction in our surroundings related to all that we do, we also find our surroundings "calling out" involuntary, spontaneous, responsive reactions from us. We look at another, they smile or frown back at us, and we "go on" with them one way or another as a result; if another cries out in pain, we cannot but respond to them in some way or another – our bodies are affected. Our embedding in this kind of involuntary, two-way responsive, social activity is of outstanding importance to us. For, through our continuous, unselfcontrolled, responsive reactions within such a flow of activity, we not only uniquely *relate* ourselves both to each other and to our circumstances, but, in continuing to responsively react, we also recreate such relations, continuously.[7]

Elsewhere (Shotter, 1980, 1984, 1993a, 1993b, 1995), I have called such continuously creative activity, "joint action," for both other people's actions and the surrounding circumstances are just as much a formative influence in what one does, as anything within oneself. In our actions, we find ourselves just as much "called" to act "into" our surrounding circumstances (already partially shaped by the previous talk-intertwined activities of others) as "out of" any of our own inner plans, or scripts, or such like – hence, the intrinsic appropriateness or relatedness of such responsive action always to its unique circumstances.

People's unavoidable, responsive, bodily embedding in their surroundings, and the way in which they "show" the nature of "their world" in their reactions, plus the way also in which we cannot be unresponsive to them, is important to us here, interested as we are in practices that might enable people to reveal the nature of their own unique inner lives to each other. For, to the extent that our responsive reactions are related to our circumstances, to how we find ourselves situated, we reveal the "shape" of our own unique "inner world," as well as our relations to it, in our spontaneous, moment by moment, practical reactions to what, bodily, we take our circumstances to be. And we do this in a whole number of ways. For instance: we reveal the practical meaning of another's frown to us, "in" our responsive reluctance to continue our relations with them; we reveal the practical meaning of a person's questions to us "in" our responsive attempts to give them adequate answers; we test our partial understanding of a person's explanation in our responsive offerings to them of possible applications or elaborations of it; we show our disturbance in not being able to make sense of another's actions "in" our being nonplussed by them, "in" our not being able "to follow" them and so on. "The fact is," says Bakhtin,

> when the listener perceives and understands the meaning (the language meaning) of speech, he [*sic*] simultaneously takes an active, responsive attitude toward it. He either agrees or disagrees with it (completely or partially), augments it, applies it, prepares for its execution, and so on. . . . Any understanding is imbued with response and necessarily elicits it in one form or another: the listener becomes the speaker. . . . Sooner or later what is heard and actively understood will find its response in the subsequent speech or behavior of the listener. (1986: 68–9)

Thus, what some "inner thing" is for us – a "difficulty" raised by a colleague's remark, say, in response to a possible "solution" proposed by us to a "problem" – is revealed, not in how we talk *about* "it" afterwards, in reflection, when no longer involved in any practical way with our colleagues, but in how we talk "of" it in the moment: "it" will necessarily "shape" the unique, moment-by-moment, responsive unfolding of our current interactions with each other. But, given our training in disattending from such phenomena, if we are to appreciate the practical meaning of these abstractions, we need a living example. Here I shall turn to Oliver Sacks's case of Dr P.

Dialogic, Responsive Relations and Their Elaboration in Sacks's Account of Dr P

The general nature of Oliver Sacks's (1985) account of Dr P – the man who mistook his wife for a hat – is well known. However, with our interest here, in the character of responsive-relational practices, attention to its details will present us with some remarkable phenomena. Indeed, I will argue, in the next section, that it can provide us with a model for a whole new practice that, as I have already mentioned, can be called a "social poetics," a practice in which our responsive understandings play a central part. For instance, straightaway, we can note that when Sacks met Dr P, he found that there "*was* something a bit odd" (1985: 8) in Dr P's way of visually relating to him: "there was," he says, "a teasing strangeness, some failure in the normal interplay of gaze and expression." Later, Sacks came to think that "he faced me with his *ears* . . . but not with his eyes" – a hypothesis born out by other evidence, as we shall see. Indeed, as Sacks notes, "instead of looking, gazing, at me, 'taking me in', in the normal way, [he] made sudden strange fixations – on my nose, on my right ear, down to my chin, up to my right eye – as if noting (even studying) these individual features, but not seeing my whole face, its changing expressions, 'me', as a whole" (1985: 8).

Indeed, as a potential sufferer of glaucoma, I have myself had a similar feeling of being depersonalized when I have had to go to have my eyes looked *at* by an opthalmologist. For on such occasions, in looking *at* my eyes, the ophthalmologist is not looking responsively at "me," but merely for possible symptoms visible in the properties of my retinas; and it is from his lack of responsiveness to me, to my changing facial expression, to my eye movements, and so on, that my feelings of depersonalization arise. So, although it is often difficult at first to say what the strangeness of an other's responsiveness to one's own being "is" (if, that is, it is strange at all), there is no doubt that one can sense its existence: Indeed, we always seem to know if there is a lack of correspondence between the outgoing way in which we respond to our circumstances, and how we expect it to be responsively returned back to us. Such discrepancies are always apparent to us, even when only very subtle nuances are involved: I make a suggestion, my friend pauses (hesitates) for less than a second, but noticeably, before agreeing to it, and I know, in that pause, that she is probably reluctant in some way, to some extent, to go along with what I propose. I question her. She says she agrees, but isn't she perhaps pretending? So I search for the meaning of her pause in what she "shows" me in her other responses to me as we go on. As Wittgenstein remarks: "It is certainly possible to be convinced by evidence that someone is in such-and-such a state of mind, that for instance, he is not [or is] pretending. But the 'evidence' here includes 'imponderable' evidence. . . . [Where] imponderable evidence includes subtleties of glance, of gesture, of tone" (1953: 228), i.e., subtleties that are nonetheless consequential. And one can become convinced of the correctness of one's initial judgment, not by being able to match the pattern of what one sees with a remembered schema in an instant, but by the degree to which one can "go on" with the person, practically, on its basis. And this was Sacks's task with Dr P: to "go on" with him to a sufficient degree, as to be able to build up a grasp of what Dr P's strange "inner world" was like, from a whole set of Dr P's responses in relation both to Sacks's probes and to other events.

In continuing his assessment of Dr P, Sacks asked him to describe some of the pictures of whole scenes in a copy of *National Geographic Magazine*. Dr P's responses were again very curious, says Sacks:

> His eyes would dart from one thing to another, picking up tiny features, individual features, as they [his eyes] had done with my face. A striking brightness, a color, a shape would arrest his attention and elicit comment – but in no case did he get the scene-as-a-whole. He failed to see the whole, seeing only details, which he spotted like blips on a radar screen. He never entered into relation with the picture as a whole – never faced, so to speak, *its* physiognomy. He had no sense whatever of a landscape or scene. (1985: 9)

Later, on a visit to his home, Sacks presents Dr P with some of his own family photographs: by and large, he recognized nobody, neither his family, his colleagues, nor his pupils. He recognized a portrait of Einstein, by picking up the characteristic hair and moustache; his brother Paul, from his square jaw and big teeth; and one or two others from their special features. But, "he approached these faces – even those near and dear – as if they were abstract puzzles or tests. He did not relate to them, he did not behold. No face was familiar to him, seen as a 'thou', being just identified as a set of features, an 'it'" (1985: 12). Indeed, Dr P had no problems with such abstract features at all. Presented by Sacks with a glove, and asked "What is this?", he described it thus: "A continuous surface . . . infolded in on itself. It appears to have . . . five outpouchings, if this is the word" (1985: 13). He could match it to an abstract schema, but he did not know how to "go on" with it: he saw no relation between it and a hand. Only later, when by accident he got it on, did he exclaim "My God, it's a glove!" Previous to that point, even when prompted by being asked if it might fit or contain a part of his own body, he was quite unable to identify it.

On the basis of this and other evidence, Sacks concluded that:

> Visually, [Dr P] was lost in a world of lifeless abstractions. . . . [He] functioned precisely as a machine functions. It wasn't that he displayed the same striking indifference to the visual world as a computer but – even more strikingly – he construed the world as a computer construes it, by means of key features and schematic relationships. The scheme might be identified – in an "identi-kit" kind of way – without the reality being grasped at all. (1985: 13–14)

Visually, Dr P was relationally "unmoved" by the things around him; they did not "call out" any responses in him linking him to his surroundings in some way. Dr P's deficit seemed to be due to right brain damage. His abstract and categorical, left brain functions seemed to be intact – a remarkable conclusion, given that "one of the most entrenched axioms or assumptions of classical neurology . . . [is] that brain damage, *any* brain damage, reduces or removes 'the abstract or categorical attitude' (in Kurt Gold-stein's term)," says Sacks (1985: 5).

Dr P's way of relating himself to his surroundings was revealed, not so much in one of Sacks's "official" tests, as in when the tests were over, and Mrs P set a meal of coffee and a spread of little cakes. Then, what was revealed was that: "Hungrily, hummingly, Dr P. started on the cakes. Swiftly, fluently, unthinkingly, melodiously, he pulled the plates towards him, and took this and that, in a great gurgling stream, an edible song of food" (1985: 15). In other words, Dr P related his activities to each other within a musical rhythm. Then, a peremptory knock at the door interrupted the flow, and Dr P seemed suddenly lost, bewildered, no longer as if at a table laden with cakes. However, his wife poured him some coffee and, in responding to the smell (earlier, he had shown he could recognize a rose by its smell), *he became related to his circumstances again;*[8] the melody of eating resumed. As a result of this "accidental" but crucial observation, Sacks sug-gests that Dr P had – without realizing it, of course – come to compensate for his "deficit" by making music (which had been at the center of life) his whole life: "I think that music, for him, had taken the place of [the visual] image. He had no body-image, he had body-music: this is why he could move and act as fluently as he did, but came to a total, confused stop if the 'inner music' stopped" (1985: 17). Indeed, if his students sat still, he could not recognize them; while if they moved, he would cry, "That's Karl, I know his body-music" (1985: 17) – just as, of course, we recognize people from their "voice-music" over the telephone, or the deaf-blind Helen Keller could reputedly recognize people by their "hand-shake-music" up to two years after first meeting them. But without access to the "musicality" of people and things, their body-music, the "rhythms" that "called out" from him his next step, so to speak, Dr P was lost; he did not know his "way about" in his surroundings.

Thus, about Dr P, Sacks concludes that ". . . he could not make a cogni-tive judgment, though he was prolific in cognitive hypotheses. A judgment is intuitive, personal, comprehensive, and concrete – we 'see' how things stand, in relation to one another and oneself. It was precisely this seeing, this relating, that Dr P. lacked" (1985: 17). As Wittgenstein puts it, the understanding that he lacked is precisely "that understanding which con-sists in 'seeing connections' " (1953: no. 122).

The Practice of a Social Poetics

There is something very special, then, in Sacks's way of relating himself to Dr P. With our interest in new, relational practices for coming to an under-standing of the unique "inner worlds" of other individuals, Sacks's conduct (and his account of it) illustrates a number of important points for us. For the fact is that, as a result of his responsive involvements with Dr P, Sacks comes to a grasp of an "inner world" that is, as he himself says, so strange that, literally, it is all but unimaginable to him. And furthermore, he tells us of it! How is this possible? How can Sacks be "told" by Dr P of a world to which he has never before had access? And how can he convey a "sense" of that strange reality to us? For, as he says after his first meeting with Dr P in his consulting room, "I could make no sense of what had occurred, in terms of conventional neurology (or neuropsychology)" (1985: 10). And he had, he says, to think again, and "to see [Dr P again] in his own familiar habitat, at home" (1985: 10). But even then, after giving him a number of standard tests at home, "the testing . . . told me nothing about Dr P's inner world," he says (1985: 14). Or at least, the tests only told him negatively what Dr P could not do. What they did not do, is tell him positively how Dr P nonetheless still managed to relate himself to his circumstances in some way. Yet clearly, Sacks did gain some access to it: indeed, as we have seen, it was the eating "hummingly" episode that was crucial (and I will return to it in a moment).

So what is Sacks doing here, what is his practice, both in his relations to Dr P and in his relations to us, his readers? Clearly, he begins by paying attention to that in Dr P's behavior which "moves" or "touches" him in some way, directly; he attends to Dr P's strange way of relating himself to him. Thus Sacks begins by bringing into the foreground – both in his relations to Dr P and in his relations to us, his readers – what those, in their search for regularities and causes, would usually leave in the background. That is, he adopts a prospective-relational stance toward both Dr P and us. Taken together, all these moves, along with his use of contrasts and comparisons, and his use of a first-person, nondisciplinary-dialogical style of writing, contribute toward the practice, as I have already suggested, of a "social poetics."

Let me emphasize the importance of first-person expressions here, and their function in the expression of people's unique inner worlds: Sacks writes in the first-person, out from within his own involvements with Dr P, talking both of Dr P's responses and reactions to his (Sacks's) behavior, and of his own evaluative reactions to Dr P's behavior. He talks of the "teasing strangeness" (1985: 8) of Dr P's gaze, of Dr P's "seeming baffled" (1985: 9) in the shoe episode, and so on, and, by the use of various "as if" constructions, Sacks also gives us a "sense" of what these strange involvements were "like" for him. Let me list some of these "as if" constructions: Dr P's looking at Sacks's face was "as if [Dr P was] noting (even studying) [my] individual features, but not seeing my whole face . . ." (1985: 8); while his looking at a beach scene was "as if the absence of features in the actual picture had driven him to imagine the river and the terrace and the colored parasols" (1985: 10); or, "he functioned precisely as a machine functions" (1985: 13–14); and so on. These metaphorical "as-if" constructions enable us to rehearse what such circumstances might be like for us; they allow us to relate something very unfamiliar to us to what is familiar.

Here, then, Sacks has no way of telling us "precisely" what his initial experience with Dr P actually was. Indeed, he did not himself know its nature. Yet he does have some access to it: his initial access to it, as I have already mentioned, is as a "strangeness" that begins with his finding Dr P's way of looking at him odd. But what the particular nature of that strangeness "is" is not at first clear: "I'm not sure that I fully realized [its nature] at the time," says Sacks (1985: 8). Yet, vague and unformulated though its nature was, Sacks clearly noticed it as "a failure in the normal interplay of gaze and expression," a perturbation, a difference in the taken-for-granted, background flow of responsiveness usual between normal people. It was a unique beginning, a sense of a radical otherness at play in him that Sacks had never encountered before, a "first time" event.[9]

I draw attention to the initial importance of Sacks's living, embodied sense of Dr P's "strange" style of interacting, to point to the way in which it hermeneutically "set the scene," so to speak, for the whole of the rest of Sacks's investigation of Dr P's strange "inner world." For, just as in our other encounters with other unique individuals – where, from their vague smiles, frowns, hesitations, and puzzled looks, etc., as well as what they say to us, we must come to a precise grasp of their meaning – so here too, beginning with this initial, embodied sense of Dr P's oddness, Sacks must come to a precise grasp of the meaning of Dr P's responses to him. He must try to make the vague, global, indeterminate way in which Dr P's behavior initially "moves" him, more determinate in some way. And this is possible, for although the evidence involved is "imponderable" (see Wittgenstein's comments above), from within his involvement with Dr P, Sacks already knows its "oddness" to be of a special, consequential kind. Thus, he must try to relate the way he finds himself "moved" or "moving" in response to Dr P's strangeness, to what is familiar to him. And it is from within that "odd" involvement that he begins to explore the details of its nature, by testing and interrogating Dr P in both some well-known ways and, as we have seen, in some "accidental" ways also.

It is this emphasis on the living, embodied, gestural aspect of people's social practices, and the direct and immediate, sensuous responses that they call out of us, that gives us a clue as to how non-informational, "poetic" events can give us access to worlds utterly unfamiliar to us. Their function is not so much to help us see, in contemplation, the supposedly true nature of what a certain thing or event actually *is*, as with drawing our attention, practically, to the *possible* relations and connections such things or events might have with other aspects of our lives. And it was to the "musical" dimension in Dr P's life that Sacks's attention was drawn. For, as he had realized, Dr P's immediate visual world consisted only of unrelated, lifeless fragments that failed to "call out" any living responses from him; for him, these were aspects of an "external" world that he had to approach "as if they were abstract puzzles or tests" (1985: 12). Dr P's "inner world," the world of connections and relations relevant to him in living out his life, was only revealed to Sacks in the eating "hummingly" episode. Only there did Sacks identify the auditory nature of the ongoing "stream of life," so to speak, within which the meaningful events of Dr P's life had their being.

This was the event which enabled Sacks to compare and to relate Dr P's responses to those of others in both his tests and in everyday circumstances.

It is at this point that Wittgenstein's (1953) methods of philosophizing become relevant. Aware that we often fail to notice the momentary particularities of our own immediate circumstances, aware that we tend to see the world just as much through our words as through our eyes – that we "tend to predicate of the thing what lies in the method of representing it" (1953: no. 104) – he wants to divert us away from describing our particular, practical activities as we *think* they *must* be (in theory); and, through the "poetic" form of his remarks, draw our attention to "observations which no one has doubted, but which have escaped remark only because they are always before our eyes" (1953: no. 415). In other words, rather than us being concerned to see everything through our discipline's eyes (through its *gaze*), he wants us to notice or to attend to how we actually do (or could) in fact "go on" with each other in our daily lives, *in practice* – something that usually escapes our notice.

Thus the focus on the particular and the practical, and the calling into question of classical, disciplinary assumptions, that is a part of Sacks's practice in interacting with Dr P, also characterizes the radical nature of Wittgenstein's own approach. Like Sacks, he also uses words continually outside the confines of any particular, already established language games. But even more radically than Sacks, he wants to break the grip upon us of various already established disciplinary forms of life – with their associated regimented ways of talking and conventions of significance – so that we become more open to seeing other possibilities. By his vague and indeterminate usages, by his surprising combinations, his comparisons and juxtapositions, the discontinuities and gaps he opens up, he "deconstructs" already-determined and taken-for-granted meanings, and shows us, for instance, that we are often "dazzled by the ideal and therefore fail to see the actual use of [a word] clearly" (1953: no. 100). Its unique, practical meaning can only be grasped from its unique use, at a unique moment, in the unique context of its occurrence.

This is something that we all already in fact know to be the case in practice, but which we continually forget as soon as we ask ourselves about the meaning of our words. It is by his "arranging of what we have always known" (1953: no. 109) into new arrangements, by his "assembling reminders" (1953: no. 127), that he "leads" us into seeing new connections and relations between things that we had not noticed before. He aims to produce in his talk (his writings) what he calls "a perspicuous representation," a form of talk that "produces just that understanding which consists in 'seeing connections' " (1953: no. 122) – something, that is, of the form of a new poetic image. This image can then be further elaborated and related to the rest of our lives by means of comparisons. Indeed, this is Wittgenstein's (1953) aim in his talk of "language-games:" "The language-games are . . . set up as *objects of comparison* which are meant to throw light on the facts of language by way not only of similarities, but also of dissimilarities" (no. 130). Such comparisons will help "to establish an order in our knowledge of the use of language: an order with a particular end in view; one out of many possible orders; not *the* order" (no. 132).

The importance of *comparisons* in elaborating the relational understandings of everyday, cannot be overemphasized (Shotter, 1995). Situated within the "strange" responsive "movement" flowing between himself and Dr P, Sacks uses such comparisons to create yet further differences, yet further responsive "movements," that work to identify the *relation* of Dr P's "strange" responses to ones more familiar to him (Hermans and Kempen, 1993). Thus Sacks, by hermeneutically relating all the fragments he gathers into a meaningful whole, succeeds in "placing" them in an intelligible relation, ultimately, to the rest of his own knowledge of both neurology in particular, and people in general. Unlike our attempts, as disciplinary professionals, to "place" something within a closed theoretical framework or system, this method of investigation, Sacks's method, is endlessly open to extension. As long as we can find or invent new ways of relating to others, we can elicit yet other distinctive reactions and responses from them, and apply yet further images and metaphors in terms of which to talk of their nature. Indeed, as we "move" from functioning within one way of relating to an other – as we cross the boundaries between different "forms of life," to use Wittgenstein's (1953) term – we can experience the changed wants, desires, and temptations, as well as the different ways of handling, looking, and evaluating, associated with each. Each new elaboration, each new way of relationally responding, serves to "fill out" yet more connections and relations between the initially puzzling event and aspects of people's lives better known to us. And this is how Sacks treated Dr P's talk: as bodily "gesturing" or "pointing toward" significant aspects of his "inner world."

Such methods, then, do the opposite of what we might expect of scientists, logicians, or philosophers: they first create an indeterminacy where before there were determinate meanings, and direct our attention to new possibilities that can at first only be "sensed," vaguely. But we can now perhaps see why, given what we said above about the nature of a *social poetics*, Wittgenstein's methods contribute toward our goal: for although they do not provide us with any new *theories* as to the nature of our words, they do provide us with a new *practice*. That is, instead of helping us "find" or "discover" something already existing, but supposedly hidden *behind* appearances, they help us grasp something new, as yet unseen, that can be sensed *in* the emerging articulation of the appearances unfolding before our very eyes (or ears). And in these circumstances, the problems facing us "are solved, not by giving new information, but by arranging what we have always known" (1953: no. 109). We find in our current ways of "going on" with each other (as a social group) possibilities for relating ourselves to each other in new ways, possibilities for new social practices. Thus Wittgenstein's methods "move" us, professionally, toward a new way of "looking over" the "play" of appearances unfolding before us, such that, instead of seeing them as related to each other in terms of certain *theoretical assumptions*, we see them in terms of the connections and relations they might actually make, the roles they might play in our lives. His similes draw to our attention things with which we are already in fact conversant, in practice, but of which we need to be reminded: "How hard I find it," he says, "to see what is *right in front of my eyes*" (Wittgenstein, 1980a: 39).

Indeed, the form of speaking and writing here is not unconnected with science fiction, with imagining distortions and transformations of the human form. Indeed, Sacks himself says of writing of such figures as Dr P and of others, that they are like "travellers to unimaginable lands – lands of which otherwise we would have no conception. This is why their lives and journeys seem to me to have a quality of the fabulous . . . [and] I feel compelled to speak of tales and fables as well as cases . . . [and my friend] Luria liked to speak here of 'romantic science' " (Sacks, 1985: xi).

Conclusions

I began by raising the question as to what is involved, not simply in *talking* as a social constructionist, but in *living* as one. And I want to end by suggesting that, following Wittgenstein, as far as our investigations are concerned, our task is not that of finding the single, Archimedean standpoint from which to construct a final, true theory of everything. What I want to suggest is that it is not to do with finding any new theories at all, rather it is to do with creating new ways of acting, new practices within which to capture – to notice and characterize linguistically – the character of the *living* moments in which meaning making occurs. Our ways of acting, or forms of life, are primary and do not, and cannot, receive their justification or rationale from any theories that we might have of them. They are themselves the source (the grounds) of all the justifications we might offer for specific actions, for the task of such justifications is to sustain our forms of life in existence (Mills, 1940). Indeed, to repeat, as Wittgenstein puts it, a theoretical picture often "stands in the way of us seeing the use of [a] word as it is" (1953: no. 305) – we need to be sensitive to the changing sensuous influences actually at work on us, moment-by-moment, in our ordinary, everyday conversational interactions with each other. For, "conversation flows on, the application and interpretation of words, and only in its course do words have their meaning" (Wittgenstein, 1981: no. 135); and "what *we* [i.e., those who follow his methods] do is to bring words back from their metaphysical to their everyday use" (1953: no. 116). That is, we point out, not the explicit, conventional, cognitive, representational meanings of people's words, but meanings of a quite different kind: those implicit in people's unique, sensed, responsive reactions to their surroundings. Thus my aim in this chapter has been to try to articulate the nature of the relational practices involved in investigating these fleeting, momentary, responsive meanings.

Given their special nature, the turn to a poetics is not accidental, for it involves grasping the unique, only-once-occurrent nature of the most fleeting, momentary, fragmentary phenomena, without, so to speak, ever stepping out from within the momentary flow of their unfolding. Realizing the difficulty of this task, Wittgenstein remarks: "Perhaps what is inexpressible (what I find mysterious and am not able to express) is the background against which whatever I could express has its meaning" (1980a: 16). Yet he is convinced that without some grasp of the nature of this background flow of activity, we have no hope of coming to any understanding of our ordinary, everyday activities: "How could human behavior be described?" he asks. "Surely only by showing the actions of a variety of humans, as they are all mixed up together. Not what *one* man is doing *now*, but the whole hurly-burly, is the background against which we see an action, and it determines our judgment, our concepts, and our reactions," he replies (Wittgenstein, 1980b: no. 629).

In other words, to the extent that we are never not in contact in some way with our surroundings, we are never not involved in two, two-way flows of activity: (i) in one, activity outgoing from ourselves calls out responses or replies from our surroundings, and (ii) in the other, activity outgoing from our surroundings calls out responses from us. For Volosinov (1986) and Bakhtin (1986), this not only means that the unbroken flow of responsive activity always has a *dialogical* quality to it, but also, that the meaning of people's words can never be wholly "inside" any of them as individuals: "If experience does have a meaning, if it is susceptible of being understood and interpreted, then it must have existence in the material of actual, real signs.... Outside that material there is no experience as such.... Thus there is no leap involved between inner and outer experience and its expression, no crossing over from one qualitative realm of reality to another ... nowhere in its entire course does the process go outside the material of signs" (Volosinov, 1986: 28). But also, Volosinov adds, "*the situation [always] enters into the utterance as an essential constitutive part of the structure of its import.* Consequently, a behavioral utterance as a meaningful whole is comprised of two parts: (1) the part realized or actualized in words and (2) the assumed part" (1976: 100; original emphasis) – or, as Wittgenstein would put it, a part that is "said" and a part that is only "shown" in the utterance.

The relational, responsive, dialogic meaning of a sign, a word, an expression, is thus something that is produced, uniquely, in the practical unfolding of the concrete relations *between* particular people, in relation to their actual circumstances, over time. "To understand another person's utterance means to orient oneself with respect to it, to find the proper place for it in the corresponding context. For each word of the utterance that we are in the process of understanding, we, as it were, lay down a set of our own answering words. The greater their number and weight, the deeper and more substantial our understanding will be" (Volosinov, 1986: 102). Finding ourselves "moved" in a vague, ill-understood fashion in our initial response to a person, we further differentiate, supplement, and elaborate its nature in our further replies to their replies, until eventually, we find their responses "making sense" to us – our later responses making clear to us what the meaning of our initial, vague response "must" have been.

With this, we arrive at a most surprising conclusion: in this responsive, relational, dialogical view of our inner lives, the "things" supposedly contained "in" them are not to be found "inside" us as individuals at all, but "in" the continuously unfolding relations occurring between ourselves and others (or an otherness), in our surroundings. Indeed, we cannot as individuals (easily) hide the contents of our "inner" lives wholly inside ourselves, for, whether we like it or not, we "display" them in the unfolding "movement" of our living out our lives, responsively, amongst others. Our embodied embeddedness in this living flow of responsive activity is ineradicable; we cannot but be immersed in it. "Only in the stream of thought and life do words [and our other activities] have meaning" (Wittgenstein, 1981: no. 173).

Notes

1 Vygotsky also makes a similar point in proposing that: ". . . awareness and deliberate control appear only during a very advanced stage in the development of a mental function, after it has been used and practiced unconsciously and spontaneously. In order to subject a function to intellectual and volitional control we must first possess it" (1986: 168).

2 But see Sampson (this volume), who draws both on Bourdieu (1977, 1980) and Dreyfus's (1991) account of Heidegger's *Being and Time* (1962).

3 The idea of a *social poetics* has been developed in collaboration with a colleague, Dr Arlene M. Katz (see Katz and Shotter, 1996).

4 And, Foucault claims, there is no escape from such rules, even through the device of producing a commentary on them: "There is no question of there being one category, fixed for all time, reserved for fundamental or creative discourse, and another for those which reiterate, expound and comment. . . . Play . . . in the form of commentary . . . is nothing more than the reappearance, word for word . . . of the text commented on. . . . Commentary averts the chance element of discourse by giving it its due: it gives us the opportunity to say something other than the text itself, but on condition that it is the text itself which is uttered and, in some ways, finalized" (1972: 220, 221). Here, clearly, I disagree. It is the move to more *poetic* forms of talk that moves us out from under the domination of established discourses.

5 Indeed, we can find the origins of this stance in Descartes's search in his second meditation – the revealing subtitle of which is: "The nature of the human mind, and how it is better known than the body" – for the "one thing, however slight, that is certain and unshakable" (1986: 16), to function as the Archimedean point for the rest of his intellectual endeavors. He finds it, of course, in his certainty that what he is, is "a thing that thinks" (1986: 19). With this as a sure basis, he feels able to claim, without a doubt, that: "I now know that even bodies are not strictly perceived by the sense or the faculty of imagination but by the intellect alone, and that this perception derives not from their being touched or seen but from their being understood; and in view of this I plainly know that I can achieve an easier and more evident perception of my own mind than of anything else" (1986: 22–3). And it is this "disembodied," unresponsive-to-the-other stance that we all have had to learn to embody if we want to be accounted properly professional in our academic dealings, both with those we study and with our fellow professionals.

6 I say non- or pre-disciplinary, as this form of talk, by definition, must be non-exclusionary.

7 That is, we recreate, reinscribe, or sustain in existence certain forms of relation, thus to stabilize and *establish* them, while also leaving open the possibility of creating entirely new forms.

8. Sacks (1985: 15) says the smell "brought him back to reality."
9 Later, he does discover the existence of other similar cases. However, we should not allow the strangeness of Dr P's case to mislead us into thinking that this makes it a special case, *sui generis*. For, in coming to a grasp of *anyone's* unique, "inner world," we always come to a grasp of something to which we have never before had access. As Garfinkel puts it, our encounters with others are always for yet "another first time" (1967: 9). What makes Dr P's case special, is the way in which Sacks had to set about elaborating and supplementing his initial responsive reaction to Dr P to finally make sense of it.

References

Bakhtin, M.M. (1984) *Problems of Dostoevsky's Poetics* (ed. and trans. Caryl Emerson). Minneapolis, MN: University of Minnesota Press.

Bakhtin, M.M. (1986) *Speech Genres and Other Late Essays* (trans. Vern W. McGee). Austin, TX: University of Texas Press.

Bakhtin, M.M. (1993) *Toward a Philosophy of the Act* (trans. Vadim Lianpunov, ed. Michael Holquist). Austin, TX: University of Texas Press.

Bourdieu, P. (1977) *Outline of a Theory of Practice*. Cambridge: Cambridge University Press.

Bourdieu, P. (1980) *The Logic of Practice*. Stanford, CA: Stanford University Press.

Descartes, R. (1986) *Meditations on First Philosophy: With Selections from Objections and Replies* (trans. J. Cottingham, with an introduction by B. Williams). Cambridge: Cambridge University Press.

Dreyfus, H.L. (1991) *Being-in-the-World: A Commentary of Heidegger's Being and Time, Division 1*. Cambridge, MA: MIT Press.

Foucault, M. (1972) Appendix: "The discourse on language," in M. Foucault, *Archaeology of Knowledge*, (trans. A.M. Sheridan). New York: Pantheon Books. pp. 221–37.

Foucault, M. (1973) *The Birth of the Clinic: An Archaeology of Medical Perception*. New York: Vintage Books.

Foucault, M. (1979) *Discipline and Punish: The Birth of the Prison* (trans. A.M. Sheridan). Harmondsworth: Penguin.

Garfinkel, H. (1967) *Studies in Ethnomethodology*. Englewood Cliffs, NJ: Prentice-Hall.

Heidegger, M. (1962) *Being and Time*, (trans. John Macquarrie and Edward Robinson). Oxford: Blackwell.

Hermans, H.J.M. and Kempen, H.J.G. (1993) *The Dialogical Self: Meaning as Movement*. New York: Academic Press.

Katz, A.M. and Shotter, J. (1996) "Hearing the patient's voice: toward a social poetics in diagnostic interviews," *Social Science and Medicine*, 46: 919–31.

Kuhn, T.S. (1970) *The Structure of Scientific Revolutions* (2nd edn). Chicago: University of Chicago Press.

Mills, C.W. (1940) "Situated actions and vocabularies of motive," *American Sociological Review*, 5: 904–13.

Sacks, O. (1985) *The Man Who Mistook His Wife for a Hat*. London: Duckworth.

Shotter, J. (1980) "Action, joint action, and intentionality," in M. Brenner (ed.), *The Structure of Action*. Oxford: Blackwell. pp. 28–65.

Shotter, J. (1984) *Social Accountability and Selfhood*. Oxford: Blackwell.

Shotter, J. (1993a) *Cultural Politics of Everyday Life: Social Constructionism, Rhetoric, and Knowing of the Third Kind*. Milton Keynes: Open University Press.

Shotter, J. (1993b) *Conversational Realities: Constructing Life through Language*. London: Sage.

Shotter, J. (1995) "Joint action, shared intentionality, and the ethics of conversation," *Theory & Psychology*, 5: 49–73.

Volosinov, V.N. (1976) *Freudianism: A Critical Sketch*. Bloomington, IN and Indianapolis: Indiana University Press.

Volosinov, V.N. (1986) *Marxism and the Philosophy of Language* (trans. L. Matejka and I.R. Titunik). Cambridge, MA: Harvard University Press.

Vygotsky, L.S. (1986) *Thought and Language* (translation revised by Alex Kozulin). Cambridge, MA: MIT Press.

Wittgenstein, L. (1953) *Philosophical Investigations*. Oxford: Blackwell.

Wittgenstein, L. (1980a) *Remarks on the Philosophy of Psychology* (vols 1 and 2). Oxford: Blackwell.

Wittgenstein, L. (1980b) *Culture and Value* (trans. P. Winch, with an introduction by G. Von Wright). Oxford: Blackwell.

Wittgenstein, L. (1981) *Zettel* (2nd edn) (eds G.E.M. Anscombe and G.H.V. Wright). Oxford: Blackwell.

3

Feminism and Psychoanalysis Consider Sexuality and the Symbolic Order: Would Social Construction Join Us?

Kareen Ror Malone

à une dame dans sa quarantaine

"If you sleep with dogs, you wake up with fleas." While this typically unsolicited admonition applies to most, it has left psychology unscathed. For all of its encounters with questions of subjectivity, psychology's disciplinary canon consistently dodges a serious theorization of the subjects it so assiduously studies. Still, with each theoretical challenge to the dominant paradigm, new possibilities for thinking subjectivity offer themselves. With this possibility in mind, the following essay engages three alternative frameworks that have infiltrated mainstream psychological discourse. The first, social construction, has become an interlocutor to lively debates in psychological theory and psychotherapy, and, due to its influence, cultural effects on subjectivity are now given more consideration. Providing a second framework, feminist psychologists have made it a little more difficult to ignore sexist practices and theories within the discipline. Although many feminists in psychology stick to an empiricist agenda, feminism has generated any number of theoretical questions that would undermine psychology's conventional strategies of research and its usual notions of subjectivity (Morawski, 1994). The third, psychoanalysis, is a longtime companion to psychology; it is both incorporated into the discipline, in bits and pieces, and disparaged as unsuitable to psychology's scientific aspirations (Frosh, 1989). Less traditional psychologists are often wary of the mechanistic view of human nature associated with psychoanalysis, and its innovations to psychology's understanding of subjectivity are often overlooked. Of immediate interest, there are points at which the challenges of feminism, psychoanalysis, and social construction intersect, most significantly over the assertion that representational practices are essential to the understanding of subjectivity.

Of the three, feminism attends most closely to the ways in which culture and history inscribe women and regulate the meanings of gender. Social construction is, at first glance, concerned with more general structures of representation. Looks, however, can be deceiving. The effects of gender are so fundamental that any feminist deconstruction of gender typically implicates general functions within representation (Gallop, 1982). Thus both frameworks provide psychology with emerging models for a conception of subjectivity whose grounds would reside in the processes of representation: a subjectivity inhabited by language (and thus history, narrative, and culture).

One could argue that feminism broadens the scope of any social constructionist revision of what it means to be a subject. The sorts of problems that vex feminism gear its theories toward an explicit address of issues such as embodiment, materiality, and sexual difference. Since feminists are also attuned to the manner in which gender and the body are *constructed*, feminism offers a rich mix of approaches to the conceptualization of the interface between the body and representation. Despite the mismatch, psychoanalysis and feminism mingle at those points where cultural practices that institute gender and sexuality cross the intimate particularity of the body (whatever that might be). In recognition of this overlap, any number of feminists are aligned with a variety of psychoanalytic schools, e.g., Jane Flax (1990) or Jacqueline Rose (1986). Both psychoanalysis and feminism could contribute to the most radical aims of social construction, i.e., the possibility of re-conceiving (or of conceiving at all) the structure of subjectivity – as psychology might study that subjectivity. Both psychoanalysis and feminism add the dimension of the body in all its howl and glory.

Although it is often addressed to issues raised by social construction, the following draws on the contributions of psychoanalysis and feminism for a fuller articulation of the vicissitudes of representation in the constitution of subjectivity. If subjectivity is profoundly tied to representational practices, one must theorize the absence of any simple correspondence between subjective desire and its symbolization. There is always more to say, you said more than you wanted, you couldn't say what you wanted. You keep talking. This intricate entanglement between desire and speech poses a question that is absolutely essential to many feminist and psychoanalytic projects and it is one that is key to the aims of social construction. Certainly social construction understands that we talk, and that such speaking constitutes the world of perception and meaning. I am not sure if social construction fully inquires into why we talk and what we are talking about.

To ferret out the "subject" of speaking, I start with Lacanian psychoanalysis on the question of subjectivity. As becomes apparent, the Lacanian speaking subject is inconceivable without its splicing into the Other – Symbolic Other, the Other of the Real, the Imaginary Other. The various formations of the Other as constitutive of subjectivity and desire also appear in another guise within a theoretical debate within feminism, referred to as the "sex wars." Ostensively over censorship and pornography, the "sex wars" repeatedly bring attention to the place of the body and desire in its relationship to cultural representations. Within this context, feminism must (and does) confront the question of the Other, the Other as the locus of the signifier, as the Other sex, and in women's encounters with the otherness of our embodiment.

Contemporary Psychoanalysis: Why Bother with Lacan?

Representation and Subjectivity

In *The Pleasure of the Text*, Roland Barthes, a well-known French literary critic, circles a distinction between *plaisir* and *jouissance*, or, as translated, between pleasure and bliss. ". . . I need to distinguish euphoria, fulfillment, comfort (the feeling of repletion when culture penetrates freely), from shock, disturbance, even loss, which are proper to ecstasy, to bliss" (Barthes, 1975: 19). The first form of pleasure connotes an enjoyment that might be called satisfaction, or at least the satisfaction we gain from satisfaction. Here body and signification are at one; there is no disharmony, loss, or lack. The latter form of enjoyment (bliss) is revealed, for instance, in that peculiar alliance between an enjoyment, which is nearly unbearable, and the anxiety which reveals its investments. This enjoyment, also wrought by a signifier or representational structure, is a bit more treacherous. With the second form, one may be forced to ask, "Who is doing the enjoying?" (Miller, 1991). In other words, the complicity between representation and the body is ordered differently.

Barthes's overall project is the articulation of how a text serves as a sort of body that "thinks" us. For Barthes, at least, one cannot think of this textual body without broaching the issue of pleasure. Pleasure drives reading; its measure is something Barthes refers to as "my body." "The pleasure of the text is that moment when my body pursues its own ideas – for my body does not have the same ideas that I do" (Barthes, 1975: 17). The autonomous responses of one's body suggest that any registration of text, including the social order itself, e.g., gender, is not confined to conscious apprehension or denotative meaning. There is some operation of the text which exceeds our grasp but which, in a sense, gives us the text itself. Once any analysis of language extends beyond reality as referent or conscious intention, one must interrogate, like Barthes, the nature of this opacity or surplus within language. There is more than one way to conceive of this dimension of otherness in speech: as body, as the unconscious, as culture.

Obviously texts possess a historical weight which skews them in particular directions and which exceeds individual consciousness. Cultural context intervenes upon our most intimate responses to any given signifier. Moreover, history clearly plays a part in the determination of "whose" signifiers see the light of day. But this broader contextualization is not what Barthes is talking about when he invokes the body. The body seems to function as a kind of placeholder or limit which reveals itself as "pleasure." It serves as a boundary of consciousness whether in the form of transgression or repetition. We experience such pleasures when we are lost in the sound of another's voice, absolutely incensed by an attack on our signifiers, lulled by imbecile nursery rhythms. How is it that texts, or more prosaically, narratives, induce belief, satisfaction, hatred, and bliss (Silverman, 1992)? How do texts read our bodies?

A portion of this question is answered by understanding the strategies by which a text legitimizes itself, or is legitimated by other practices within a given historical period, or serves as a sort of reiteration of historically sedimented knowledge (see Benhabib et al., 1995; Gergen, 1989). But such answers, as important as they may be, do not take up the full complexity of our relationships to texts; they skirt Barthes's central concern, namely that of the imbrication of body, pleasure, and text, or in Lacanian lexicon, the relationship between *jouissance* and the signifier. From a number of vantage points, clarifying the relationship between the body, *jouissance*, and the signifier is a precarious endeavor. There are suspicions that the results of such a project would resurrect ideologically suspect categories of the body. Since the manner in which we conceptualize emotion, desire or affect often depends upon a prediscursive or pre-reflective ground, how to theorize the body as an autonomous field of effects without returning to an essentialist model is uncharted territory.

An investigation of *jouissance* and corporeality would not constitute a thoughtless return to a sort of troublesome essentialism. Rather it is a reopening of the question of what sutures being and meaning – what gives meaning its punch – without teleological categories which would reify the conjunction. Even if the play of the signifier overrides the prediscursive, an emphasis on *jouissance* would require that one take up questions of affect and impassioned desire, especially as these dimensions infiltrate the social field. Otherwise, in order to motivate speaking, one may be forced to resort to a pragmatically motivated agenda. One may understand this pragmatism in terms of intersubjectivity and context, i.e., the pragmatic use of speech is communicative rather than self-interested. This is a significant change in focus – although it leaves a certain residue of subjectivity untheorized – in that such a subject would be the "floating" aftereffect of its appearance in a given situation. To combat this relativism, some import political or philosophical categories to position the subject and endow it with qualities that transcend context. The reservation a more Lacanian view might pose would be directed to another dimension of this "constructed" subjectivity, the implicit cognitivism that undergirds the "communicative" subject. By this I mean an emphasis on the powers of consciousness such that anything that may exceed known significations is *in theory* at the subject's disposal. It may be unknown but it is not repressed, and there is little mention of repetition compulsions and inexplicable bodily desires. It appears that, once we discover culture or context, we discover it "in our heads." We think in metaphors of negotiation or the generation of new narratives as if we come into a context as unified bodies whose investments exist on the same plane as narrative itself.

Sometimes, by evoking the subject as a performance, we attempt to elude a model of subjectivity that is based on rational consciousness and cognition – mirror images of the scientist/psychologist. Performative subjectivity is imagined through the tropes of irony and play. Yet avoiding anxiety by introducing an unbreachable distance between subject and object is not just a trademark of "objectivist" discourses; it might well come into play in the evocation of subjectivity as ironic performance. The "objectivist" division between subject and object is perhaps repeated in the ironic distance between the enunciation and the place of the enunciator. How can we theorize when/where the subject is truly "at stake" in her utterance? What gives context its coherence or makes it fall away as irrelevant. Slavoi Zizek, Lacanian cultural theorist, makes a similar point with respect to the limits of any deconstructive analysis:

> Yet it seems as if the poetic style itself, the style of continuous ironic self-commentary and self-distance, the way of constantly subverting what one was supposed to say literally, exists only to embellish some basic theoretical presuppositions. This is why "poststructuralist" commentaries often produce . . . an endless quasi-poetical variation of the same theoretical assumption. . . . The problem with de-construction, then, is not that it renounces a strict theoretical formulation and yields to flabby poeticism. It is, on the contrary, that its position is *"too theoretical"* (in the sense of a theory which excludes the truth dimension; that is, which does not affect the place from which we speak). (Zizek, 1987: 33)

Pursuing the question of *jouissance* safeguards against relegating irrationality, affects, and the body to the disciplinary dustbin. Articulating the structures that produce *jouissance* allows one to specify ways in which bodies resist signification (as a transformative moment or a recalcitrant one). Thus the question of *jouissance* may further illuminate how a subject responds to conflicting identities as opposed to disassociated identities. It would also provide an antidote to the way in which thinking through social construction and subjectivity can lean on more cognitive frameworks.

Thinking through the body may also implicate other tenets within social construction and mainstream psychology. In attempting to reconstruct a subject, from whatever perspective, it might be in our interest to imagine not only a less reified subject but also a less self-transparent one. For Lacan, this less transparent and probably less flexible subject finds its (indeterminate) genesis in an opacity that marks the subject's inauguration into representation. Put prosaically, the signifiers that I "start with," whether cultural or familial, are a mystery to me. How they are given is not necessarily how they are received. Consequently, one's induction into symbolizing or into the field of the Other is not, for Lacanians, a smooth transition. The balance of such encounters inevitably leaves us with too much and too little. However, this is not the old hack that reality and language don't correspond. This is a new hack. Lacan suggests·that representation and subjectivity do not correspond *even as representation is the only vehicle for the subject's being.*

Subjectivity and the Errant Surplus in Speaking

Lacan frames the disjunction of subjectivity in one of his trademark aphorisms, "Desire is the Desire of the Other" (Lacan, 1977a). He means many things by this phrase. The Other is the locus of the signifier, the place of words, culture, conventions, and the like. It is, thus, that which shapes the trajectories of what I can desire. But, as Willy Apollon (1988) notes, this locus is always embodied (this is also Foucault's insight: the Symbolic Order is always a practice). As a result, there is more. In fantasy and in actual relations, questions of identity, recognition, and desire traverse symbolic exchange. The eruption of these moments often mark blind spots in the Symbolic process itself. Am I ever recognized for what I am? Why do I care? What makes my style different from another's style? Why do I keep asking the same question? Why am I not satisfied with the answer?

Put simply, the supersession of one's desire by the desire of the Other echoes the earlier quotation from Roland Barthes: any text is more to us than we can intend. This assertion can be taken beyond the evident elusiveness of language itself and beyond broader cultural effects. This excess can be found in what was previously designated by the categories of pleasure and bliss. A text covers and evokes the signifier's blind reach across the body. Such enjoyment motivates one's readings of texts and one's participation in narratives. I cannot write the text that you will read. You cannot write the text that you will read. There is a gap.

The recalcitrance of the signifier, its indeterminate excess, refers to any number of dimensions. The fact that representation forms interlocking and contradictory networks of meaning contributes to the transformative possibilities of signification. However, the body's surprise landing in these networks as (made to be) differentially sexed, as subject to the logic of the signifier, as eventually hooked to the signifier both secures and blocks meaning. Subjects begin as objects of the Other's networks of meanings, of the Other's fantasies, of the Other's *jouissance*, of the Other's demand. The signifier bears within it a certain imperative, to be this or that (girl or boy are two likely requests), and this imperative bears upon being. I mean here that the "issue" of the signifier cannot be extricated from the intersubjective and corporeal structures that we rather too cavalierly categorize as matters of love, sex, and desire. These matters reflect the intrication between signifier and body whereby meaning attains being through *jouissance*.

> Actually he [Lacan] is looking at the direct connection between the unconscious and the body. He says that unconscious thought comes first to the body. This connection is precisely what he is going to call *jouissance*, insofar as *jouissance* has to do with the signifier and at the same time is linked to the rims of the body. . . . When you present the unconscious as work, you say blind non-thinking work.
>
> So, it takes a second level of description. Blind and non-thinking work. And work for what? Then you define the unconscious as work for jouissance. The new thing that Lacan introduces is to consider the signifier not as an agent that produces signification, which is the classical Lacan. The central problem in *Television* is how come the signifier produces an effect of *jouissance*, a direct effect which you experience? You can't say that you don't experience it in the body. (Miller, 1990: 23)

In essence, Lacan postulates "another scene" of signification which "glues" and breaks into our daily conversations. The other scene serves as a motivational matrix that makes "communicating" itself absolute even if its forms are particular *per* culture, family, and individual. Thus, it is curious that social construction in the USA shows so little interest in Lacanian psychoanalysis or in psychoanalysis in general. If Lacanian psychoanalysis could offer social construction further theoretical tools to conceptualize the logic of the signifier in its relation to the Other, it would appear as important an ally as cultural studies, poststructuralism, linguistics, or discourse analysis. Psychoanalysis theorizes intersubjectivity through transference, is dubbed a "talking cure," and is guided fundamentally by speech, i.e., say whatever comes to mind. Psychoanalysis also theorizes another domain, the domain of enjoyment, pleasure, and bliss. If, for Lacan, the human dimension is founded on our status as speaking, we exist as speaking beings with desiring libidinal bodies. These bodies, too, must be explicated.

Feminism and the Question of Sexuality

The Encounter with the Other: Feminist Theory, Lacan, and Sexual Difference

Although second-wave feminism initially addressed gender equality in terms proper to the public domain, the nature of gender inequality pushed feminism to consider more deeply the meaning of sexuality within patriarchy. This shift toward what some might refer to as the private sphere complicates feminist theory in that feminism must now conceive its aims beyond those articulated by liberalism (rights) or Marxism (modes of production). If sexual imagery and indeed sexuality itself play some sort of role in the oppression of women, then one has to ask what sex is such that it lurks so shamelessly in the shadows of power.

Currently one thinks of sex as a constructed set of signifiers complicit with power. As a set of discourse–power relationships, sex criss-crosses the body in a manner analogous to our inscription through race and class. It appears in certain contexts and disappears in others. The Lacanian wager would be a bit different. It would suggest that there is some autonomy to the sexual field both with respect to sexual difference and with respect to sexuality itself. It is here that Lacan resembles radical feminists. We don't have sex for biological reasons or because we find it economically feasible (e.g., marriage) or because of certain specific cultural imperatives (go forth and flounder). Rather sex represents a kind of simpleton's solution to particular impasses in our encounter with the Other. As derivatives of this encounter, sex, race, and class may all intersect with what it means to face difference and impossibility (Cornell, 1993; Miller, 1994). Sex and sexual difference are the prototypic rituals by which the impasses of the Other are marked on the bodily subject. Although the Lacanian Other is defined as the locus of the signifier, sex and sexual difference are spawned by the signifier not only in what it produces (discursive practices) but in what the signifier cannot say (the Real). Lacan's annoying reminder, "there is no sexual relation," marks the impossibility of negotiating the relationship with the Other. What, in fact, does the desire in your eyes mean? In a defense of non-monogamous relationships, Pat Califia makes this point more crudely:

> You are as alone in a simultaneous orgasm as you are sitting home while your lover goes out on a date. . . . Each of us has impossible fantasies of devouring or absorbing the loved one; of splitting twinning, loving mirror images of ourselves; or of becoming an appendage of the adored Other, since she will not damage or sever a part of herself. This infantile kind of love . . . [asks for] the . . . reassurance a loving Other provides, but not the threat of rejection or the unpredictability of another consciousness. . . . This irrational hunger cannot be appeased by possessiveness. Like the national deficit, it has to be lived with. (1994: 201)

The national deficit that interests Califia reflects a structural impasse that marks the Other as Other. This most certainly means that the Symbolic Order (representation) can not say it all – another interpretation always awaits. The impasse also reveals itself, in Califia's domain, as a corporeal appeal. An appeal for a whole body, an appeal for recognition from the other, *an appeal to know the jouissance of the Other.*

These interrelated and asymmetrical moments that define our relationship to the Other operate in the medium of the signifier. I strike a bargain in order to identify with the signifier, woman. As defined by the signifier, I am "alienated." My body is subject to the strictures of the Symbolic Order. I am excluded from certain forms of bodily pleasure and encouraged to experience others. Christened by the signifier, I also exist as a subject who may enjoy the conjunction of that signifier (woman) with a vast array of other signifiers. It is not in the nature of the signifier to refer to something but rather to represent the subject for other signifiers – the possibilities are, in theory, endless. However, we presumably recognize that neither culture (history) nor the body allow for endless discursive play. Sometimes, I cannot respond to the desire of the Other (Dunand, 1995).

There is some opacity; the signifier cannot signify adequately one's encounter with the Other. There is an indeterminate moment that refers to our existence as objects for the Other. At this moment, we are not subjects of desire but desire's subjects or, in the worst case scenario, its victims (Fink, 1990). This means that the signifier, woman, and any place it may occupy within signification does not and cannot resolve the impasses of my desire constituted through the desire of the Other. This failure in the signification of woman does not involve simply alienation but also involves impossibility, impossibilities which may have as much to do with my being a woman as what can be signified.

At a structural level, the impossibilities of desire specifically impact the question of sexuality, sexual difference and its relationship to power. One could argue that myths of sexuality, such as rape myths and myths of complementarity (me Tarzan, you Jane), are partially motivated by the denial of the impasses of the Other. Lacanians call such reigning cultural myths of sex the path of the *norm-male* or *nor-male* (Ragland, 1995). These myths may bolster our narcissism and organize reality, but they are idealized and deceptive tyrannies that foster aggression and oppression. From this perspective, certain power dynamics within a patriarchally determined sexuality would have to be traced to issues inherent to sexuality itself rather than being referred to broader power inequities.

If, as psychologists, we are going to query fully the import of representation, we may find its structure answers to our encounter with the Other and is corporeally instantiated. This move, as a question of the body, difference and the Other, implicates sex and sexual difference. In many respects, social construction is rather reserved in its deconstruction of sexuality itself (e.g., Tiefer, 1995), and although there is a great interest in the problem of difference, difference is neutered. In stark contrast, one can navigate the feminist spectrum, from Andrea Dworkin to Pat Califia, and encounter a certain unerring presence to sex. Mandy Merck (1993), for example, sees Dworkin's portrayal of the brutality of sex as narrated from the viewpoint of the child, i.e., as a sort of replaying, not only of the patriarchy but of other overwhelming encounters with whatever it is that sex means. The failure of *Intercourse* (Dworkin, 1987) to adequately account for historical and literary context in its analysis of heterosexual intercourse is not a failure of scholarship but instead intimates a focus on *another scene* of sex.

In *Intercourse*, Dworkin is most obviously interested in the penis as a power tool of larger society yet the text incessantly slides into more nebulous territories, e.g., bodily boundaries, penetration, splitting, fusions, hatred, and love. From the (far) other end, Pat Califia (1994), in her self-interested separation of social power and power in sex, explicitly foregrounds the ways in which sexual relationships repeat issues of dependence, trauma, and otherness. One does not, however, have to choose between Dworkin or Califia, seeing such structures in sex as merely aftershocks of the patriarchy or making them an insoluble deficit that simply provides us with a pleasant pastime.

The testaments of feminist heterosexuals in a special issue of *Feminism and Psychology* (Kitzinger and Perkins, 1992) suggest that sexually explicit ventures in our discipline are still difficult to broach. When romantic aspirations involving asymmetrical power relations were recounted in that volume, they were cast as "unsound fantasies" or considered the atavistic habits of an earlier, now transcended heterosexuality (Bartky, 1992; Gill and Walker, 1992). Constructionist minded feminists seemed most preoccupied with deconstructing labels and binaries that surround sexual identity (Crawford, 1992; Gergen, 1992). In a number of contributions (but not all), the political and psychological ends that earmark feminism were seemingly replicated in bedroom activities, especially in the invocation of a more egalitarian sexuality (e.g., Rowland, 1992). If it is otherwise, if sex possesses an autonomy outside of such political definitions, little about such matters was expressed – at least by the feminists included in this issue. This is not to say that a number of critical questions were not entertained relating to child-rearing, lesbian feminism, a bit on race, and heterosexual privilege. Still, it looks like the politically recalcitrant questions about Eros are being

Status:	; NTRB:04-23-00
Request date:	03-10-00 04:10PM
Author:	bayer betty m and harre rom
Title:	reconstructing the psychological subject: bodies,
	practices and technologies
Publ. Place & Date:	London,England Sage 1998
ISBN:	
Patron name:	Stedman, James M. (210) 567-4768
Acquisition method:	ILL request letter
Supplier:	Texas A&M at Corpus Christi
Process date:	03-22-00 11:23AM
Level of Service (Regular, Priority, Rush): regular
Federal Express ($12 extra)?:
Payment (give credit card or UTHSCSA account and exp. date, or say "cash"):
Needed by:	03-24-00
Note:	li:8036291

left to lesbian sadomasochists, radical feminists outside of psychology, and those who are committed to psychoanalysis (e.g., Benjamin, 1980).

The feminist theorization of sexuality has taken a number of unexpected turns in its effort to fully confront the range of meanings that are constitutive of sex and gender. At times, this has meant that feminism conceives the nature of reciprocal sexual relationships. Feminist flirtations with lesbian sexuality as a kind of signifier of sex and its emphasis on mother–daughter relations in its psychoanalytic branches represent efforts to "uncross" the power differential that marks the sexual divide (Flax, 1990). Shere Hite's promotion of masturbatory pleasures and clitoral stimulation fall into the same category (Gallop, 1988; Segal, 1993). At the multifaceted interface between the theorization of sex and feminist goals, a lively debate on the role of sexual imagery has evolved. This debate has been dubbed, during the height of its acrimony, the "sex wars" (not, you will notice, the war between the sexes which, in a way, it recalls). Although the debate is most often seen as split between radical anti-porn feminists and their libertarian counterparts, it also encompasses a series of less-attended-to yet interesting questions about the nature of sexuality and representation.

Firstly, there is some question about the significance of theorizing sexuality at all. Do we (they), in fact, spend too much time talking about sex, sexual imagery, pornography, and desire? Perhaps we (they) should address, once again, women and poverty, child care, and dwindling abortion rights (Freccero, 1990). For those in feminism who believe that a radical interrogation of sexuality is one of its more critical tasks, there are striking differences in how this question of sex is approached. For many within radical feminism, current notions of gender and sex are considered the foundation of all unequal power relationships in much the same way that Marx might consider modes of production to be the foundation of all inequality (MacKinnon, 1987). Typically, in this branch of feminism, there is a clear analogy between the position of men in the bedroom and the position of men in society. (Men are on top.) For Andrea Dworkin, at least, the very act of penetration constitutes women as dis-empowered. Women are defined by a certain violation of our (their) boundaries; the moment of Eros is the moment when the woman's body renders itself "breachable" (Dworkin, 1987). There is "a virtual synthesis of intimacy and state policy, the private and the public, the penis and the rule of men" (Dworkin, 1987: 158).

Many in radical feminism regard pornography as the propaganda of women's pervasive sexual subordination. Given this belief, one obvious strategy of intervention is to attack vigorously the legal and illegal distribution of pornography and disparage forms of sexuality that replicate the power–sex association that undergirds patriarchy. In this respect, feminists such as MacKinnon have been incredibly active. Their work is influential in the legal realm, where they have crafted legislation restricting pornography as a civil rights infringement on women (Gilbert, 1993). Many current analyses of advertising, pornography, and rape bear the imprint of a radical feminist analysis (e.g., Koss, 1993). Such feminists have articulated an alternative social position on a number of women's issues, in which the objectification of women is approached in terms of its implied horizon of sexual exploitation.

In reaction to the success of this feminist analysis of sexuality, there has been the predictable patriarchal backlash. Both men and women have chastised radical feminism for ruining sex while impugning women's ability to make sexual choices. The motivations for such criticisms are numerous, from the desire to maintain the sexual status quo to gaining stature from bashing feminism, e.g., Camille Paglia (Gallop et al., 1990). There have been, however, some fairly important exchanges within feminism over the analysis of sex offered by radical feminists. These exchanges have resulted in excellent feminist theorizing, for example, in the classic, *Pleasure and Danger* (Vance, 1984). More importantly, such debate pushes feminism to examine thoroughly the stakes of sexual desire.

Within the MacKinnon view, women's sexual desire is absolutely produced by the reigning culture. We cannot even begin to imagine what sex is about (except domination) until gender inequality is eradicated. Other feminisms argue that we must begin with the phenomenology of desire itself. If, in the name of a feminist agenda, we deny those desires of women that make us uncomfortable, we are failing in our most radical mission; we are supporting the more general repressiveness of the patriarchy (Valverde, 1987). At the far end, those lesbian sadomasochists that give many feminists fits suggest that desire derives from an autonomous realm. It is supported by fantasy and is far removed from other arenas of social oppression. Sexual desire is about something else. Insofar as sex implicates power (and it is disingenuous for sadomasochistic lesbians to assert otherwise), we should claim and explore that power rather than flee from it. In between there are a number of voices that propose that we examine what desire is all about before we encourage legislation which outlaws forms of sexual expressions (Cowie, 1993).

Spoils of the Sex Wars

All feminist parties to the "sex wars" debate seem to agree on the terms of the controversy in that certain aspects of sexuality repeatedly figure in the analysis of the relationship of power and desjre. In both camps, there is a presumed relationship between sexual desire and the law. In one case, sex "executes" the law; it is an instrument of bodily compliance. Of course, those within radical feminism see this connection as a matter of "conditioning" (through pornography) or compulsion (through economics). There is no question of "enjoying" the law and its imposition. Radical feminism seems to subscribe to the notion that we can be utterly usurped by the patriarchal law, which is why they see fantasy as privatized ideology.[1] The perceptive observation that the law must obtain the consent of the body is magnified into a conflation between law and enjoyment. In a way, the move is comparable to certain importations of Foucault which emphasize the omnivorous appetite of discursive practices. Such readings may not give adequate consideration to Foucault's concern with resistance to and complicity with power – a concern tied to the body.

Those who dispute the aims of radical feminism with respect to sex, also typically claim a relationship between law and sex. For those most ardent opponents, women who defend sadomasochism (S/M), sex is obviously inextricable from law and its transgression. Scenes are about obedience and disobedience, compliance and refusal. Here one blatantly asserts that the only way "to do" law is to enjoy it. At the very least, S/M reveals the hidden investment of the law, showing us the "hard-on" under the judge's robe (Califia, 1994: 163). Within this second view, the dynamics between law and desire are accorded a significant psychological component that is irreducible to the social dimension while at the same time subverting it. As a result, proponents of S/M sometimes appear to be re-staging the most onerous features of the patriarchy while simultaneously proclaiming themselves "sex radicals." This is an audacious and not altogether convincing claim.

Robert Samuels (1993), touches upon a number of the forces at play in sadomasochistic desire in his Lacanian analysis of perversion. Samuels refers sadomasochistic dynamics to certain structures that define our encounter with the Other. In a sense, the perverse moment re-enacts a supersession of one's body/need/desire by the Symbolic Other, e.g., Be a girl! Be a boy! By the time we are old enough to "play" this game, it is our self-conscious awareness which is superseded. S/M renders this Symbolic supersession as a matter of enjoyment. At this point it would be helpful to recall Barthes's seemingly innocent remark about the pleasure of the text: i.e., bliss extends us beyond our boundaries. In S/M, one is toying with a *mise en scène* that orchestrates the re-inscription of our bodies through an absolute subordination to the Symbolic Other of the law. Everything that I've read of this erotic pastime indicates that its practitioners know very precisely what they are doing – from arbitrary role reversal, to insulting imperatives, to a preoccupation with uniforms. They mimic the Symbolic Order. Thus, in a sense, S/M eroticizes law as enforcement by reproducing its subjective structure. This may be what is viewed as part of S/M's radicality: they take the judge's erection seriously.

Still, the sadist does more than give the masochist "cathartic relief." She gets off herself, and that's the rub. Protestations to the contrary, sadists as well as masochists get their thrills from this particular type of encounter. Seen as a complicity of pleasures, S/M renders the law impotent. So, in a sense, sadomasochistic lesbians are right; they do subvert the law rather than simply replicate it. The law becomes merely a matter of enjoyment; the judge is just masturbating. In the process, law loses its relation to limit and structure. The law may be an Imposter but the fact of law isn't (Lacan, 1977b). Thus, it is important to question the degree to which the sadomasochistic "revelation" of *jouissance* is not merely absorbed into itself. Said another way, is *jouissance* sufficient in itself to "re-construct" the subject and alter her place in the Symbolic Order? It is interesting that the "sex wars" bring one closer to these sorts of questions than does social construction, at least with respect to the complicated relation of law and the body. But this complicated relation is a matter of some significance. The law is, in part, the mandate of the signifier. *Insofar as language is performative, it is always bound to the law.* The law's imbrication into the domains of sex and power is not, consequently, a matter of little (or no) interest to social construction. It is a vehicle by which social construction can consider the signifier and the body, e.g., the concept of *jouissance.* More importantly, it is a vehicle whereby social construction can consider power, the signifier, and the body.

Besides their address to the issues of law and the body, the warring sides of the sex debates share another preoccupation, namely that of the nature of fantasy and image in their relationship to desire. This preoccupation also obviously concerns processes of representation. On the one hand, feminist challenges to pornography imply that (re)presentations of sexuality are significant factors in the maintenance of actual sexual behavior. Fantasy is assumed to possess enormous power. For many, sexual fantasies cultivated by pornography reproduce patriarchal power. Some feminist criticisms of the anti-pornography feminists contest this tendency to rely on the power of fantasy without really theorizing the nature of fantasy. Elizabeth Wilson (1993) argues that such feminisms suffer from a fundamentalism that we usually associate with conservative religious thinking, a sort of moral correspondence theory wherein what we imagine is an unambiguous prelude to what we are about to do.

As an arm of the patriarchy, fantasy is assumed to replicate two realities. First it repeats or represents the reality of the social order. In the second instance, it directly reflects the desires of whatever figure is staged as the protagonist. For others like Wilson, fantasy as a representational practice can not simply mirror political realities or a self-identical desire (modeled on volition). Fantasy itself is sutured by repressed cross-identifications that preclude any simple demarcation of who is in charge. Thus it is not merely a product of a singular ego or of "actual" power relations. In the following, Lynne Segal quotes the French psychoanalysts, Laplanche and Pontalis:

> In fantasy the subject . . . cannot be assigned any fixed place in it (hence the danger, in treatment, of any interpretations which attempt to do so). As a result, the subject, although always present in fantasy, may be so in a de-subjectivized form, that is to say, in the very syntax of the sequence in question. (1993: 70–1)

Segal's point is to challenge any simple reading of pornographic fantasy. If we are de-centered, it is difficult to come from one place. This is an important consideration for social construction as well. It suggests that certain representational practices may, in themselves, situate us in more than one position, that is, we are not merely de-centered by a multiplicity of voices/narratives. Rather the very process of narration reveals a disjunctive subjectivity that is founded in the Other. For Lacanians, the placeholder of power (who is in charge) is denoted by the expression, "agent," but agent is certainly *not* reducible to a self-transparent and thus self-interested individual (Ragland, 1995). Agent is a place in a structure, perhaps held by the object, perhaps held by the Symbolic Order. In fantasy, the "agent" is the object. As noted previously, for Lacanians, our "world" is not only determined by the limits of language. We emerge as desiring beings from the Symbolic Other (language), but we are equally indebted for our being to the Other's *jouissance* and the Other's desire. As children and adults, we cannot always read the Other's *jouissance* or its desire. It "falls out" of the intersubjective/languaged net. Put another way, we can be claimed by what we can't read. Fantasy, as opposed to cognition, is an attempt to find our place in the Other as objects of *jouissance* (S. Sowecke, personal communication, 3 May 1995). The question we pose to the Other on this score is as answerable as arriving at a set procedure that will assure you of immediate sexual gratification from your partner. So, instead, we have fantasies.

> Introducing a libidinal logic into meaning whose syntax is that of the sexual divide, *jouissance* is both fragile and rigid – what Lacan calls the essence of the human, and of which Colette Soler will say, "There are certainly . . . biological bodies of different genders, and signifiers related to sex: man and woman, father and mother, as well as all those which erect sexual ideals, such as 'virgin,' 'whore,' 'wife,' and so forth. None of these inscribes the object which would annul the sexual lack, and they all fail to compensate for the hole, for the partner of *jouissance* is unapproachable in language." (Ragland, 1995: 148)

The operation of fantasy as that which (re)produces the kind of object we are for the Other serves to suggest that all representational structures may, to some degree, entail an excess that binds representation without being reducible to it. As feminism in its most disparate forms suggests, the juncture between representation and desire is charged with questions of sexual difference and power. This excess, whether at the level of narcissism or more primitive modes of *jouissance* (our being as objects), both clogs the relation between desire and representation as well as motivates that relationship. Furthermore, entertaining questions about *jouissance* and the body probably requires that we seriously consider the issue of the ontogenesis of the subject even if we eschew old-fashioned narratives of development. If we inhabit a languaged reality, our subjectivity must find its genesis in the locus of the signifier (the Other in Lacanese). It may be time to theorize our relation with this Other. Is our de-centered genesis to be based simply in a formalist conception of language or does that encounter give birth to a more complexly structured subjectivity?

This Knot which is the Subject

The above wanderings about Lacanian psychoanalysis and feminism reflect a conviction that both pursuits offer social construction new avenues for thinking through subjectivity. Social construction may unduly limit itself if it relies too heavily on sociological formations as cultural context and upon cognitive models as the kernel of subjectivity. Despite the extremely radical challenge social construction presents to traditional psychology, it can, in its framing of culture and subject, subscribe to a certain unexamined rationality wherein the body is just an adaptive perceptual apparatus, an uncomplicated pleasure, an inscriptive surface, or an undifferentiated biological potential. (Did I cover all the bases?) Social construction can go further. There is an interstice between corporeality and representation where even psychoanalysis and feminism cross paths. I would suggest that social construction join the adventure.

Note

1 One could as easily argue the opposite, that fantasy is where ideology does not work (Segal, 1993).

References

Apollon, W. (1988) "What's At Stake in the Freudian Clinic," *Newsletters of the Freudian Field*, 2: 27–45.
Barthes, R. (1975) *The Pleasure of the Text* (trans. R. Howard). New York: Hill and Wang.
Bartky, S. (1992) "Hypathia unbound: a confession," *Feminism and Psychology*, 2: 426–8.
Benhabib, S., Butler, J., Cornell, D. and Fraser, N. (1995) *Feminist Contentions*. New York: Routledge.
Benjamin, J. (1980) "The bonds of love," *Feminist Studies*, 6: 144–74.
Califia, P. (1994) *Sex Radicals*. Pittsburgh: Cleis Press.
Cornell, D. (1993) *Transformations*. New York: Routledge.
Cowie, E. (1993) "Pornography and fantasy: psychoanalytic perspectives," in L. Segal and M. McIntosh (eds), *Sex Exposed: Sexuality and the Pornography Debate*. Brunswick, NJ: Rutgers. pp. 132–54.
Crawford, M. (1992) "Identity, passing, and subversion," *Feminism and Psychology*, 2: 429–31.
Dunand, A. (1995) "The end of analysis (II)," in R. Feldstein, B. Fink, and M. Jaanus (eds), *Reading Seminar XI*. Albany, NY: State University of New York Press. pp. 251–8.
Dworkin, A. (1987) *Intercourse*. New York: Free Press.
Fink, B. (1990) "Alienation and separation: logical moments in Lacan's dialectic of desire," *Newsletter of the Freudian Field*, 4: 78–119.
Flax, J. (1990) *Thinking in Fragments*. Berkeley, CA: University of California Press.
Freccero, C. (1990) "Notes of a post-sex wars theorizer," in M. Hirsch and E.F. Keller (eds), *Conflicts in Feminism*. New York: Routledge. pp. 305–25.
Frosh, S. (1989) *Psychoanalysis and Psychology: Minding the Gap*. New York: New York University Press.
Gallop, J. (1982) *The Daughter's Seduction: Feminism and Psychoanalysis*. Ithaca, NY: Cornell University Press.
Gallop, J. (1988) *Thinking Through the Body*. New York: Columbia University Press.
Gallop, J., Hirsch, M., and Miller, N.K. (1990) "Criticizing feminist criticism," in M. Hirsch and E.F. Keller (eds), *Conflicts in Feminism*. New York: Routledge. pp. 349–69.
Gergen, K. (1989) "Warranting voice and the elaboration of the self," in J. Shotter and K. Gergen (eds), *Texts of Identity*. London: Sage. pp. 70–81.
Gergen, M. (1992) "Unbundling our binaries – genders, sexualities, desires," *Feminism and Psychology*, 2: 447–9.
Gilbert, H. (1993) "So long as it's not sex and violence: Andrea Dworkin's *Mercy*," in L. Segal and M. McIntosh (eds), *Sex Exposed: Sexuality and the Pornography Debate*. Brunswick, NJ: Rutgers. pp. 216–32.

Gill, R. and Walker, R. (1992) "Heterosexuality, feminism, contradiction: on being young, white, heterosexual feminists in the 1990's," *Feminism and Psychology*, 2: 453–6.

Kitzinger, C. and Perkins, R. (1992) "Heterosexuality," special issue of *Feminism and Psychology*, 2(3).

Koss, M.P. (1993) "Rape: scope, impact, interventions, and public policy responses," *American Psychologist*, 48: 1062–70.

Lacan, J. (1977a) "The agency of the letter," in *Ecrits* (trans. Alan Sheridan). New York: Norton. (Original work published 1966.)

Lacan, J. (1977b) "The subversion of the subject and the dialectic of desire," in *Ecrits* (trans. Alan Sheridan). New York: Norton. (Original work published 1966.)

MacKinnon, C. (1987) *Feminism Unmodified*. Cambridge, MA: Harvard University Press.

Merck, M. (1993) *Perversions*. New York: Routledge.

Miller, J.-A. (1990) "A reading of some details in *Television* in dialogue with the audience, Barnard College, New York," *Newsletter of the Freudian Field*, 4: 4–30.

Miller, J.-A. (1991) "The analytic experience: means, ends, and results," in E. Ragland and M. Brachers (eds), *Lacan and the Subject of Language*. New York: Routledge. pp. 83–99.

Miller, J.-A. (1994) "Extimité," in M. Bracher, M. Alcorn, R. Corthell, and F. Massardier-Kenney (eds), *Lacanian Theory of Discourse*. New York: New York University Press. pp. 74–87.

Morawski, J.G. (1994) *Practicing Feminisms, Reconstructing Psychology: Notes on a Liminal Science*. Ann Arbor: University of Michigan Press.

Ragland, E. (1995) *Essays on the Pleasures of Death: From Freud to Lacan*. New York: Routledge.

Rose, J. (1986) *Sexuality in the Field of Vision*. London: Verso.

Rowland, R. (1992) "Radical feminist heterosexuality: the personal and the political," *Feminism and Psychology*, 2: 459–63.

Samuels, R. (1993) *Between Philosophy and Psychoanalysis*. New York: Routledge.

Segal, L. (1993) "Sweet sorrows, painful pleasures: pornography and the perils of heterosexual desire," in L. Segal and M. McIntosh (eds), *Sex Exposed: Sexuality and the Pornography Debate*. Brunswick, NJ: Rutgers. pp. 65–91.

Silverman, K. (1992) *Male Subjectivity at the Margins*. New York: Routledge.

Tiefer, L. (1995) *Sex is not a Natural Act and Other Essays*. Boulder, CO: Westview.

Valverde, M. (1987) *Sex, Power, and Pleasure*. Philadelphia: New Society Publishers.

Vance, C. (ed.) (1984) *Pleasure and Danger*. Boston: Routledge and Kegan Paul.

Wilson, E. (1993) "Feminist fundamentalism: the shifting politics and sex and gender," in L. Segal and M. McIntosh (eds), *Sex Exposed: Sexuality and the Pornography Debate*. Brunswick, NJ: Rutgers. pp. 15–28.

Zizek, S. (1987) "Why Lacan is not a post-structuralist," *Newsletter of the Freudian Field*, 1: 31–9.

4

Two Ways to Talk about Change: "The Child" of the Sublime Versus Radical Pedagogy

Ben Bradley

"What awful lives children live!" he said, waving his hand at her as he
crossed the room. "Don't they, Rose?" "Yes," said Rose. "And they can't
tell anybody," she added. (Woolf, 1937: 129)

It is one of the shocks of late acquaintance with an etymological dictionary
that, according to its roots, psychology means study of (-ology) the mind
(psyche). For the discipline's history is marked by a series of announce-
ments *denying* that the manifold breathings of soul and spirit and mind wit-
nessed in any of those more or less vivid idiosyncratic struggles that give
direction to each small complex of actual un-normalized, wintery, moral,
existential life could ever form the proper focus of psychological investigation. "I believe we can write a psychology," wrote J.B. Watson (1913) at
a seminal instant, based on the "elimination of states of consciousness as
proper objects of investigation," a subject in which we "never use the terms
consciousness, mental states, mind, content."

Truly Watson's words echo down the century. As behaviorism has given
way to cognitive science and artificial intelligence, a new orthodoxy has
emerged. Once again personal experience and the complex vagaries of
mental life are sidelined, this time in favor of modeling the processes that
are supposed to give rise to human behavior on the capacities of the computer (Bradley, 1993a; Gardner, 1985; Pylyshyn, 1984; Searle, 1992). Even
the movement calling itself social constructionism denies mind. The constructionist castigates both behavioral and cognitive approaches as blind to
their own cultural investments. But claims to be studying consciousness or
experience fall foul of the same critique. Talk about the mind is artifact of
cultural forces, an epiphenomenon shaped by the conventions of discourse.
Discourse is real. Everything else is relative to discourse. So subjective
reality, personal experience, mind is not real. And we remain to be delivered from the absurdity of an intellectual discipline that habitually disowns
its defining topic of inquiry.

We are the hollow men
We are the stuffed men.
(Eliot, 1963)

No wonder that, like the guy in the street, psychologists are confused about how to promote human welfare. About politics. About coming together to lift social oppression. About psychology's failure to be "one of the most revolutionary projects ever conceived by the mind of man" (Miller, 1969). For in the end it can only be change in the whole culture that will determine whether psychology has lived up to its revolutionary potential. And while the cultural guardians of mind make believe that mind and experience is unreal, there can be no recourse to the consideration of detailed circumstantial personal experience as a goad to cultural change. If experiences are ruled out, then the experience of oppression is ruled out.

After all, it is not for academics to decide what the problems of working-class people, of women, of black people, of children, might be. Rather, it is for the academic to find out about and respond to the issues as experienced by such groups themselves (Parker and Spears, 1996; Stanley, 1990). If our assumptions and our pedagogy allow no space for the expression of the only data that might clue us in to our collective sickness of soul, the repressive tolerance that masquerades as freedom of speech wins out and there can be no reconstruction of psychology as a practice of emancipation.

This chapter argues that the denial of mind is a symptom of a deep and unremarked bulwark that conserves psychology in its current form and so betrays the ambitions of all those who try to reinvent the discipline or to give it greater social utility. This bulwark comprises the shared and individual existential determinants that create a psychological language with a structure consonant with what literary critics call the Romantic sublime (Bradley, 1993b; see next two sections, below). Like what James called "healthy-mindedness," the sublime fosters a temperament in which the tendency to see things uncritically is like a water of crystallization in which the psychologist's character is set (cf. Bradley, 1991). Such a temperament often makes the practice of the discipline like a type of religion,

> a religion in which good, even the good of this world's life, is regarded as the essential thing for a rational being to attend to. This religion directs [the psychologist] to settle scores with the more evil aspects of the universe by systematically declining to lay them to heart or make much of them, by studiously ignoring them in reflective calculations, or even, on occasion, by denying outright that they exist. Evil is a disease; and worry over disease is itself an additional form of disease, which only adds to the original complaint. (After James, 1903: 109)

Despite countless claims to have founded new paradigms or to have revolutionized theory, the sublime goes on maintaining divisions crucial to the social *status quo*: adult from child, mind from body, professional life from home-life, pedagogy from research. Whether in the architecture of the lecture-hall or the design of the laboratory-experiment, on the TV chat-show, or in the most arcane annals of theory, psychologists' language promotes a form of transcendence which both denies their own subjectivities and blinds them to the subjectivities of others. Simultaneously it locks psychology into a child-centered form of developmental explanation that is inimical to promotion of the social weal (Kessen, 1979, 1990).

Hence among the compost of facts to which the typical degree course introduces students of psychology, there will be little to worry them about fighting social inequality or ending social and psychological repression. Students may learn much about personality, the nervous system, statistical analysis, the simplest kind of visual illusion, and infant communication. However, they are unlikely to learn anything that obliges them to think seriously about poverty, alienation, domestic violence, war, starvation, and ecological destruction. Such facts may concern them as private citizens. But they will hear that, "as scientists, . . . [psychologists] have no special obligation to solve social problems" (Miller, 1969: 1063).

Grounds for Ignoring Social Problems

What are the grounds of this shocking doctrine? In what follows, I canvass three possibilities.

First is the linguistic and political quietism fertilizing the assumption that discussions of human development should primarily be discussions of the individual's past. Human development is not some change that needs to be collectively struggled for in the here and now. It is something idealized that has always already been fixed by history, in the dim of evolutionary conjecture, at the masqued ball of eggs with sperm, in a blooming buzzing confusion of statements about "the child" (Bradley, 1989; Kessen, 1979; see next section).

Second is the idea that psychological knowledge must be based in a series of procedures that distance the knower from the subject-matter under investigation. If scientific knowledge is to be objective, it must be value-free and, hence, strictly quarantined from moral and political discussion.

We are increasingly reminded that science is a form of transcendence involving a flight from the uncertainties prompted by cultural difference. Scholars like Bordo (1989) and Keller (1985) have shown how the pursuit of objectivity in the writings of Descartes and Bacon served to suppress personhood and the cultural anxieties of the moment as irrelevant to pure reason, making the isolated monologic intellect the true deity of the modern era.[1] But, while this argument has been made for the natural sciences in general, its applicability and significance for the science of mental life have not so far been explored.

Yet this is an argument peculiarly relevant to the study of mind. For the great discoveries of natural science traditionally concern phenomena that exist on a different scale from their human investigators, where there is naturally a high degree of isolation of the phenomenon from the observer: "We are too small to influence the starts in their courses, and too large to care about anything but the mass effects of molecules, atoms and electrons" (Wiener, 1948: 189–90). Natural scientists can therefore easily afford to ignore events which might be of the greatest significance from the point of view of an observer conforming to the scale of existence of atoms or stars themselves. But in psychology, the coupling between observer and observed is far harder to minimize.

Psychologists have not the natural advantage of looking down on their subjects, as from the cold heights of eternity and ubiquity. Yet they have maintained this elevated vantage-point for more than a century and with such success that the identification of the psychologist with the natural scientist is now taken for granted both inside and outside the discipline (John, 1986). Until we understand how the psychologist's separation from their subject-matter is achieved, we can be in no position to talk of changing the discipline (see next section).

Following on from and sustaining this is, third, the idea that psychology can be lived, taught, and researched without reference to the dynamics of personal experiences for teacher, student, or subject, however nodal these experiences may be acknowledged to be within the individual's private self-understanding. This is the insight that informs Georges Devereux's (1968) reconstruction of the behavioral sciences on the grounds of a relational methodology that draws out the psychoanalytic resource of the "counter-transference." For Devereux, the anxieties, fantasies and feelings occasioned in *the researcher* by their research with other people – far from being discounted or denied, as with the sublime – were the royal road to understanding (Bradley, 1993b; Bradley and Selby, 1996).

This paper asks what parallel method is available for *teachers* of psychology who recognize as counter-transferential the existence of the blindnesses and oppressions that structure even the most liberal educational discourse. How to access the "distortions in pure intersubjectivity" which prevent the designers of (counter)cultural praxis from being able to establish an ideal situation for garnering speech (Habermas, 1970)? How to develop a pedagogy that will move the psychological community on from expert talk on "the child" or "the brain" or "the gene" to take up a critical, politically active stance to current social arrangements (see section after next)?

Time in Developmental Explanation

In psychology, it has been said, we live forwards, but must understand backwards. However, the successes of evolutionary explanation in biology have encouraged developmentalists to overlook this truism and thereby to commit a version of what philosophers call the genetic fallacy.

In philosophy the genetic fallacy is the mistake of allowing the question "How come?" to pre-empt the question "What?" It is the mistake of thinking that the power of knowledge can be justified, explained away, or nullified by an account of its history. For example, a scientist might justify the predictive power of a conclusion by giving an account of the rigorous procedures which led to the conclusion. A social constructionist might call an argument into question because it is the product of particular historical, of cultural circumstances that could have been otherwise (Gergen, 1985: 272; cf. Lavine, 1962). Both arguments commit the genetic fallacy, the fallacy of forgetting that the primary value or meaning of an event has no necessary connection with its genesis in history or its causal explanation.

In psychology, genetic fallacies have their own peculiar form. They arise from as what James (1878) called "the appeal to the polyp." The analysis of an experience's chronology and historical "origin" takes the place of the analysis of the meaning of that experience. This is an error because one cannot judge the developmental significance of something until one has analysed what that something is in its grown form. Thus James complained that religious experience is often pooh-poohed in psychology because it is said by experts to be caused by certain (mal)functions of the brain or oddities of sexual experience in childhood. Questions of quiddity are displaced by "how come?" From this it follows that the first step in any developmental analysis must be to describe the collective *fruits* of the human psychogenetic process in maturity, however glorious or inglorious these fruits may be.

By their fruits shall ye know them, not by their roots. (James, 1903: 25)

In psychology, early is not necessarily deep. For we must contrast what occurs at the start of life, which, being at so great a historical distance, may now be of little relevance to the adult's actual experience, with what lies "under an especially heavy weight of repression" in that experience, repression which the infant does not have the maturity to register (Winnicott, 1957). Yet development has become synonymous with ontogeny in psychology (Morss, 1990). Almost as a principle of logic, and despite compelling evidence (e.g., Kaye, 1982), the first few years of life are thought to determine what follows. The past determines the present. This relationship is also presumed to predict the future of course, therefore removing it from the equation: the future being taken to be determined by the present and therefore like the present in being determined by the past (Figure 4.1).

"The principal content of American psychology is developmental psychology: what happened to you earlier is the cause of what happened to you later. That's the basic theory: our history is our causality. We don't even separate history as story from history as cause. So you have to go back to childhood to get at why you are the way you are," write Hillman and Ventura (1993: 17). Or further. To our genes, to our evolutionary history, to a species-specific mechanism in the brain, to conceptual DNA – billiard-ball causality being the only acceptable explanation.

What gets lost in the genetic approach is any sense of the many difficulties inherent in understanding the present in its own right. Yet, the meaning we give to the past emerges from the dynamics of the present (cf. James, 1890;

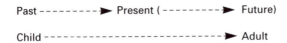

Figure 4.1   *The genetic conception of developmental time*

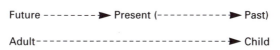

Figure 4.2 *The meaning of the present depends on what is yet to happen*

Freud, 1899).[2] And the way we understand the present gets part of its quality from what we make of the future (Michael, 1996).[3] See Figure 4.2. Thus we are likely to be critical of the past if we are dissatisfied with the present and want things to change in the future. On the other hand, if we are content for things to continue as they are, then we are likely to be content to describe the past, not criticize it. Only when we recognize the contested quality of the present as it bears on the future will we recognize that the meaning of the past, and of child development, is not fixed but radically ambiguous (Bradley, 1989, Ch. 10).

"Children are our future" say the bumper-stickers. "Child is father to the man!" enthuse the psychologists. No. Man is father to the child. And until we have some way to define and change the ways that adult relationships constitute "the infant" as topic of inquiry, we may as well bracket off the study of the child in attempts to understand the possibilities and constraints of human progress. After all, one thing certain about early childhood is that, once we have subtracted immediate experience, the meaning of an individual's infancy will very much depend on what happens to that infant in the world that governs its later life. We come across a bunch of abused children. One becomes a prominent physicist. A second suicides. The third becomes a repeat-abuser. The fourth becomes an agent of change. We cannot see until later what was significant about the abuse in each case. Indeed, in many cases of mature intelligence, it may not be helpful to think particular abuse had *any* particular effect (as Levett, 1992, uses her data to show).

Or imagine that I am producing a sentence. You won't know what this sentence means until my last word. The meaning of what we say at a religious or political meeting, or write in this book, depends in an important part on what later succeeds. Likewise, much of the excitement of watching a sporting contest, a piece of theater, of reading a book, of attending a course is the excitement of not knowing the extent to which what has been learned by the end of the event will make changes in the way one sees things now. "The truth is what is destined to be found out in an ideal community of inquirers" (Peirce, 1882).

A developmental psychology in the spirit of Peirce and Thoreau, of Tracey Chapman and Luce Irigaray, of William Blake, Mary Wollstonecraft (1792) and Erasmus Darwin (1803), of Luxemburg and Kierkegaard (Cupitt, 1983)? Then we would see the present as a time when what has happened hitherto could be re-understood and transformed in the light of what might better happen in future. In this spirit, development would refer less to the ladder of stages that each individual is supposed to have climbed to attain maturity, than to the personal, collective, and institutional changes which are prerequisites for the transition to a more rational and equitable use of resources, minimization of destructive conflicts, and the enlargement of the realm of freedom (e.g., Marcuse, 1969).

But how are we to move toward such a developmental discipline? A first step, if psychologists are to overcome the genetic fallacy, is to find an alternative to the subject-position from which we traditionally view human behavior. The next section presents a reading of Charles Darwin's work to illustrate the poetic that creates this traditional subject-position. Darwin pioneered a way of discussing human behavior without reference to the varieties of individual experience. His language sets the scientist above moral and political debate and makes psychological development the analog of biological evolution. I suggest that the form of Darwin's language makes psychologists heirs to the Romantic sublime.

How Darwin Lost his Awe

When Darwin grew old, he took up his pen to write a memoir for his family by recollecting his "development of mind." In a life of widely acclaimed scientific achievement, he records one odd regret. He had lost his taste for beauty. Trying to describe his growing "disgust" for music, fine art, and Shakespeare, and his attenuated response to Nature, he connected it with the decline in his belief in God. He had become uncomfortably numb, "a kind of machine for grinding general laws out of large collections of facts" (Darwin, 1958: 139). And he explained his previous love of Nature, of Art, and of God as manifestations of a sense in his brain that had long since "atrophied" his sense of awe, or what he more rigorously called his sense of "sublimity" (1958: 91).

This section is in five parts. The first part outlines the three phases of the sublime as found in Romantic poetry and links them to Darwin's (1859) project in *On the Origin of Species*. The next two parts analyse Darwin's writings to illustrate his attitude to Nature before and after he had constructed his theory of evolution. The fourth part shows how the sublime position from which Darwin's theory views human behavior results in a pedagogy of the expert, distanced from others' experience. The final part links this position to an idealizing emphasis on the past in developmental psychology.

Analysis of the Sublime

The idea of the sublime was common in Darwin's youth (Manier, 1978). It particularly referred to the subjective consequences of awe produced by the overwhelming power of Nature. Kant was its pre-eminent philosopher. For Kant (1790), the inability of Mind to represent the infinity or unattainability of Nature, leads Mind to posit a new transcendent realm of meaning, ultimately undefinable – the sublime. It was as if the classical age of the Enlightenment had driven God ever further from immediate human experience to create the space in which the sublime came into its own. The sublime was a victory snatched from reason's defeat, a paradoxical affirmation of the boundlessness of the human spirit, arising from a confrontation with human limitations.

The dynamics of the sublime are typified in a passage of Wordsworth's *Prelude* (1805). Striving to cross the backbone of the Alps with a friend, the young Wordsworth got lost. Suddenly they found themselves on the brink of a great gorge. All at once they were confronted with immeasurable height, tumultuous sound, brightness, storm, torrents falling from black drizzling crags – "the giddy prospect of the raving stream." It proves too much for Wordsworth. His senses are usurped by Nature. But, through the struggle for expression that later gives rise to the poetry of the *Prelude*, there is revealed to him another order of meaning: the sublime.

> I was lost;
> Halted without an effort to break through;
> But to my conscious soul I now can say –
> 'I recognise thy glory:' in such strength
> Of usurpation, when the light of sense
> Goes out, but with a flash that has revealed
> The invisible world, doth greatness make abode,
> There harbours; whether we be young or old,
> Our destiny, our being's heart and home,
> Is with infinitude, and only there . . .

The poet's personal experience of an infinite Nature has overpowered his senses, stunned him into passivity. But, in retrospect, this experience creates a faith in the author's own boundlessness, *his own* exaltation to the spectra of infinitude.

Criticism of Wordsworth by fellow Romantics like Keats and Blake, whilst recognizing his achievements as a poet, deplored Wordsworth's philosophy. In Keats's (1819) phrase, Wordsworth's sublime was self-aggrandizing: an "egotistical" sublime. Modern critics of the Romantic sublime have taken a more psychological approach (e.g., Bloom, 1973). Preeminent amongst them is Thomas Weiskel (1976).

Weiskel parses the sublime diachronically: dissecting production of poetry such as Wordsworth's into a sequence of three phases. Phase one is of habitual perception: smooth fit between inner and outer, Mind and World. So, before losing their path, the *Prelude* tells of an unbroken harmony between observers and observed as they were contentedly clambering upwards among the unfolding Alps: "What'er in this wide circuit we beheld,/Or heard, was fitted to our unripe state/Of intellect and heart."

Phase two is a knock-out. The subject is overcome by uncertainty. Correspondence breaks down and we are drowned in the dread that doubt first brings. Sense is overwhelmed. Suddenly, as in the Gondo Gorge, the cosmic explorer is astonished, overawed, humiliated by a scene or text. Or "like stout Cortez, when with wondering eyes/He star'd at the Pacific, and all his Men/Look'd at each other with a wild surmise/Silent on a Peak in Darien" (Keats, 1817).

In phase three, Mind recovers the balance of inner with outer by constituting a fresh relation between itself and the object. Here the very indeterminacy which erupted in phase two is taken as symbolizing the mind's relation to a transcendent order (Weiskel, 1976: 24). Previously, baulked, the author rebounds to decide that his own soul, his own destiny is "with infinitude."

The implication I draw from Weiskel is that the mental attitude depicted by the mature Wordsworth is of the same ilk as the attitude to reality of the modern scientist (cf. Clifford and Marcus, 1986).[4] And what makes that attitude? What happens to a certain kind of mind whenever its objects or signifiers begin to crystallize too distinctly, to stand out in too sharp a relief from the continuities which normally subdue them? As if warned, the mind will begin to "spread its thoughts," to avert the lingering which could deepen into obsessive fixation (Weiskel, 1976: 29). The Romantic sublime rescues Mind from an excess of meaning, as experienced by Wordsworth in the Gondo Gorge. It puts a stress on continuity. It stretches significance out across the world, as if all were one.

The uniqueness of distinct sensible impressions is suppressed in favor of the writer's own will to understand. Wordsworth's is a poetry in which awe at Nature's alien grandeur has been transformed to bespeak the grandeur of the author's own vision of humanity, of his great destiny. A Nature that had seemed at first too different, too active, overwhelmingly powerful, has been reduced to an illustration of Wordsworth's own philosophy. The sublime melts the formal otherness of things, reducing them to material or substance. The formal properties of the perceived particular are cancelled and replaced by their universal "significance," values assessed and assigned by the author's mind (Weiskel, 1976: 59).

Modern psychology is indebted to Darwin for just such a transformation of its subject-matter. The new "view of things" that Darwin's (1859) *Origin* bequeathed to the study of mental life justified the materialistic gradualism that James (1890: 152) damned in his eloquent but doomed rearguard action against what he called "mind-stuff" theories. "*Natura non facit saltum*" was Darwin's (1859) favorite theoretical maxim. And if Nature doesn't make leaps, then a Darwinian psychology can recognize no differences of kind in its treatment of the phenomena that come under its investigation. A Darwinian psychology can give no sense that the "nerve-world" may differ in quality from the "mind-world."[5] Hence consciousness, says James, "is an illegitimate birth in any philosophy that starts without it, and yet professes to explain all facts by continuous evolution." Either it must have been there from the beginning at the big bang ("the appeal to the polyp") or it is beyond the reach of Darwinian explanation.[6]

Darwin's poetic, the life he led, the language he wrote, was just as much informed by a poetic of the three-phase sublime as Wordsworth's. But Darwin's success went beyond Wordsworth's. For he adapted the sublime to new uses, uses that enabled him to avoid in the name of Science the kind of political skulduggery and ecclesiastical furore that had sunk the work of previous evolutionary writers.[7] Darwin's work was vehicle for a Victorian imperialism that, in order to justify itself, needed to remake the history of the world in its own image, with scientific rather than moral argument as ultimate arbiter. Most crucially, the poetic Charles Darwin developed allowed Victorian science to challenge a central narrative of Western culture, the Genesis stories of Creation, at its most sensitive point, the dynamics and origin of spirit and the highest human faculties, without seeming so to do. As Beer (1983: 8, 51) writes, "it was essential to Darwin's project that it should be accepted not as invention, but description." Thus, at first sight, Darwin's *Origin* seemed merely to be reporting in a culture-cleansed way an objective array of dry facts. But, Beer goes on, "evolutionary theory is first a form of imaginative history. It cannot be experimentally demonstrated sufficiently in any present moment." Hence, read more critically, the *Origin* is primarily a work of imagination. Frequently Darwin is forced to ask his readers to imagine a scenario from the past so that he can illustrate a point (e.g., 1859: 90). In fact, the culminating illustration in his famous chapter on Natural Selection is both abstract and entirely imaginary. It takes the form of a long commentary on a family-tree of "the species of a genus large in its own country" (see Figure 4.3).

The next four subsections of this essay link the imaginative dynamic underlying Darwin's mature view of Nature (including the human mind) to the sublime. In the first, it is shown how Darwin was overwhelmed by the grandeur of Nature. The next discusses the way that Darwin was led to distance himself from this experience by seeing Nature as produced by scientific laws which were themselves supremely grand. The penultimate subsection links the imperial theoretical position Darwin adopts to his use of an expert voice. Finally, it is shown how the denial of others' experience and a developmental emphasis on the past are corrollaries of the subject-position Darwin devised, and, by implication, of any psychology which takes up a similar model of science in commenting on human behavior.

The Grandeur of the Brazilian Rain Forest

The first step in drawing a parallel between Wordsworth's sublime and the work of Darwin is to show that Darwin's initial experience of Nature was, like Wordsworth in the Gondo Gorge, one of awe. I draw my evidence from Darwin's diary of his voyage in the *Beagle*.

In his autobiography Darwin described the months leading up to HMS *Beagle*'s departure as "the most miserable I ever spent." Waiting in Plymouth Sound, he was constantly sea-sick, cramped, lonely, and spasmodically subject to terrifying heart attacks (now thought to be psychosomatic; Bowlby, 1990). The only thing that did not fail to excite Darwin's anticipation was the grandeur of the scenery he expected to see. After escaping the *Beagle* one day for a walk along the Plymouth cliffs, he wrote:

> There is no pleasure equal to that which fine scenery & exercise creates, it is to this I look forward with more enthusiasm than any other part of the voyage. (December 1831; Darwin, 1988: 15)

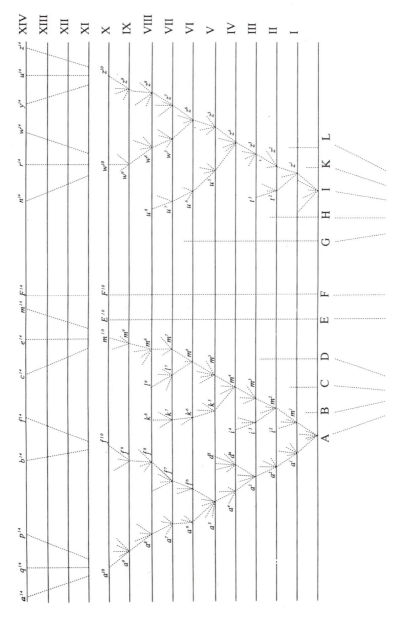

Figure 4.3   *"Let A to L represent the species of a genus large in its own country; these species are supposed to resemble each other in unequal degrees, as is so generally the case in nature, and as is represented in the diagram by the letters standing at unequal distances"* (Darwin, 1859: 116).

The first months of 1832 saw Darwin record the many vexations of the *Beagle*'s crossing of the Atlantic. Yet one senses a rising undercurrent of expectation. He was re-reading the German explorer Humboldt's *Personal Narrative*:

> The night does its best to soothe our sorrow; the air is still and deliciously warm . . . Already I can understand Humboldt's enthusiasm about the tropical nights; the sky is so clear & lofty, & stars innumerable shine so bright, that like little moons, they cast their glitter on the waves. (6 January, 1832; Darwin, 1988: 22)

The Cape Verde Islands gave him a glimpse of the expected glory, but the glimpse soon faded. Two weeks later, on the isle of Fernando, he was carping vociferously. Its forest was very beautiful and "ought to have satisfied me. But I am sure all the grandeur of the Tropics has not yet been seen by me. We had no gaudy birds, no humming birds, no large flowers . . ." (19 February, 1832; Darwin, 1988: 36). Finally, in Bahia, he got his fill:

> 28th [February 1832] . . . About 11 o'clock we entered the bay of All Saints, on the northern side of which is situated the town of Bahia . . . It would be difficult [to] imagine, before seeing this view, any thing so magnificent. . . . The town is fairly embosomed in a luxuriant wood & situated on a steep bank overlooks the calm waters of the great bay of All Saints. . . . But these beauties are as nothing compared to the Vegetation; I believe from what I have seen Humboldt's glorious descriptions are & will for ever be unparalleled: but even he with his dark blue skies & the rare union of poetry which he so strongly displays when writing on tropical scenery, with all this falls far short of the truth. The delight one experiences in such times bewilders the mind; if the eye attempts to follow the flight of a gaudy butterfly, it is arrested by some strange tree or fruit; if watching an insect one forgets it in the strange flower it is crawling over. . . . The mind is a chaos of delight, out of which a world of future & more quiet pleasure will arise. I am at present fit only to read Humboldt; he like another sun illumines everything I behold. (Darwin, 1988: 37–8)

Notwithstanding a further four years of adventure, the Brazilian rain forest kept its place as Darwin's touchstone for natural grandeur. Returning in 1836 for a last glimpse of tropical America, Darwin (1988: 377) found that his awe for tropical scenery "had not decreased even in the slightest degree . . . epithet after epithet is found too weak to convey to those who have not had an opportunity of experiencing these sensations, a true picture of the mind" (Darwin, 1988: 378). This sounds like phase two of the Romantic sublime. Darwin is overawed by the infinite grandeur of the forest. He is knocked out. Words fail him. Yet he looks forward to creating a world of future and more quiet pleasure out of this extraordinary knock-out blow. He seeks a "mechanism" that will explain and thereby contain the unsettling chaos of delight, a mechanism that he was later to dub "sublimely grand" (Desmond and Moore, 1991: 330).

The Grandeur of "My Theory"

I now trace how Darwin was led to elevate himself above the experience of awe at Nature's profusion by recasting Nature as subject to the reign of scientific laws. Darwin's experience in the jungle set in motion not just a subjective but a literary dynamic. Darwin first expressed the jungle's extra-ordinariness, not in scientific terms, but as overwhelming his capacities for poetic language. Nature was an even greater text than Humboldt! Darwin's two decades of slog towards constructing the argument that finally found form in the quickly written *Origin* of 1859, can be seen, therefore, as at least partly esthetic or literary in character. This is the third phase in Darwin's long haul towards constructing for the Victorians a new kind of psycho-logical sublime.

Hence Darwin fought his battle on two fronts. First, he sought a way of explaining the teeming generations of Nature by fixed laws, thereby intel-lectually and imaginatively to reappropriate what at first was so over-whelming – to fight nature on nature's own ground, as Bloom (1973: 9) describes it. But Nature is never just Nature, where authorship is concerned. It is always something represented in a certain way. To fight against Nature is equally to fight against the way one's literary precursors have represented Nature. So Darwin had to do more than devise laws. He had to recast the huge weight of anthropocentric theology and poetic myth-making that shrouded pre-evolutionary understandings of human origins. He had to find a way to write against the grain of a language that valued design and took for granted godhead, in order to express his theories of production (Beer and Martins, 1990: 168).

Witness in this regard the *Origin*'s (1859: 489–90) final paragraph. It starts by inviting us to contemplate an English hedgerow, an entangled bank, a bank described as a complex web of affinities, an interdependent multitude of contrasting species, birds and birdsong, insects flitting, and worms crawl-ing through the damp earth. Here is the Brazilian jungle again, but attenu-ated, without the brilliance, modulated to a more prosaic English key. Matter of factly, and in the same breath, we are told that this multiplicity has all been produced by the fixed action of natural laws "acting around us." The laws are enumerated. Prominent amongst them being "a Ratio of Increase so high as to lead to a Struggle for Life, and as a consequence, Natural Selection, entailing Divergence of Character and the Extinction of less-improved forms." At the last, lest we think that Darwin's reworking of the Bible's Genesis stories had drained the cosmos of its glory, we are invited to reconsider:

> Thus, from the war of nature, from famine and death, the most exalted object which we are capable of conceiving, namely, the production of the higher animals, directly follows. There is a grandeur in this view of life, with its several powers, having been originally breathed into a few forms or into one; and that, whilst this planet has gone cycling on according to fixed laws of gravity, from so simple a beginning endless forms most beautiful and most wonderful have been, and are being, evolved. (1859: 90)

Here is Darwin, grasping subjectively to reappropriate the awe which had him aghast in the Brazilian undergrowth. Here the chaotic profusion of the rain forest is at last subsumed and made as one by the reign of laws dis-covered through science. No longer would he be overwhelmed by what he had once called the grandeur of Nature. Darwin now claims that the grandeur attaches to "my theory," *his own* "view of things." The *Origin*'s rationality and imagery had contained and conquered what had seemed in the jungle so super-significant as to be tantamount to proof of God's existence. By extending the reign of natural laws, he reasserted the continuities that the exotic forest had shaken. At the same time, his language recast the religious poetry to which his text was heir: the herb yielding seed after its kind, the fowls that may fly above the earth, and the creeping thing that creepeth upon the earth. Life begins, as in the Bible, with powers being breathed into the dust of the ground. There is even a hint of the Gospel story, with famine and death leading to "the most exalted object we are capable of conceiving."

Darwin's law took the place of the law of Creation. His was a genius which had out-guessed the immortals. Meek he might be, but his vision transcended even the greatest heights of previous authorship.

> Authors of the highest eminence seem to be fully satisfied with the view that each species has been independently created. To my mind it accords better with what we know of the laws impressed on matter by the Creator, that the production and extinction of the past and present inhabitants of the world should have been due to secondary causes, like those determining the birth and death of the individual. When I view all beings not as special creations, but as the lineal descendants of some few beings which lived long before the first bed of the Silurian system was deposited, they seem to me to become ennobled . . . Etc. (1859: 488–9)

Like Keats's (1820) Apollo, "knowledge enormous" had put him on a footing with God.

Pedagogy as a Cult of the Expert

While Darwin's awe at Nature was triggered by the chaotic profusion of the jungle, it also evinced the liveliness of his imagination. A key theme in the *Origin* is Darwin's aim to reshape this dynamic in his readers, to repress the sensitivity of the imagination when confronted by sensual excess and to tame our wonder at the infinite complexity and perfections of Nature.

> He who will go thus far, if he find on finishing this treatise that large bodies of facts, otherwise inexplicable, can be explained by the theory of descent, ought not to hesitate to go further, and to admit that a structure even as perfect as the eye of an eagle might be formed by natural selection, although in this case he does not know the transitional grades. *His reason ought to conquer his imagination*; . . . (1859: 188; emphasis added)

We must not look at organic being "as a savage looks at a ship, as at something wholly beyond his comprehension." Rather, we should invoke our faith in the ubiquitous reign of natural law, even where we have no supporting evidence!

This maneuver is adopted time and again in the *Origin*. Right from the start, Darwin tells us that, to prove his case, he would have to publish a vast host of facts "with references" as evidence. This he is unable to do for want of space. Time and again he tells us that he has the necessary long arrays of dry facts.

He has spent twenty years gathering them. But their publication is delayed. In the meantime, he writes, "I must trust to the reader reposing some confidence in my accuracy" (1859: 2). From then on we constantly meet such sentences as "I can only repeat my assurance that I do not speak without good evidence."[8]

This way of writing sets up a crucial dynamic in the reader. Each reader is led to retrace Darwin's path to his sublime. Awe at Nature is to give way to an interest in the accumulation of objective data that are grist for scientific law. To achieve this end, Darwin's book sets up a strong cult of the expert. Right from his opening discussion of the breeding of distinct varieties of domesticated animals like pigeons, sheep, and horses, Darwin introduces the idea that there is an enormous gap between the differences visible to an educated and an uneducated eye, differences which, he adds disarmingly, in deference to pigeon-fanciers, "I for one have vainly attempted to appreciate."

In the same way, when Darwin quotes others, as he often does, these are ushered in with some laudatory phrase, as "the highest authority, Prof. Dana," "the most eminent geologists" and other such "highly competent judges." On the principle that only the best associate with the best, we end up thinking that, as an expert on his chosen topic, evolution, Darwin must be an impeccable source. Our dependence on Darwin's expertise is endlessly solicited as, paragraph after paragraph, we are given, not evidence, but Darwin's reading of the evidence. It is this which accounts for the omnipresence in the *Origin* of the first person singular that amused his contemporaries (Gaull, 1979): "I strongly suspect," "I believe," "I cannot enter here into the details necessary to support this view . . . but I can see no reason to doubt that." We get the impression, as Butler (1880) complained, that Darwin has come up with the idea of evolution *de novo*, solely by congress with the rocks, without reference to forerunners, though his notebooks show this to be far from the case (Bradley, 1994).

Darwin is not debating his topic with others. He is a gifted and highly trained judge, a solitary observer, a genius even, who has been "much struck with certain facts" (1859: 1). He has looked long and hard at Nature and he is telling what he sees, namely, "that all the forms of life, ancient and recent, make together one grand system; for all are connected by generation" (1859: 344). In the process, he turns what was formerly his defect, his incapacity to make sense of the profusion of Nature, into his chief advantage. Again and again he stresses that his readers are profoundly ignorant of the many aspects of Nature that most directly bear on his theory. "It deserves especial notice that the more important questions are those on which we are confessedly ignorant; nor do we know how ignorant we are" (1859: 466). But he, Darwin, has transcended our ignorance. He has perceived the one grand system. Given our ignorance and his expertise, it is hard to gainsay him.

Repercussions for Modern Psychology

Historians have increasingly stressed that the success of the *Origin* can be seen as carried forward by a great sea-change in the politics of the educated public and in scientific opinion about a whole range of issues, including Mind. Gruber and Barrett (1974) and Desmond and Moore (1991), for example, show how anxious Darwin was about inciting the moral indignation of his peers with his heterodox views during the seventeen years between his first writing them down and his first publishing them. In this regard, Darwin's unexpected receipt of the paper by Alfred Russel Wallace in 1858, making an independent case for evolution by natural selection, that spurred him into publishing *On the Origin of Species*, did not simply threaten to pre-empt Darwin as chief prophet of the new creed. It also suggested that, at last, the time was ripe for the safe publication of his views.

But, while Darwin's success was, from one side, merely that of the cork first brought to shore by a turning cultural tide, his long-held fear of controversy was also at the crux of *the form* of the *Origin*. Darwin's aversion to politico-philosophical debate makes a divorce between fact and value basic to the book's construction, not to mention that of its more overtly psychological sequels (Darwin, 1872, 1877). This divorce is achieved by the apparent immediacy of Darwin's contacts with Nature, for example, the way that he is repeatedly and directly "struck" by "great classes of fact." Darwin believed that unmediated observation of the kind at which he excelled could effectively bypass any need for philosophical debate. No one would have to puzzle over the constitution of human knowledge if "He who understands baboon would do more toward metaphysics than Locke" (Darwin, 16 August, 1838). Natural history should decide the ultimate questions of epistemology. And in natural history knowledge is simple and straightforward.

Darwin's was at bottom a materialistic doctrine. "The mind is function of body," not vice versa (Darwin, 1838). But in the *Origin*, Darwin was "very far from wishing to obtrude" his materialistic beliefs (Darwin and Darwin, 1887: 263). The *Origin* was thus, covertly, the thin end of a wedge, a wedge of which an essential aim was confessedly to inaugurate a new gradualistic psychology:

> In the distant future I see open fields for far more important researches. Psychology will be based on a new foundation, that of the necessary acquirement of each mental power and capacity by gradation. (Darwin, 1859: 488)

And it was all the more effective for being thin: the book mentions psychology just this once. Hence, while the psychological sublime aggrandizes *the subject* of inquiry, its impact on *the object* of investigation is to subjugate it to the rule of natural law and thereby to melt the threatening otherness of others. The sublime reduces the awesome mystery of (human) Nature to material or substance. It makes the mind into what James called mind-dust. This can be seen in Darwin's own psychological work. His book on emotion, for example, is very largely a comparison between the anatomy of the facial muscles that effect emotional expressions in adults, babies, animals, and the insane. How the individual experiences emotions is neither here nor there (Darwin, 1872).

How was Darwin to justify his materialism to psychologists? It was crucial that he prove "the several moral and mental faculties of man have been gradually evolved" (1901: 194). But there could be no fossils to support the assertion. The best evidence, he said, was to study the development of children, which was at least analogous to evolution. "That such evolution is at least possible ought not to be denied, for we daily see these faculties developing in every infant" (1901: 194). The child study movement was to take up this suggestion with gusto (cf. Darwin, 1877). Before long, the dominant idea in developmental psychology was Haeckel's (1874) "biogenetic law:" that ontogeny recapitulates phylogeny. And it has remained so (Morss, 1990). In making the stages of the evolution of the human species the cause of stages of child development, this law had the effect of making all information about the development of children evidence for what happened *in the past*, in evolution (Costall, 1985). Child study, like the natural history of the baboon, is a study of the ladder by which we have climbed towards the heights of human intelligence, heights upon which, in a flattering self-affirmation, the scientist reigns supreme.

Reconstructing Psychological Pedagogy

If we are to change the way the sublime leads psychologists to a stance of being above the turbulence of their own subjectivities and of treating others as objects, we must change the way that psychology is taught. The main model of pedagogy in psychology, as in higher education as a whole, is still governed by the sublime, the cult of the expert, wall-to-wall monologue. The aggrandizement of the individual knower, the expert, has as its corollary the almost complete silencing, the passivation of the expert's audience. The learner's highest goal is commonly conceived as being accurately to regurgitate the knowledge that the expert has banked in them. The very material architecture of our culture, the seats bolted down in parallel in even the newest of our lecture theaters, reinforces this "banking" model of pedagogy (Freire, 1970; on pedagogic architecture, cf. Walkerdine, 1984).

Such an attitude may work well in disciplines like biology or physics, where the focus of interest can more easily be thought of as material. But do we not need a different kind of relationship between knower and known if we are to learn about the mind? Should the knowledge we acquire in psychology not serve as a route that leads us out of passivity into active critique of the oppressions that bind and silence us? This section briefly surveys some affirmative answers that educators have devised to these questions.

Each of these answers shows a similar disestablishment of the psychologist as expert, such that the teacher is no more likely to know in advance the outcome of an educational course, and no less likely to learn from it, than any other participant. Thus ecological psychologists have built up a considerable range of participatory workshops and transformational rituals designed to awaken or reaffirm a commitment to the defense of our natural environment against the depradations of profiteers and cultural neglect (e.g., Seed et al., 1988). These techniques are just as likely to be of value to old campaigners as to initiates (Bragg, 1995).

Elsewhere Bronwyn Davies (1994) has developed a technique described by Haug (1987) into a classroom strategy she calls "collective biography." Here a group will choose to investigate a common topic: for example, the acquisition of genderedness or of the emotions of shame or guilt, or one's positioning in specific discourses such as the discourse of romantic love. Each individual then writes an account of their own idiosyncratic experiences that bear on the topic and then shares their account with the rest of the group. Once the accounts have been pooled, discussion is led to show how each individual's experiences reflect common ways of organizing experience and behavior. Students and teachers

> can examine the construction of their own biography as something at the same time experienced as personal and their own – woven out of their own body/minds – and yet visibly made out of, even determined by, materials and practices not originating from them. (Davies, 1994: 83–4)

As a result, participants are led to see which social practices need to be changed if their own personal dissatisfactions are to be alleviated. For oppressions are often so internalized within an individual that they have become a "cop in the head." We must therefore aim to help each other track down those oppressions with which more than one can identify, oppressions which can be generalized and brought into the theater of change.

Other educators have adapted theatrical techniques to this end (e.g., Griffiths, 1990). For example, my own teaching methods are based on the work of Augusto Boal. Responding to Freire's (1970: 41) insistence that the oppressed engage in reflection on their concrete situation as their means by which to enter collectively into critical and liberating dialogue that transforms action, Boal's (1974, 1992) Theater of the Oppressed was first worked out as a means by which Brazilian village folk living in a brutal military dictatorship could come up with means by which to effect social change. Boal contrasts his poetics with Aristotle. For Boal, Aristotle's *Poetics*, in which poetry is taken to be independent of politics, nevertheless constructs the first, extremely powerful poetic-political system for the intimidation of the spectator, for elimination of the "bad" or illegal tendencies of the audience (by means of catharsis). This system, he says, is still in use, not just in conventional theater, but in TV soap operas, the "news", and in Western films as well. Movies, theater, and television are united, through a common basis in Aristotelian poetics, in repression of the people's recognition of the need for social change.

As in collective biography and Seed's "Council of All Beings," Boal's poetics of the oppressed assumes that many of the deepest distortions experienced in the context of the intersubjectivity which defines any liberatory process are a product of bodily dispositions organized into collective practices. The doorway to a psychology that takes development to be party to social progress is to recognize and change these psychosomatic practices. Boal's (1974) work suggests three main techniques: Image Theater, Invisible Theater, and Forum Theater. By way of illustration I will say a few words on each.

Image Theater is a series of exercises and games designed to uncover important truths about societies and cultures without resort, in the first instance, to spoken language (though this may be added in the various "dynamizations" of the images). The participants in Image Theater make still images of their lives, feelings, experiences, oppressions; groups suggest titles or themes, and then individuals "sculpt" three-dimensional images under these titles, using their own and others' bodies as the clay. However, the image work never remains static. As with all of the Theater of the Oppressed, the frozen image is simply the starting point for or prelude to the action, which is revealed in the dynamization process, the bringing to life of the images and the discovery of whatever direction or intention is implicit in them.

Beginning with bodies rather than words draws on the fact that many of our deepest oppressions are reproduced through a symbolism that is never explicitly spoken. This is the realm of unconscious symbolism that Voloshinov (1927: 88) called "behavioral ideology" to distinguish it from those realms ruled by consciously formulated ideas: law, art, science, religion, government. Behavioral ideology, said Voloshinov, is more volatile, more sensitive and more responsive than an ideology that has undergone conscious explication. It is the site where the deepest contradictions in a culture accumulate. To raise awareness of this usually hidden realm of bodily meanings is therefore to challenge the deep political implications of our most familiar daily routines.

In teaching according to Boalian principles, I have found students raise issues rarely canvassed in traditional modules of their psychology degree. Incidents will be taken from experiences of the repressions implicit in typical family scenarios, in the difficulties of mourning, in anxieties about speaking and writing in their own voice, in disempowerment in the classroom, in the dynamics of dating (which both genders often sculpt as oppressive!), in the forbidden rituals surrounding drugs, and in dominance by research-supervisors.

The polysemy of images is a vital factor in this work. A group of individuals will perceive a whole range of different, but often intriguingly related meanings within a single image, often seeing things which the sculptors had no idea were there. Working with images, sculpting rather than talking, can also be more democratic, as it does not privilege more verbally articulate people. Image Theater can be used in the preparation of Invisible Theater or Forum Theater, and is central to the more recent therapeutic work, the subject of Boal's next book, *Méthode Boal de théâtre et de thérapie – l'arc-en-ciel du désir* (Jackson, 1992: xx).

Invisible Theater is public theater which involves the public as participants in the action without knowing it (but with a different intention from Garfinkel's, 1967). They are the "spect-actors," the active spectators, of a piece of theater, but while it is happening, and usually even after the event, they do not know that this is theater rather than "real life" (though of course it is "real life" too). For example, in Brazil, a man in Boal's group went to a shop with street frontage, with a woman friend, and started trying on women's dresses. Another actor, as part of the gathering crowd, expressed loud indignation at this "perversion," while a third actor took the cross-dresser's part – why shouldn't he wear women's clothes if he wants to . . . in no time at all a crowd is involved in heated discussion. Invisible Theater is a way of using theater to stimulate public debate, getting people to question issues in a public forum. It might be compared to agit-prop street theater, with the essential difference that the audience is free to take up any position it wants, and has no feeling of being preached at. It asks questions without dictating answers. Theater of the Oppressed is never didactic to its audience; it involves a process of learning together rather than one-way teaching. *It assumes that there is as much likelihood of the audience knowing the answers as the performers.*

Forum Theater is a theatrical game in which a problem is shown in an unsolved form, to which the audience, again spect-actors, is invited to suggest and enact solutions (e.g., Gergen and Gergen, 1996). The problem is always the symptom of an oppression, and generally involves visible oppressors and a protagonist who is oppressed. In its purest form, both actors and spect-actors will be people who are victims of the oppression under consideration; that is why they are able to offer alternative solutions, because they themselves are personally acquainted with the oppression. After one showing of the scene, which is known as "the model" (it can be a full-length play), it is shown again slightly speeded-up, and follows exactly the same course until a member of the audience shouts "Stop!", takes the place of the protagonist and tries to defeat the oppressors. The game is a form of contest between spect-actors trying to bring the play to a different end (in which the cycle of oppression is broken) and actors ostensibly making every possible effort to bring it to its original end in which oppressors triumph over the oppressed. Its aim is again to stimulate debate (in the form of action, not just words), to show alternatives, to enable people to "become protagonists in their own lives" (Jackson, 1992: xxi–xxii).

As discussed in the previous parts of this chapter, psychologists traditionally investigate development in a way that denies the possibility of future change by assuming the present to be always already fixed by dynamics set in the past. If psychology is to reconstruct its relationship to the reproduction of the present, then psychology needs to change the way it reproduces itself. It needs to create a space for experience in which subjects can become aware of the obstacles that collectively serve to impede their development. No longer can the psychologist be "the one supposed to know," imposing knowledge from above. They must find a way of accessing the "view from below." Which means they must find a way of undoing the hegemony of the sublime, in pedagogy as well as research (Bradley and Selby, 1996).

The educational strategies reviewed in this section are not intended to be exhaustive or definitive in this regard. Rather they are meant to illustrate the kinds of technique that need to come under discussion if we are to devise a lasting and effective emancipatory approach to the development of mental life.

Conclusion

This essay contrasts two ways of talking about psychological change. We may either talk about change as something that happens to an individual according to a plan that has always already been determined in the past. Or we may talk about change as something that might be collectively striven for in the present with an eye to transforming the future. Both kinds of talk have a history in the discipline (Bradley, 1994; Cahan and White, 1992). But to date, developmental psychology has been dominated by the vision of change that applies to individuals and is fixed in the past. My point has been to analyse the hegemony of the past in psychological discussions of change as a prelude to exploring the implications of seeing psychology as an emancipatory discipline that fosters collective development arising out of an analysis of the often oppressive dynamics of the present.

Why are psychologists so deaf to the voices of the downtrodden? How has it taken decades of struggle by feminists to persuade developmentalists that children widely suffer oppression and abuse? What is the subject-position psychologists traditionally adopt that has allowed them to conduct countless pieces of research on children, and to spend countless hours assessing and therapeutizing the old and the young, without finding out about the incidence of incest or the prevalence of domestic violence in contemporary society, now described as "epidemic" by the American Medical Association (Gilligan, 1994)?

I have suggested that psychologists' traditional deafness to others' oppressions has three facets. First is the fatalistic assumption that developmental explanation must take the form of a natural history of the individual's past. Second is the belief that psychological knowledge must be based in a series of procedures that distance the knower from the subject-matter under investigation. And third is the idea that psychology can be lived, taught, and researched without reference to the dynamics of personal experience in teacher, student, or subject, however nodal these experiences may be acknowledged to be within the individual's private self-understanding. Each of these characteristics can be traced to the dominance of one form of linguistic practice in psychology.

I illustrated the dynamics of this practice by analysing the approach to mind taken by Charles Darwin, widely recognized to be a founding figure in modern psychology, particularly by developmentalists (Bronfenbrenner et al., 1986). These dynamics bear a close resemblance to the dynamics of the Romantic sublime. I have argued that, until the hegemony of the sublime is broken in psychological teaching (not just research), moves to reconstruct psychology as a more efficacious means of promoting human welfare will fail. To this end, I have briefly surveyed some different ideas for the reconstruction of an emancipatory pedagogical practice in psychology, dwelling at greatest length on techniques drawn from Boal's theater of the oppressed.

I conclude that unless we change the way that psychologists reproduce the discipline in their practice, attempts at reconstruction will have little real impact in the body politic. As it stands, psychologists "have bought [their] own freedom at the cost of everyone else's soul – a truly Faustian contract" (Reicher, 1996: 237). The kinds of poetic and pedagogical changes I have argued for here would only be a first step towards revoking this contract. If psychology is really to become a powerful agent of human emancipation, further steps are needed. Thus, as soon as we organize a space in which to hear the voices of the oppressed in psychology, we immediately face the task of taking up the social and political implications of the oppressions we learn of in our work.

Around the world, a growing number of psychologists and non-psychologists are coming together to take up this challenge. For example, in July 1994, a new body called "Psychology Politics Resistance" was formed with an aim of persuading both individual psychologists and organizations of psychologists to adopt an active opposition to exploitation and oppression as a central aspect of their work and, in particular, to encourage such considerations as a key element in the education of all psychologists (see Reicher and Parker, 1993; Reicher, 1996, for PPR's other aims). Whatever the fate of this body, it points towards the minimum conditions for giving substance to the term radical ("of the root") in any forward-looking psychology of human development.

Acknowledgements

Thanks to the many people who have encouraged and criticized, facilitated, questioned, and suggested whilst I have been working out the ideas discussed in this chapter: Jane Selby, John Morss, Betty Bayer, Shep White, John Shotter, Ken Gergen, Mary Gergen, the staff of the Darwin Archive at the University Library, University of Cambridge from 1983–85, and particularly Bill Kessen, whose example, faith, and hospitality, personal and intellectual, helped when help was hard to come by.

Notes

1 On monologue and dialogue, see Bradley, 1994; Voloshinov, 1927.

2 "*Dawning* processes probably play as important a part [as *fading* ones] in giving the feeling of duration to the specious present" (James, 1890: 638).

3 "Our childhood memories show us our earliest years not as they were but as they appeared at the later periods of revival, the childhood memories did not, as people are accustomed to say, emerge; they were formed at that time. And a number of motives, which had no concern

with historical accuracy, had their part in forming them as well as in the selection of the memories themselves" (Freud, 1899: 69).

4 "One has the suspicion that the only difference between poet and scientist is that the latter, having lost their sense of style, now try to comfort themselves with the pleasant fiction that they are following rules of a quite different kind which produce a much grander and more important result, namely, the Truth" (Feyerabend, quoted in Beer, 1983: 91).

5 What had been philosophically known as the phenomena of "consciousness". (In this regard, Darwin (1859, 1872) is truly the forefather of Watson's (1913) Mind- and mental-content-denying behaviorism; Boakes, 1984.)

6 Note that it is not beyond the reach of *evolutionary* explanation, however, if such explanation is not gradualistic. Darwin's gradualism is not essential to evolutionary explanation, as argued variously by Costall (1986) and in the debate on punctuated equilibria (Maynard Smith, 1982).

7 Most notably, his grandfather Erasmus Darwin (Bradley, 1994).

8 However, as the above quotation shows, Darwin would not have been able to deny that many types of evidence, particularly that for his favorite dictum *natura non facit saltum*, could never be conclusive, but always a matter of trust.

References

Beer, G. (1983) *Darwin's Plots: Evolutionary Narrative in Darwin, George Eliot and Nineteenth-Century Fiction*. London: Routledge.
Beer, G. and Martins, H. (1990) "Introduction: rhetoric and science," *History of the Human Sciences*, 3: 163–75.
Bloom, H. (1973) *The Anxiety of Influence: A Theory of Poetry*. New York: Oxford University Press.
Boakes, R.A. (1984) *From Darwin to Behaviourism: Psychology and the Minds of Animals*. Cambridge: Cambridge University Press.
Boal, A. (1974) *Theater of the Oppressed*. New York: Urizen, 1979.
Boal, A. (1992) *Games for Actors and Non-Actors*. London: Routledge.
Bordo, S. (1989) *The Flight to Objectivity: Essays on Cartesianism and Culture*. Albany, NY: State University of New York Press.
Bowlby, J. (1990) *Charles Darwin: A Biography*. London: Hutchinson.
Bradley, B.S. (1989) *Visions of Infancy: A Critical Introduction to Child Psychology*. Cambridge: Polity Press.
Bradley, B.S. (1991) "Infancy as paradise," *Human Development*, 34: 35–54.
Bradley, B.S. (1993a) "A serpent's guide to children's 'theories of mind'," *Theory and Psychology*, 3(4): 497–521.
Bradley, B.S. (1993b) "Questioning the researcher's existence: from deconstruction to practice," in L. Mos, W. Thorngate, B. Kaplan, and H. Stam (eds), *Recent Trends in Theoretical Psychology*, vol. 3. New York: Springer-Verlag.
Bradley, B.S. (1994) "Darwin's intertextual baby: Erasmus Darwin as precursor in child psychology," *Human Development*, 37: 86–102.
Bradley, B.S. and Selby, J.M. (1996) "Therapy, consciousness raising, and revolution," in I. Parker and R. Spears (eds), *Psychology and Society: Radical Theory and Practice*. London: Pluto Press.
Bragg, E.A. (1995) "Towards ecological self: individual and shared understandings of the relationship between 'self' and 'the natural environment'." PhD dissertation, Department of Psychology and Sociology, James Cook University, Queensland, Australia.
Bronfenbrenner, U., Kessel, F., Kessen, W., and White, S. (1986) "Toward a critical social history of developmental psychology: a propaedeutic discussion," *American Psychologist*, 41: 1218–30.
Butler, S. (1880) *Unconscious Memory*. London: Murray.

Cahan, E.D. and White, S.H. (1992) "Proposals for a second psychology," *American Psychologist*, 47: 224–35.

Clifford, J. and Marcus, G.E. (1986) *Writing Culture: The Poetics and Politics of Anthropology*. Berkeley, CA: University of California Press.

Costall, A. (1985) "Specious origins? Darwinism and developmental theory," in G. Butterworth, J. Rutowska, and M. Scaife (eds), *Evolution and Developmental Psychology*. Brighton: Harvester.

Costall, A. (1986) "Evolutionary gradualism and the study of development," *Human Development*, 29: 4–11.

Cupitt, D. (1983) *The Sea of Faith*. London: BBC Publications.

Darwin, C.R. (1838) "Notebooks M & N," in H.E. Gruber and P.H. Barrett (eds), *Darwin on Man: A Psychological Study of Scientific Creativity*. London: Wildwood, 1974.

Darwin, C.R. (1859) *On the Origin of Species by Means of Natural Selection, or, the Preservation of Favoured Races in the Struggle for Life*. Cambridge, MA: Harvard University Press, 1964.

Darwin, C.R. (1872) *The Expression of the Emotions in Man and Animals*. London: Murray.

Darwin, C.R. (1877) "A biographical sketch of an infant," in H.E. Gruber and P.H. Barrett (eds), *Darwin on Man: A Psychological Study of Scientific Creativity*. London: Wildwood, 1974.

Darwin, C.R. (1901) *The Descent of Man*. London: Murray.

Darwin, C.R. (1958) *The Autobiography of Charles Darwin, 1809–1882, with Original Omissions Restored* (ed. N. Barlow). London: Collins.

Darwin, C.R. (1988) *Charles Darwin's Beagle Diary* (ed. R.W. Keynes). Cambridge: Cambridge University Press.

Darwin, C.R. and Darwin, F. (1887) *The Life and Letters of Charles Darwin, including an Autobiographical Chapter* (3 vols, ed. F. Darwin). London: Murray.

Darwin, E. (1803) *The Temple of Nature or the Origin of Society*. London: Johnson.

Davies, B. (1994) *Poststructuralist Theory and Classroom Practice*. Geelong: Deakin University Press.

Desmond, A.J. and Moore, A.J. (1991) *Darwin*. London: Michael Joseph.

Devereux, G. (1968) *From Anxiety to Method in the Behavioural Sciences*. The Hague: Mouton.

Eliot, T.S. (1963) *Collected Poems 1909–1962*. London: Faber.

Freire, P. (1970) *Pedagogy of the Oppressed*. Harmondsworth: Penguin.

Freud, S. (1899) "Screen memories," in J. Strachey (ed.), *Collected Papers*, vol. V. London: Hogarth, 1957.

Gardner, H. (1985) *The Mind's New Science: A History of the Cognitive Revolution*. New York: Basic Books.

Garfinkel, H. (1967) *Studies in Ethnomethodology*. Englewood Cliffs, NJ: Prentice-Hall.

Gaull, M. (1979) "From Wordsworth to Darwin: 'on the fields of praise'," *Wordsworth Circle*, 10: 33–48.

Gergen, K.J. (1985) "The social constructionist movement in modern psychology," *American Psychologist*, 40: 266–75.

Gergen, K. and Gergen, M. (1996) "Playing with ourselves: polyvocal and performative," presentation at conference on "Discourse and Social Practice," Adelaide, 28 February to 3 March.

Gilligan, C. (1994) "Getting civilized," *Fordham Law Review*, 63: 17–31.

Griffiths, V. (1990) "Using drama to get at gender," in L. Stanley (ed.), *Feminist Praxis: Research, Theory and Epistemology in Feminist Sociology*. London: Routledge.

Gruber, H.E. and Barrett, P.H. (eds) (1974) *Darwin on Man: A Psychological Study of Scientific Creativity*. London: Wildwood.

Habermas, J. (1970) "Toward a theory of communicative competence," in H.P. Dreitzel (ed.), *Recent Sociology*, No. 2.

Haeckel, E. (1874) *The Evolution of Man*. London: Kegan Paul.

Haug, F. (1987) *Female Sexualization*. London: Verso.

Hillman, J. and Ventura, M. (1993) *We've Had a Hundred Years of Psychotherapy and the World is Getting Worse*. San Francisco: Harper.

Jackson, A. (1992) "Introduction," in A. Boal, *Games for Actors and Non-Actors*. London: Routledge.

James, W. (1878) "Remarks on Spencer's Definition of Mind as Correspondence," in *Essays in Philosophy*. Cambridge, MA: Harvard University Press, 1978.

James, W. (1890) *The Principles of Psychology*. New York: Norton.

James, W. (1903) *The Varieties of Religious Experience: A Study in Human Nature*. Cambridge, MA: Harvard University Press, 1985.

John, I.D. (1986) " 'The scientist' as role-model for 'the psychologist'," *Australian Psychologist*, 21: 219–40.

Kant, I. (1790) "Analytic of the sublime," in *Kant's Critique of Aesthetic Judgement* (trans. J.C. Meredith). Oxford: Oxford University Press.

Kaye, K. (1982) *The Mental and Social Life of Babies: How Parents Create Persons*. Brighton: Harvester.

Keats, J. (1817) "On first looking into Chapman's Homer," in J. Barnard (ed.), *John Keats: The Complete Poems* (2nd edn). Harmondsworth: Penguin. 1976, p. 72.

Keats, J. (1819) "Letter to George and Georgiana Keats," in *The Letters of John Keats, 1814–1821*, vol. 2 (ed. H.E. Rollins). Cambridge: Cambridge University Press, 1958.

Keats, J. (1820) "The fall of Hyperion: a dream," in J. Barnard (ed.), *John Keats: The Complete Poems* (2nd edn). Harmondsworth: Penguin, 1976.

Keller, E.F. (1985) *Reflections on Science and Gender*. New Haven, CT: Yale University Press.

Kessen, W. (1979) "The American child and other cultural inventions," *American Psychologist*, 34: 815–20.

Kessen, W. (1990) *The Rise and Fall of Development*. Worcester, MA: Clark University Press.

Lavine, T.Z. (1962) "Some reflections on the genetic fallacy," *Social Research*, 29: 321–36.

Levett, E. (1992) "Adult sequelae to child abuse," PhD Dissertation, Capetown University, South Africa.

Manier, E. (1978) *The Young Darwin and His Cultural Circle*. New York: Reidl.

Marcuse, H. (1969) *An Essay on Liberation*. Boston: Beacon Press.

Maynard Smith, J. (1982) "Evolution – Sudden or Gradual?" in J. Maynard Smith (ed.), *Evolution Now: A Century after Darwin*. London: Macmillan.

Michael, M. (1996) "Pick a utopia, any utopia," in I. Parker and R. Spears (eds), *Psychology and Society: Radical Theory and Practice*. London: Pluto Press.

Miller, G.A. (1969) "Psychology as a means of promoting human welfare," *American Psychologist*, 24: 1063–75.

Morss, J.R. (1990) *The Biologising of Childhood: Developmental Psychology and the Darwinian Myth*. Hove: Erlbaum.

Parker, I. and R. Spears (eds) (1996) *Psychology and Society: Radical Theory and Practice*. London: Pluto Press.

Peirce, C.S. (1882) "How to make our ideas clear," in *Chance, Love and Logic*. New York: Barnes and Noble, 1923.

Pylyshyn, Z.W. (1984) *Computation and Cognition: Toward a Foundation for Cognitive Science*. Cambridge, MA: MIT Press.

Reicher, S. (1996) "The reactionary practice of radical psychology: revoking the Faustian contract," in I. Parker and R. Spears (eds), *Psychology and Society: Radical Theory and Practice*. London: Pluto Press.

Reicher, S. and Parker, I. (1993) "Psychology, politics, resistance: the birth of a new organisation," *Journal of Community and Applied Social Psychology*, 3: 77–80.

Searle, J. (1992) *The Rediscovery of the Mind*. Cambridge, MA: MIT Press.

Seed, J., Macy, J., Fleming, P., and Naess, A. (1988) *Thinking Like a Mountain: Towards a Council of All Beings*. Philadelphia, PA: New Society Publishers.

Stanley, L. (ed.) (1990) *Feminist Praxis: Research, Theory and Epistemology in Feminist Sociology*. London: Routledge.

Voloshinov, V.N. (1927) *Freudianism: A Marxist Critique*. New York: Academic Press, 1976.

Walkerdine, V. (1984) "Piaget and the child-centred pedagogy," in J. Henriques, W. Hollway,

C. Urwin, C. Venn, and V. Walkerdine (eds), *Changing the Subject: Psychology, Subjectivity and Social Regulation*. London: Methuen.

Watson, J.B. (1913) "Psychology as the behaviourist views it," *Psychological Review*, 20: 158–77.

Weiskel, T. (1976) *The Romantic Sublime: Studies in the Structure and Psychology of Transcendence*. Baltimore, MD: Johns Hopkins University Press.

Wiener, N. (1948) *Cybernetics, or, Control and Communication in the Animal and the Machine*. New York: Wiley.

Winnicott, D.W. (1957) "On the contribution of direct child observation to psycho-analysis," in *The Maturational Processes and the Facilitating Environment: Studies in the Theory of Emotional Development*. London: Hogarth, 1965.

Wollstonecraft, M. (1792) *Vindication of the Rights of Women*. Harmondsworth: Penguin, 1975.

Woolf, V. (1937) *The Years*. London: Hogarth Press.

Wordsworth, W. (1805) *The Prelude, Etc*. New York: Holt, Rinehart and Winston, 1954.

5

Positioning a Dialogic Reflexivity in the Practice of Feminist Supervision

Susan E. Hawes

Feminists have criticized scientific research and scientific organizations for the ways in which their theories of knowledge formation and dissemination replicate existing patriarchal structures that are considered oppressive to women. Certain postmodern and poststructuralist theories explicitly address the various aspects of implicit or latent power-controls as they are exercised in social institutions, such as research, academia, and the natural and social sciences. One purpose underlying such analyses is to apply critical textual interpretive practices, like deconstruction and genealogical critique (Foucault, 1978) to expose the contextuality and partiality of all truth claims, as well as the latent power relations exercised in particular discourses and institutionalized practices. These reflexive critical analyses are, in turn, believed to potentiate the emergence and actualization of formally marginalized discourses and practices and to open up local possibilities for resistance to dominant discourses.

This paper argues that an application of reflexivity in dialogue to a field of practical science can both "destroy the myths that cloak the exercise of power and the perpetuation of domination" (Wacquant, 1992), and enable new and local forms of power and resistance to come into parlance. Specifically, the practice of a dialogical reflexivity can be positioned within feminist emancipatory discourses as an alternative to recent egalitarian and essentialist feminist attempts to promote women's interests in pedagogy and clinical supervision.

Chipping Away at Patriarchy from the Margins

In the critiques of patriarchal social systems for their chronic and incessant oppression of women, feminists have implicated with particular assiduity numerous manifestations of hierarchy as embodiments of patriarchal dominance. Taking notable issue with the ways in which science, as it is both theorized and practiced, is rooted deeply in sexism and has ignored or distorted the experiences of women and other non-dominant groups from an alleged position of epistemological superiority (Harding, 1991), some feminists descry traditional scientific practice as an exercise in patriarchal domination. Their analyses suggest that the act of knowing becomes an act of hierarchically based privilege that reverberates throughout society. The scientist is perceived as enacting his gendered privilege by means of the symbolic and material control, possession, objectification, and dominance of the epistemological object (Keller, 1985). Certain social theorists and feminists claim that science is not so much a set of value- and context-free rules for accessing overarching truths as socially constructed and "constituted through practical activities including those of designating what reality is and deciding what counts as objectivity" (Morawski, 1994: 12). From this perspective, science and other intellectual pursuits cannot be abstracted from their historical and social contexts, for they are never completely neutral, but rather emerge from discursive activities grounded in social relations. The interpretive approach of imbedding science within culture and history is a critical stance that feminism and social constructionism share in common with Marxist theory, Hermeneutic philosophy, and late twentieth-century philosophy of science. The perspective articulated in these criticisms of science warns that the objectification exercised in the gaze of the inquirer is not disinterested, but rather effects a dominion over its object(s) by virtue of its patriarchal social currency. In other words, objectivity has been found to entail a masculine subjectivity, obfuscated by sanctioned proclamations of neutrality.

Feminist critics have demonstrated the absence of women as both objects and subjects in traditional scientific practice. They have lobbied for greater numbers of women in the sciences, and their works have advocated and actualized greater attention to women's issues and experiences. In these movements into the academy there has been an assumption of institutionally sanctioned power, about which feminists hold a tension between suspicion and desire. Turning their critical practice back upon themselves as purveyors of power/knowledge in the academy, they have also sought to understand and attend to women's distinctive needs in traditional learning settings, by both theorizing the nature of these needs and altering traditional practices of knowledge transmission. As a springboard into a proposed postmodern feminist approach to clinical supervision, liberal and constructionist feminist theories will be briefly explored here for their strengths and limitations in pedagogical and supervisory practices in clinical psychology.

Equality, Voice, and Liberationist Pedagogies

The constructionist and liberal feminist approaches to pedagogy and supervision have attempted to disrupt what amounts to a persistent replication of repression and control by dominant patriarchal forms in the practice of social science. Egalitarian and standpoint theorists hold that women's state will be improved with equal access to power, when their distinctive natures are given voice and empowered; they also privilege women's interpretive access to reality (Harding, 1991; Tong, 1989). In the context of pedagogy, these models assert that women may have learning needs that differ from those associated with and institutionally supported in men, and that traditional learning opportunities frustrate or stifle women's educational development (Hayes, 1989; Tisdell, 1993). Some have called for more egalitarian, collaborative, and experienced-based learning opportunities for women that challenge traditional patriarchal hierarchies of knowledge generation (Cinchy et al., 1985), and have achieved some influence in the feminist literature in education.

Belenky et al.'s (1986) qualitative inquiry, *Women's Ways of Knowing*, inferred that the women they interviewed had a preference for "connected learning," that is, opportunities for linking their own individual experiences and thoughts with those of other learners, and that women believed the quality of their relationships to be a central influence on their learning potential (Hayes, 1989). Elizabeth Hayes, in this egalitarian tradition, asserts that a feminist pedagogy should emphasize "a collaborative, participatory teaching–learning process that engages learners in the creation of knowledge based on personal experience that can be used as the basis for individual change and social action" (1989: 56).

Laurie Finke (1993) describes feminists' attempts to apply the work of Paulo Freire to the education of women by making learning a "practice of freedom," through both the use of egalitarian classrooms and the development of new pedagogies that are "participatory, experiential, and non-hierarchical." She notes that the crucial concepts within a liberatory pedagogy have been "empowerment," "student voice," "dialogue," and "critical thinking." It has been observed that feminist pedagogues, in their desire to avoid reproducing white male privilege in their classrooms, generally share a concern for facilitating women's senses of personal power to effect change in their lives and for creating a learning context that emphasizes relationship and connection (Tisdell, 1993).

The supervision of trainees in clinical psychology is a pedagogic field that has received relatively little attention in the feminist literature. Although traditionally hierarchical in form, supervision also may be seen to reflect a "woman's touch": mentoring through supportive inquiry, therapeutic role-modeling, and non-intrusive consultation. At the same time, however, the traditional clinical supervisor is viewed as one who has knowledge that he or she provides or transfers to the humble novitiate. The authority embodied by the supervisor, however subtly or explicitly enacted in the transactions between the two participants in clinical supervision, is derived from both the local institution sustaining the relationship as well as the institutionalized traditions of western professionalism. In addition, it is sustained by parallel institutions, such as our legal system. What are understood as the charges of the supervisee (training, the care of clientele, etc.) belong in fact to the supervisor. The pedagogical transactions, deemed appropriate to the task of training the supervisee, have traditionally and unquestioningly been derived first and foremost from the disciplinary needs and assumptions of the individual supervisor and his or her professional context.

Constructivist psychotherapists, feminists, and liberationists have eschewed the traditional notions of locating expertise only in persons with socially sanctioned authority and of learning as a unidirectional transaction, in which knowledge flows from knower to the learner. They criticize such modernist assumptions of objectified knowledge and the artificial privilege that is replicated in hierarchically organized relationships, and have developed counter models of supervision that are explicitly collaborative and that assume a non-centrality of clinical expertise (Anderson and Goolishian, 1991a, 1991b; Lax, 1992). Hawes describes collaboration in supervision in the following way:

> Collaboration in the supervisory process can be understood to include at least three defining characteristics: bidirectionality, noncentrality of expertise, and circularity in modeling practices. These characteristics speak to the reciprocity of interpersonal obligations, the absence of rigidly enacted hierarchy in a working relationship, and an outcome or object that is a shared construction of every participant. (1993: 4)

In these models, the supervisor assumes a "non-expert" stance, recognizing that knowledge comes in many forms, from many sources, and is not exclusively possessed by the supervisor (Anderson and Goolishian, 1991a, 1991b; Lax, 1992). She or he maintains a stance of posing questions rather than providing answers, in the hope of co-creating opportunities for the supervisee to discover his or her own interpretations of clinical phenomena, and encouraging creativity, authenticity, and candidness in the supervisee. Feminist supervisors are drawn to collaborative models because these do not replicate male privilege through hierarchy and knowledge entitlements. They emphasize a relational foundation for learning, do not assume that their supervisees must do as they do, think as they think, in order to learn, and seek to foster a clinician's discovery of her own distinct "voice." This model places both supervisor and supervisee in reciprocal and mutually beneficial positions of learner and knowledge-bearer, in which the supervisor is seen as having as much to learn from the supervisory dialogue as the supervisee. Such a collaborative supervision can have at least three positive implications:

> (1) it meets with favor from mature students (Gandolfo and Brown, 1987; Singer, Peterson, Magidson, 1992), (2) women in particular appear to benefit more from collaborative working relations than hierarchical ones (Cinchy et al., 1985; Holloway et al., 1989), (3) both supervisor and supervisee are challenged to move beyond their present knowledge states (Anderson and Goolishian, 1991a, 1991b; Lax, 1992). (Hawes, 1993: 6)

Such notions of diminished power differentials or an equal playing field in the supervisory relationship invite simplistic applications by practitioners, who may naively overlook the paradox in supervisor–supervisee equality. Critics of constructionist and egalitarian feminist approaches to pedagogy and supervision have attempted to elucidate the paradoxical outcomes of similar liberationist approaches, noting, for one, that these reformist projects have been developed by using the same political and social means responsible for the social forms that they have striven to revise, that is, by means of enlightenment liberatory rules of competition, rationality, and equal opportunity. Most of these critics, coming from postmodern and poststructuralist feminist orientations, have alerted us to the ways in which the rules of difference and similarity under the guise of equalization may also smack of patriarchal whitewashing. Morawski (1994), for example, has exposed the erasure of "femininity" latent in the equalizing concept of androgeny, as well as its potential to deny socially arranged (not freely chosen) aspects of gender identity. She states:

> What was introduced as the possibility of a flexible, enabling, and even gender-free personhood revealed an uncomfortable resemblance to conventional masculinity. . . . Androgeny appeared at once to maintain gender dualisms and to perpetuate a state of cultural ideals favoring a particular type of social agency: that of a cognitively flexible, independent, and self-contained individual. (Morawski, 1994: 45)

The Constitution of Power and Subjectivity

Postmodern and poststructuralist feminists in particular have sought to countermand the silencing of women's experiences and subjectivities by critically examining the role of language and discourses in "constituting knowledge, together with the social practices, forms of subjectivity and power relations that inhere in such knowledges and the relations between them" (Weedon, 1987: 108). They attempt to expose the latent oppressive nature of cultural institutions, such as the sciences, by reading between the lines of dominant discourses to discover positions of resistance, and by revealing the social interests contained in even our most commonsense notions (Flax, 1991; Hare-Mustin and Marecek, 1990; Hawes, 1994; Weedon, 1987). Many hope thereby to elucidate the multiplicity and complexity in social relations of knowledge production, allowing room for marginalized discourses to have voice and to engage in open contestation with or resistances to dominant sites of power. As Weedon has stated,

> For feminists, the attempt to understand power in all its forms is of central importance. The failure to understand the multiplicity of power relations . . . will render an analysis blind to the range of points of resistance inherent in the network of power relations, a blindness that impedes resistance. (1987: 124)

Poststructuralist feminists understand power as present in all discursive transactions, as "a relation . . . [that] inheres in difference and is a dynamic of control and lack of control between discourses and the subjects constituted by discourses who are their agents" (Weedon, 1987: 113). Positively stated, poststructuralism is "a way of conceptualizing the relationship between language, social institutions and individual consciousness that focuses on how power is exercised and on the possibilities of change" (Weedon, 1987). Based on the works of Michel Foucault, this approach to social analysis examines the social interests and implicit power elements contained within the myriad structures of social practice (Foucault, 1978). A poststructuralist feminist focuses her critical gaze upon those institutions and practices that, appearing to be neutral and free from ideological bias, tacitly harbor and exercise power over subjects within range of their influence. She would ask,

> what were the most immediate, the most local power relations at work? How did they make possible these kinds of discourse, and conversely, how were these discourses used to support power relations? How was the action of these power relations modified by their very exercise, entailing a strengthening of some terms and a weakening of others, with effects of resistance and counterinvestments, so that there has never existed one type of stable subjugation, given once and for all? How were these power relations linked to one another according to the logic of a great strategy. (Weedon, 1987: 97)

Chris Weedon (1987) understands poststructuralism's implications for social change as lying in Michel Foucault's discursive critique of multiple sites of power, which facilitates "mobile and transitory points of resistance, producing cleavages in a society that shifts about, fracturing unities and effecting regroupings" (Foucault, 1979: 96). Foucault is not interested in creating yet another overarching system of truth and potential domination, but rather seeks to "question over and over again what is postulated as self-evident, to disturb people's mental habits . . . to dissipate what is familiar and accepted" (Foucault, in Kritzman, 1988: 265). The program of action that emerges from feminist readings of Foucault is one of resistance, "a resistance that is locally, not universally grounded" (Hekman, 1990: 182). Thus, if we are to come to an awareness of what we are doing in our doing of it, and to open up opportunities for alternatives, we must ourselves become reflexively aware of the character of our own practices.

A Dialogical Reflexivity in Practice

Reflexivity has become a crucial concept in postmodern theory-making and practice. Because postmodernists insist that all knowledge emerges *discursively in social relations* and, by extension, that knowledge is partial and multiplicitous, they must then turn their critical gaze back upon themselves as a means of assessing the contexts which engender and constrain their own discursive range. European theorists of the social sciences have asserted for hundreds of years that human attempts to describe the experience of other humans necessarily involve reflexivity, in that we are using the very human, historically-located processes that we are trying to understand (Gadamer, 1975). We cannot remove ourselves from an equation in which we are a part. Rather, our own enculturated processes of interpretation need to be embraced as both the objects and mediators of our investigations.

Gadamer's (1975) descriptions of reflexive processes have been the inspiration for the model of reflexivity to be promoted here. His articulation of prejudice and tradition as necessary "fore-structures" of understanding posits all epistemologies as "rooted, contextual and historical" and thus requiring critique and reflexive examination in order to grasp their horizons (Hekman, 1990). He included both the natural and social sciences in this rootedness. Critical reason, for Gadamer, or the ability to distinguish between "legitimate and illegitimate prejudices" (the nearest one can get to "the truth") involves the inquirer in an ongoing self-critical activity that extends beyond the self to include the historical, social, and moral context that is the horizon of that individual's potential understanding (Gadamer, 1975). Genuine understanding, for Gadamer, always involves new under-standing, that is, a knowledge that comes from a fusion of horizons, a "meeting of the contextual understanding of the interpreter with that of the interpreted" (Hekman, 1990). The hermeneutic process of interpretation requires reflexivity, a process of turning one's gaze back upon oneself for the purpose of permitting the other to become known through a dialogical process of differentiation.

The hermeneutic agenda of examining one's preunderstandings, while on the surface similar to an exploration of "countertransference" or irrational biases, differs in its emphasis on recognizing the cultural, historical, and social relational influences on one's assumptions or perceptions of truth or reality. It is not about self-reflection in the service of the ego:

> For Gadamer, philosophical hermeneutics is not an attempt to recover an indi-vidual "self" from the proliferation of discourses, but the preservation of a level of discourse that is ultimately selfless. On his model, the philosophical appropri-ation of texts is not a "becoming self" but a "becoming other." It is not a reflec-tive recovery of the desire to be, but a response to a question, that is, the question of the subject matter of the historical tradition. That subject matter is, of course, we ourselves. But our identity is not fixed in eternity, it is instead the continuity of our becoming-other in every response, in every application of the preunder-standing that we have of ourselves in new and unpredictable situations. (Aylesworth, 1991: 81)

Implicit in Gadamer's writing on hermeneutic analysis is also a notion of responsibility or ethic, that is, an expectation that the inquirer is obliged to allow the other to question his or her horizon of preunderstandings (Gadamer, 1975). In this tradition, reflexivity is not solipsistic, but historical, critical, and committed.

Another important account of reflexivity in social analysis is Bourdieu's (1992). He focuses only initially upon the individual characteristics of the individual research, such as class, gender and ethnicity. The substance of a reflexive analysis moves beyond the person in order to discover the "social and intellectual unconscious embedded in analytic tools and operations," taking into account the possible intellectual stances available to the researcher given her or his academic field. Unlike most postmodern theorists, Bourdieu also considers the biasing impact of intellectualism itself that, Wacquant states, "entices us to construe the world as a spectacle, as a set of significations to be interpreted rather than as concrete problems to be solved practically" (Wacquant, 1992: 39). He shares with Gadamer and Foucault the view that reflexive social analysis frees those engaged in the practice to see themselves and their world in ways previously unavailable to them. Bourdieu has been understood to use reflexive social analysis to "denaturalize and defatalize the social world, that is, to destroy the myths that cloak the exercise of power and the perpetuation of domination" (Wacquant, 1992: 72). This deconstructive activity may have consequences for practical experience:

> I believe that when sociology remains at a highly abstract and formal level, it contributes nothing. When it gets down to the nitty gritty of real life, however, it is an instrument that people can apply to themselves for quasi-clinical purposes. . . . When you apply reflexive sociology to yourself, you open up the possibility of identifying true sites of freedom, and thus of building small scale, modest, practical morals in keeping with the scope of human freedom which, in my opinion, is not that large. (Bourdieu, 1992: 199)

Postmodern feminism reflexively applies discourse critique to feminist theories, with the purpose of revealing the ways in which many attempts at change contain within them subtle or hidden reinforcement of existing patriarchal discourses. Morawski, for example, in her recent book, *Practicing Feminisms, Reconstructing Psychology*, explores innovative applications of reflexive feminism to research psychology, presenting

> the ways in which psychological investigations are altered by acknowledging the observer, the subject, and the relations between observer and subject as conscious and self-conscious agents in the making of science. (1994: 6)

Morawski explores the pitfalls of empiricist feminist research, revealing latent patriarchal meanings hidden within scientific method (Morawski, 1990, 1994). She specifically addresses the ways in which androgyny research is a case in which social relations are replicated on multiple levels in the work of the scientist. She articulates how a shift in "authorial control" of gender moved first from the subjects perceptions to the psychologist, with his superior concepts and technologies, then, with the introduction of the concept of androgyny, to the "feminist-informed researchers, " creating a new source of work and identity for aspiring female scientists. She goes on to state:

> The androgyny concept offered new social roles that supplanted older, certainly derogatory, images of the female scientist, the woman who thinks like a man, with a more becoming form of gendered personality, the independent woman worker who is also gentle and receptive. Androgyny altered more than the social relations among certain scientific workers: It afforded a new expert perspective on society. It reconfirmed that psychological science commands a penetrating gaze on popular life. . . . (Morawski, 1990: 169)

Hare-Mustin and Marecek (1990) demonstrate how the meanings made of gender difference by feminists are multiple and shifting, carrying hidden social interests and at times contradictory social implications. After exploring the overt and covert meanings in feminist biases towards finding difference or similarity between the genders, they conclude,

> What we see as the alpha [difference] and beta [similarity] bias have similar assumptive frameworks despite their diverse emphases. Both take the male as the

standard of comparison. Both construct gender as attributes of individuals, not as the ongoing relations of men and women. Neither effectively challenges the gender hierarchy, and ultimately neither transcends the status quo. They are changes within the larger system of assumptions, but they leave the system itself unchanged. (1990: 54)

They recommend that a deconstructive critique of conceptual oppositions, such as gender, be used to subvert latent domination of women in the social construction of gender meanings, asserting that there can be no one right view of gender. The view that gender is multiple and shifting potentiates the accommodation of variation and likeness, and necessarily involves an awareness of what Gadamer (1975) calls "effective history" and Foucault recognizes as the power in discourse.

Jill Morawski, as well as Rachel Hare-Mustin and Jeanne Marecek, move criticism recursively beyond the object of their inquiries back upon themselves as purveyors of knowledge within specific fields. Morawski concurs with Sue Wilkinson that there is a need for "reflexivity in feminist psychology that is not only personal and functional, that not only assures self-consciousness and methodological revisions, but that also demands 'a discipline or subdiscipline to explain its own form and influence' " (1994: 124). It is critical that the reflexive practitioner look for power not simply as internally-residing attributes of persons, but as imbedded in all social relations. When we identify dominance only in the person or persons of those engaged in benefiting most from the effects of a dominant discourse, we perpetrate the same kind of misuse of power that we have eschewed in others, by our having re-enacted a dichotomous rather than capillary process of understanding. For example, the prevalent dichotomy of perpetrator/victim, while permitting the assignment of blame and innocence within a discourse of justice, suggests resolution only within that dichotomy (the vanquishing of either the perpetrator's or the victim's subjectivity) and occludes the marginalized sources of power in the abusing relationship, as well as the social disciplines maintained by a monologic discourse in which one side of the dichotomy must always be disciplined.

Reflexively Considering Collaboration in Supervision

If we concur with poststructuralism that power is capillary and contiguous with social relationships, and we hold with Foucault that power is "tolerable only on condition that it masks a substantial part of itself. Its success is proportional to its ability to hide its own mechanisms" (Foucault, 1979: 98), then we must ask ourselves, as Morawski, Hare-Mustin and Marecek have done in their critiques of feminist empiricism, where the power "goes" when we speak of collaborative and egalitarian relationships in the context of a collaborative supervision, a relationship that is explicitly socially sanctioned as hierarchical. My concern here is to explore the possible conflicting desires and social demands within a feminist clinical supervision that are rarely articulated or worked. For example, how is the engendering of power in a person of lower status accomplished via an *exchange* of practical knowledge that concomitantly disguises the power in the person of higher status within a purported *discourse of equality*. I would like to suggest that, rather than attempting to erase power differences within the supervision relationship, defiance of an explicit social hierarchy and mutual empowerment may be facilitated through an explicitly dialogic reflexivity that openly unpacks the many ways in which power is manifest between supervisor and supervisee.

When supervision is understood as an area of practical reason, its predominantly moral obligations come to light (Hawes, 1993). The supervisor is located in a professional role that requires her or him to use judgment not only to ascertain the "best" interests of the client but to evaluate judgments and actions of the supervisee. In this kind of practice, moral reasoning emerges as an historically located discourse from within a specific set of social relations, and it is into this discursive community that a supervisee is being inducted. The consensual validation of truth claims or the "goodness" of certain decisions made within the context of supervision with a trainee are located not only between the more local, supervisee–supervisor relationship but within a larger set of community relations, and has ramifications that extend to that community. Specifically the supervisory relationship is not simply dyadic, but multiadic, that is, the supervisee, the client, and the professional community are all represented by the supervisor. The supervisor is expected to hold allegiance to multiple "clients:" she or he instructs, evaluates, and fosters and facilitates the personal agency in the supervisee, manages the safe and effective treatment of the client, is responsible for the fiscal and ethical health of her or his particular agency, and promotes the viability of the profession. In addition to all these, a feminist supervisor is also carrying her political commitment to women's personal and social needs. These "clients" do not always have the same needs, and the supervisor may find her or himself in a bind between nurturing a desire for colleagueship in a supervisee and directing the treatment of a faltering therapy. In such an instance, the collaboration dissolves, because the supervisor is fully responsible for the outcomes of his or her supervisees' cases and must be in a position at any time to "take over" ownership of the therapy process from the supervisee.

Thus, a supervisor's assumption of a "non-expert" status under these conditions could be constituted as a breach of responsibility or minimally a misrepresentation of self by his or her many "clients." What does it mean when a supervisor both is legally and ethically responsible for the supervisee's client and describes that responsibility as "shared" or equal? Does a supervisee really desire "training" from someone no more empowered than she? Does she seek to deny the social powers and disciplinary implications attributed to the practice she is being trained to perform? As Finke, considering feminist pedagogy, notes, "[r]egardless of our attempts to de-center our authority as teachers, we must evaluate our students and must do so from the position of a 'subject supposed to know' " (1993: 17–18). Whether or not one questions the modernist assumptions represented in these views of supervision, that does not dismiss the existence of culturally defined moral obligations and their influence on the pragmatics of professional psychology training, nor are we necessarily furthered in a liberationist agenda when we disguise our desire for power by diminishing the power in those we explicitly seek to become like.

Specifically, does the implementation of equality in settings of knowledge transferal mean the absence of power differences, or merely erased power? I propose that power in collaborative structures merely goes underground, negatively present in a discourse of "no power differences" or equality. One cannot suspend the impact of centuries of enlightened authority carried by socially constructed disciplines by wishing it away (Foucault, 1979). Moreover, it is not a comfort to see feminist supervisors and educators, as members of a marginalized group in hard-won positions of authority, uncritically either feigning or desiring oneness with a group less powerful than they. Must one erase power in oneself to allow another to experience it? This kind of approach to power makes the error of assuming that power is a finite object that persons have or do not have, rather than understanding power as taking place in discourses, as Foucault does. Remember, he sees power as relational and "capillary," that is, operating "at the lowest extremities of the social body in everyday social practices" (Frasier, 1989: 18). Power, then, is manifest in supervision in the discursive regimes that constrain that practice.

The disavowal of power differences in a collaborative relationship does not mean that power and the struggle for control do not impact on the persons and relations involved; quite the contrary. The traditions of Radical and Marxist feminisms, as well as more recent feminist poststructuralism and postmodernism (Harding, 1991; Tong, 1989; Weedon, 1987) have long sought to expose the ways in which a patriarchal culture masks the oppression of marginal groups in the languages and relational structures of our customs and institutions. Hermeneutic philosopher, Hans-Georg Gadamer (1975) has suggested that the unexamined preunderstandings and power relations in social institutions that happen "behind the backs" of the participants and their resulting interpretive distortions are more insidious for their invisibility. Morawski (1990) and the authors of *Making a Difference* (Hare-Mustin and Marecek, 1990) have elucidated the ways in which feminists may overlook the ways in which their small victories replicate dominant macrostructures. Donna Haraway alerts feminists to their replication of patriarchal domination or colonialization through projections of unity and universality onto the descriptive categories we call ourselves:

> There is nothing about being "female" that naturally binds women. . . . None of "us" have any longer the symbolic or material capability of dictating the shape of reality to any of "them." Or at least "we" cannot claim innocence from practicing such dominations. White women, including socialist feminists, discovered (i.e., were forced kicking and screaming to notice) the non-innocence of the category "woman." (1991: 157)

Laurie Finke accuses liberal pedagogues' attempts to promote non-authoritarian learning environments of "mystifying the very forms of authority they sought to exorcise, authority that is both institutionally and psychically embedded in the social relations of education" (1993: 7). The erasure of power in a purportedly egalitarian supervision makes it difficult if not impossible for a supervisee to express her or his experiences of the supervisor's power (Hawes, 1993). Indeed, an insidious double bind may be encountered in purported egalitarian supervision, when the application of power is simultaneously disavowed or denied. Systemic theories have observed that individuals, who are dependent upon some others for an understanding of the boundaries of their existence, can become pathologically confused when their reality is paradoxically construed. A child, for example, who is told by her parent that she is "free to choose" while simultaneously communicating to her through other means that she could never make a good choice on her own, may thus find herself unable to act, mistrustful of her own capacity to understand. By extension, a "collaborative" supervisory relationship can set up a similar double bind for

> the supervisee who is on the one hand told her voice is equal in the discussion and at the same time knows that she is being evaluated by the supervisor for her capacities as a therapist or psychologist. Supervisees in such a situation may become hypervigilant in their efforts to collaborate in the ways their supervisors seem, inexplicably, to want them to. (Hawes, 1993: 7)

Finally, supervision that does not address the multiple forms of power differences in the supervisory relationship does not prepare supervisees to address differences in power that inhere in the therapeutic relationship. For instance, is the supervisee prepared to reflexively critique the layers of social implications her feminism may have within a context that discursively and, at times, practically, endows her with influence over her client? As is the case with supervisor and supervisee, a therapist's role surrounds her with suggestions of having something she can transfer to her client, be that an experience or a skill, that in turn suggests, however illusory or constructed, differences in power both within and outside the therapeutic dyad. Further, are therapeutic goals free of disciplinary implications for a client and what would it mean for the therapist to consider these in dialogue with her clients?

Dialogic Reflexivity

A feminist hope of providing supervision in ways that avoid uncritically replicating patriarchal systems of domination may approximate that goal by integrating some of the dialogical reflexive processes described above into the supervisory discourse, and by eschewing the words "collaborative" and "egalitarian." Dialogic reflexivity is defined here as a process of explicitly turning one's critical gaze back on oneself as well as the professional, historical, and cultural discourses that empower and constrain one's capacities to think and act in the context of a relationship. In the supervisory relationship, then, there are two processes of reflexive practice: one that is performed in the private thoughts of the participants, and the other that is practiced in the dialogue between them. The objects of this reflexivity would not only be the personal and interpersonal horizons of the subjects engaged in the dialogue, but would extend to the larger historical, cultural, and institutional social relations in which they are each inextricably embedded.

These feminist supervisors would retain their socially sanctioned (and professionally mandated) authority for the maintenance of supervisory boundaries, the protection of the supervisee's clients from damaging errors in practice, and the advocacy for the supervisee's training experience. Indeed, the supervisor's responsibility is here extended to assume the introduction to and training in reflexive analysis. However, in contrast to traditional uses of power in supervision, the supervisor's authority itself would be introduced into the actual supervisory dialogue as an object of critical reflection. Throughout the supervisory relationship, the access to and uses of power would be discursive themes actively elicited and supported by the supervisor. Power relations, the exercise and resistance to power, would be explicitly tracked from the perspective that they can take on multiple and shifting forms in both participants.

It is very important that dialogic reflexivity not be confused with more individualistic uses of the term, reflexivity, that is, those analyses limited to therapist or supervisor countertransference, or with a self-critique limited only to the "personal" power issues of the analyst. For example, reflexivity that involves a supervisor and supervisee in the examination solely of intrapsychic material is a common occurrence in psychoanalytic supervision, and systemic therapy's exploration of parallel processes that may occur between the therapy and the supervisory relationship could also be considered reflexive. Both of these approaches are important versions of reflexivity, but they tend not to turn the critical gaze, beyond the individual or local system involved in treatment, to consider the social contexts and power relations affecting both the clients' and the professional's discursive freedoms and constraints. The version of a reflexive feminist supervision proposed here would involve the explicit engagement in and modeling of a reflexive critique that encompassed the self, the particular supervisory relationship, the institutional context in which the supervision takes place, the social implications of therapeutic and psychological practice, and the multiple, shifting ways in which power is exercised and contested in each of these domains. It has been proposed that,

> A reflexive supervision would involve some of the following processes: (1) the bringing of as many involved discourses onto the table for discussion as one is able, thereby examining and entertaining a multiplicity of perspectives; (2) all truth claims would be contextualized within their social milieu and examined for their social impact or their power to constrain or oppress, liberate or illuminate; (3) both the supervisor and supervisee would be engaged in a dialogue that enhances the questioning of their own assumptions and the opening up to the differences in the other; (4) overt and inobvious power relations and differentials

would be openly unpacked, critiqued and attempts made to understand their implications. (Hawes, 1993: 8)

The supervisor's engagement in this kind of clinical reflexivity has the potential to impact upon all her or his "clients," mentioned above. Within the supervisory dyad, a different kind of discourse between the pair is facilitated, one in which each is encouraged to interpret their actions in new and potentially transformative ways. Dialogic reflexivity engages each in an act of responsibility for recognizing the complexity and partiality of the ways in which they approach a therapeutic issue, and leaving themselves open to being questioned by the text of the other (Gadamer, 1975). The supervisor's commitment to dialogic reflexivity leaves room for the supervisee to address and take responsibility for the range and limits of her or his own authority. It would be important for a supervisor at the outset to initiate a dialogue with the supervisee in which each explores the meanings she confers upon therapeutic change in our culture, power relations, and their relationship to supervision. The supervisor voices a commitment to attending to her or his constructions of the relationship, its changing discursive forms and power relations, and bringing those into the dialogue. At the same time, she or he invites the supervisee to assume the difficult task of articulating resistance and responsibility in the supervision relationship. The supervisor openly acknowledges that she or he anticipates that power is going to manifest itself varyingly as potentiality, creativity, dominance, and suppression throughout their relationship, and that it will enhance their work to attend to the overt and, when possible, the latent forms these take.

The modeling of reflexive practice should also extend to the supervisee's therapeutic work with clients, as well as the critical exploration of psychology's emancipatory and disciplinary limitations in this culture. Within the context of ever-increasing calls for psychological practice to be responsive to the needs of diverse and marginalized social groups, dialogic reflexivity in supervision models a process that enhances a professional's capacity to allow herself to be changed by the social horizon of another. Thus, there is potential for both the client and the therapist to engage in reconceptualizing themselves and each other, by locally reconsidering the psychological subject in its multiple meanings. In keeping with Foucault's notion that power and the resistance to power are present everywhere and have not a single reference point (Weedon, 1987), the reflexive practitioner seeks to uncover sites of hidden power in the "reverse discourses" of otherwise marginalized groups, thereby making access to resistance more possible for individual members of those groups. Hawes asserts that,

[b]y its very insistence on the role of implicit oppressive power relations hidden in dominant discourses and its assertion that the intentional engagement in deconstructing these discourses is empowering, a reflexive stance entertains a view of people that is less patronizing, patriarchal and pathologizing. (1994: 8)

Such an engagement in critical reflexive dialogue can further move the psychologist beyond the horizons of her or his own discipline. An invitation to explore the multiple shifting discursive contexts legitimizing one's domain of authority can break down the seeming boundaries between fields of knowledge and practice for the clinical psychologist. In my practice I have found that I consider the tensions between my horizon as a psychologist and those particular to my clients, and that I feel obligated to place my assumptions under that same respectful scrutiny as I do theirs. Thus I often find myself both violating and reinventing the discursive boundaries between my "field" and those of social architects, physicians, seers, agitators, judges, teachers, confessors, and charlatans. More aware, now, of the social and historical rootedness of my understanding, I am no longer innocent of the implications my understanding may have for others.

The practitioner of a dialogic reflexivity, because she or he examines not only her individual prejudgments but those of her social and professional milieu, will find that the ways in which she understands her professional role and its social implications will be subject to change and ongoing revision. We have become more aware that our roles as professional scientists are hardly innocent of political intentions or consequences. Aylesworth notes Gadamer's view that "the human sciences, insofar as they comprise a body of methods and techniques, are not distinguishable from technology and its totalizing agenda" (Aylesworth, 1991). Foucault, too, has targeted the social sciences for their roles in perpetuating a modernist discursive regime. Practitioners of psychology are currently under heightened pressure to shift allegiance from the humanistic social agenda of the early part of this century to that of the marketplace, and are thus in terrible need of skills in practical reasoning and social critique.

For example, we are prone, in our press to discover new venues of practice in order to survive, to promote psychologists as simple technicians in specialized domains, such as drug treatment, quality assurance research, and managed health care, which in turn only passively contribute to what appear to be overwhelming social forces. Corporate forces in managed health care have constructed a new vision of the health professional as laborer, and have divided the discipline of health care into "responsibility" by individuals (and local communities) and "control" by corporations under the auspices of "management." While we are easily led to see the changes in our society's vision of health care as a monolithic force, a postmodern critique can reveal the partiality, complexity and contradictions in the social relations of contemporary health care. The nature of the corporate diminishment of professional psychologists' cultural currency is no more unified than the possible points of resistance, a perspective that we should nurture as a means of preventing abdication or blind accommodation. From the vantage point described in this essay, we may be more effective if we assume "mobile and transitory points of resistance, producing cleavages in a society that shifts about, fracturing unities and effecting regroupings" (Foucault, 1979: 96). To do so, we need to engage in the kind of reflexive personal and social critique outlined above, and to accomplish this, as Bourdieu advocates, "as a collective enterprise rather than the burden of the lone academic" or practitioner (Wacquant, 1992). Thus it behooves those of us who train practitioners to train them to be reflexive in both their clinical and supervisory endeavors for the sake of all their various and shifting "clients."

Feminists, fortified by some of the postmodernist ideas of Gadamer, Foucault, and Bourdieu, have promoted a commitment to reflexive critical analyses as means to elucidating latent discourses that privilege dominant social groups and limit the scope of emancipatory theory. It has been argued here that a dialogic reflexivity, the practice of turning one's gaze, critically and responsibly back upon one's self, one's institutional and social milieu, and one's professional role, can have a vital place in the performance of clinical supervision. Rather than eschewing power in the person of the supervisor, which only creates illusions of equality in a hierarchically structured social domain, power in its various, shifting manifestations is turned into an object of dialogic analysis within the supervisory relationship. The discovery and unpacking of the workings of power and authority in each member of the dyad has the potential to empower formerly marginalized discourses and to create points of resistance within hierarchical systems, which then have implications for learning in a supervisory relationship, for the supervisee's clients, and for the profession of clinical practice.

References

Anderson, H. and Goolishian, H. (1991a) "Supervision as collaborative conversation: questions and reflections," in H. Brandau (ed.), *Von der Supervision zur systemischen Vision*. Salzburg: Otto Muller Verlag. pp. 180–205.

Anderson, H. and Goolishian, H. (1991b) "The client is the expert: a not-knowing approach to therapy," in unpublished collection of papers by the Houston-Galveston Family Institute (ed.), *A Collaborative Language Systems Approach to Therapy: New Directions in Theory and Practice*. Houston, TX.

Aylesworth, G.E. (1991) "Dialogue, text, narrative: confronting Gadamer and Ricoeur," in H.J. Silverman (ed.), *Gadamer and Hermeneutics: Science, Culture, Literature*. New York: Routledge. pp. 63–81.

Belenky, M.F., Cinchy, B.M., Goldberger, N.R., and Tarule, J.M. (1986) *Women's Ways of Knowing: The Development of Self, Voice, and Mind*. New York: Basic Books.

Bourdieu, P. (1992) "The purpose of reflexive sociology" (The Chicago Workshop), in P. Bourdieu and L.J.D. Wacquant, *An Initiation to Reflexive Sociology*. Chicago: University of Chicago Press. pp. 61–216.

Cinchy, B.M., Belenky, M.F., Goldberger, N., and Tarule, J.M. (1985) "Connected education for women," *Journal of Education*, 16: 28–45.

Finke, L. (1993) "Knowledge as bait: feminism, voice, and the pedagogical unconscious," *College English*, 55: 7–27.

Flax, J. (1991) *Thinking Fragments: Psychoanalysis, Feminism, and Postmodernism in the Contemporary West*. Berkeley, CA: University of California Press.

Foucault, M. (1978) *The History of Sexuality, Volume I: An Introduction* (trans. Robert Hurley). New York: Random House.

Foucault, M. (1979) *Discipline and Punish: The Birth of the Prison*. New York: Random House.

Frasier, N. (1989) *Unruly Practices: Power, Discourse and Gender in Contemporary Social Theory*. Minneapolis, MN: University of Minnesota Press.

Gadamer, H.G. (1975) *Truth and Method*. New York: Continuum.

Gandolfo, R. and Brown, R. (1987) "Psychology intern ratings of actual and ideal supervision of psychotherapy," *Journal of Training and Practice in Professional Psychology*, 1: 15–28.

Haraway, D. (1991) *Simians, Cyborgs, and Women: The Reinvention of Nature.* New York: Routledge.

Harding, S. (1991) *Whose Science? Whose Knowledge? Thinking from Women's Lives.* Ithaca, NY: Cornell University Press.

Hare-Mustin, R. and Marecek, J. (1990) *Making a Difference: Psychology and Construction of Gender.* New Haven, CT: Yale University Press.

Hawes, S. (1993) "Reflexivity and collaboration in the supervisory process: a role for feminist poststructuralist theories in the training of professional psychologists," paper presented to the National Council of Schools and Programs in Professional Psychology, winter meeting, La Jolla, CA.

Hawes, S. (1994) "Applying a feminist critique to academic presentations: more reflexive practices." Unpublished manuscript, Antioch New England Graduate School.

Hayes, E. (1989) "Insights from women's experiences for teaching and learning," *New Directions For Adult and Continuing Education,* 43: 55–66.

Hekman, S.J. (1990) *Gender and Knowledge: Elements of a Postmodern Feminism.* Boston: Northeastern University Press.

Holloway, E.L., Freund, R.D., Gardiner, S.L., Nelson, M.L., and Walker, B.R. (1989) "Relation of power and involvement to theoretical orientation in supervision: an analysis of discourse," *Journal of Counseling Psychology,* 16 (1): 88–102.

Keller, E.F. (1985) *Reflections on Gender and Science.* New Haven, CT: Yale University Press.

Kritzman, L. (ed.) (1988) *Michel Foucault: Politics, Philosophy, Culture.* New York: Routledge.

Lax, W. (1992) "Postmodern thinking in a clinical practice," in K. Gergen and S. McNamee (eds), *Social Constructionism in Therapeutic Process.* London: Sage. pp. 114–36.

Morawski, J. (1990) "Toward the unimagined: feminism and epistemology in psychology," in R.T. Hare-Mustin and J. Marecek (eds), *Making a Difference: Psychology and Construction of Gender.* New Haven, CT: Yale University Press. pp. 150–83.

Morawski, J. (1994) *Practicing Feminisms, Reconstructing Psychology: Notes on a Liminal Science.* Ann Arbor, MI: University of Michigan Press.

Singer, D., Peterson, R., and Magidson, E. (1992) "The self, the student, and the core curriculum: learning from the inside out," in R. Peterson, J. McHolland, R. Bent, E. Davis-Russell, G. Edwall, K. Polite, D. Singer, and G. Stricker (eds), *The Core Curriculum in Professional Psychology.* Washington, DC: American Psychological Association. pp. 133–40.

Tisdell, E.J. (1993) "Feminism and adult learning: power, pedagogy, and praxis," *New Directions for Adult and Continuing Education,* 57: 91–103.

Tong, R. (1989) *Feminist Thought: A Comprehensive Introduction.* Boulder, CO: Westview Press.

Wacquant, L.J.D. (1992) "Toward a social praxeology: the structure and logic of Bourdieu's sociology," in P. Bourdieu and L.J.D. Wacquant, *An Initiation to Reflexive Sociology.* Chicago: University of Chicago Press. pp. 1–59.

Weedon, C. (1987) *Feminist Practice and Poststructuralist Theory.* Oxford: Basil Blackwell.

6

The Ordinary, the Original, and the Believable in Psychology's Construction of the Person

Kenneth J. Gergen

The psychological subject is pre-eminently a textual being, born of a confluence of discursive practices. In generating the sense of a subject to be elucidated, the investigator can scarcely escape tradition; to do so would be to fail in achieving intelligibility. Yet, molding character from the available repositories of discourse is a precarious undertaking. Accounts of character – what it is to be a coherent and identifiable person – are first of all possessions of the populace. They are central constituents of ordinary language conventions and, as a result, intimately intertwined in daily patterns of human relationship. Thus, when people speak of their intentions, beliefs, wants, hopes, fears, and the like, they are not only generating and solidifying agreements concerning the ontology of personal being, they are also carrying out patterns of relationship in which such terms are essential integers. (The utterance "I adore you" not only asserts the condition of adoration to be a central essence of human beings, but simultaneously participates in a form of relatedness that equally determines what it is to be human.) The psychologist's position is thus precarious in two senses: first with respect to his/her symbiotic relationship with the existing language communities, and second with respect to the life forms that such writing may either disturb or destroy.[1]

It is the question of achieving intelligibility that is the chief focus of the present paper. The textual construction of the person is critical not only for novelists, biographers, and autobiographers; it is also of pivotal importance to historians, political scientists, legal theorists, philosophers of knowledge, psychologists, and many others. All are challenged with the problem of rendering in words a sense of recognition, a sense that "I know and understand the person whereof they speak." At the same time, in all these cases the writer is faced with a subtle but consequential problem: he or she must rely on the discursive forestructure supplied by the culture and yet perishes by its repetition. The writer must rely on the existing argots of understanding or cease to be intelligible. To write of someone who "feels pickle" or who "wishes in the horizontal" fails in the cooperative achievement of making sense. At the same time, to reproduce the existing forestructure is to fail in generating moments of distinction – a sense that the subject is significant, worthy of distinction in the ongoing hurly-burly of daily activity. If the writer does not estrange the audience from the commonplace, voice is lost. At worst, the writer simply expands the domain of tedium.

How is it then that the professional psychologist, as a writer, navigates between the shoals of the banal and the absurd, making claims about human nature that are simultaneously acceptable to and at variance with common opinion? The problem is interesting from several standpoints. While rhetorical analysis has traditionally centered on the writing of fiction, the fiction writer occupies a very specialized role within the culture. And, although this role does undergo historical change, it has long been defined in terms of its liberty. That is, violations of the rules of common intelligibility are anticipated – or even desired for the forms of entertainment, enlightenment, or escape which they allow. Thus, along with other rhetorical processes, analyses of character formulation in fictional writing may be misleading if generalized to other forms of literary construction. Indeed, as rhetorical consciousness has expanded in recent years, analysts have become increasingly concerned with the literary dimensions of the human sciences. Hayden White's *Tropics of Discourse* (1978), Donald McClosky's *The Rhetoric of Economics* (1985), Bruno Latour's *Science in Action* (1987), and James Clifford and George Marcus's *Writing Culture* (1986), along with sociological works by Bryan Green (*Literary Methods and Sociological Theory* (1988)) and Richard Harvey Brown (*Society as Text* (1971)), and the psychiatrically oriented writings of Donald Spence (*Narrative Truth and Historical Truth* (1982)) and Patrick Mahony (*Freud as a Writer* (1987)), are among the most visible works of this genre. The present analysis extends this line of endeavor to inquire, most particularly, into the scientific psychologist's construct of character.[2]

In light of the role played by scientific psychology within the culture, such an excursion takes on special significance. For as traditionally reasoned, the rigorous and objective study of mental processes should ultimately lend itself to an enhanced quality of cultural life. With greater knowledge of the emotions, thought processes, memory, motivation, personality dispositions, and the like, we should be able to make more informed decisions concerning educational practices, child rearing, career choice, and a host of other matters including the care and prevention of mental disorders. In effect, scientific accounts of mental processes are candidates for truth status, and to achieve truth is to claim superiority over (and thus to marginalize) all competing forms of discourse. Yet, regardless of the extent and rigor of the research practices, the resulting account is a textual achievement. No less than the novelist, the psychologist must employ techniques of literary construction to render scientific accounts acceptable. Most importantly, to the extent that such techniques dominate the scientific account, observational practices – regardless of rigor – cease to make an imprint on the rendering. Methods of experimentation, systematic measurement, and sophisticated statistical devices lose their power, both to possess the text and to warrant its truth. They neither control the discursive rendering of "the subject", nor do they justify it. Thus, to penetrate the textual devices for creating the subject within the psychological literature simultaneously undermines the objectivity of such accounts and serves as a means for liberating otherwise-marginalized discourses.

The present attempt is not to assay the full range of rhetorical techniques in current use. More modestly I shall outline three sources of constraint in the writings of professional psychology and the way in which these constraints enter into the fashioning of the person. I will direct attention first to issues deriving from the psychologist's membership in the culture at large, then to problems emerging within the scientific subculture, and finally to the textual character of laboratory practice. To echo the initial refrain, my special concern in each case is with the psychologist's attempt as scientist, to equilibrate between the opposing necessities of conventionality and originality.

Creating the Subject in Cultural Context

The psychologist's ultimate challenge is to present a compelling picture of human functioning to an audience whose lifelong effort has been that of functioning humanly. For the most part, people are relatively secure in their "knowledge of people" and will cite their everyday adequacies as proof of their discernment. Of course, professional psychologists are no less members of the culture at large, and as a result they share in the common conceptions of the person. It is indeed just this background which enables them ultimately to meet the challenge of intelligibility. In the same way that the seventeenth-century vicar Robert Burton could turn commonsense beliefs in melancholy into a 500-page treatise on the causes and cures of this affliction (1977), psychologists of today enter the laboratory already committed to the belief that persons possess rational thought, emotion, memory, and the like. The culture's ontology of personhood is seldom brought into question, and thus the psychologist's accounts are typically congenial to the surrounding ethos.[3]

It is in this context that one is sensitized to the subtle shifts in the professional construction of the person occurring over the past century. As I have tried to describe elsewhere, nineteenth-century romanticism revitalized and refashioned the medieval "reality of the deep interior" (Gergen, 1991). That is, the literary, musical, architectural, and artistic ventures of the time conspired to define the person in terms of a deep energic force, often equated with soul and rooted in both the spiritual and natural world. It was the expressions of the deep interior, whether in terms of inspiration, devotion, grief, or moral commitment, that gave personal existence its significance. These suppositions are, of course, reflected in the character of major protagonists of romantic novels. And in psychology, it is this cultural context that served both to stimulate and to render intelligible Freud's theory of the unconscious. Without the forestructure of romantic discourse (see Whyte's (1960) *The Unconscious Before Freud*), psychoanalytic theory could have neither been penned nor proliferated.

Yet, in the twentieth century, as romanticism has been replaced by the Zeitgeist of modernity, the deep interior recedes from view. In modern psychology curricula, Freudian theory receives but scant attention (often viewed as a historic relic or relevant only to circumscribed problems of mental health). In the scientific laboratories Freudian theory is remarkable for its absence. For in the modernist culture, we find a prevalent return to Enlightenment assumptions of human functioning. Within the present century, the deep interior as the core around which character is constructed has largely been replaced by what we believe to be the more accessible processes of observation and reason. That is, persons are rendered intelligible as persons primarily by virtue of their experiences and thoughts. It is reason and observation that, in the modernist vein, lead to essential knowledge or understanding, not only in the domains of science, but also in the visual arts, architecture, music, dance, and so on. And it is on the powers of reason and observation that we can rely for continued progress and prosperity.[4]

The psychological sciences have drawn from this same repository of cultural beliefs in their fashioning of the twentieth-century being. The two most central lines of research within the mainstream have explored, first, the process of learning (through observation) and, second, information processing (the character of thought). The works of J.B. Watson, Ivan Pavlov (as popularized within the USA), B.F. Skinner, and Clark Hull were canonical texts within the former realm. All were concerned with the processes by which individuals acquire knowledge of the world or learn to adapt to the world as it is. All served to inform the reader that the individual is defined in terms of his/her capacities to know (through experience) and adjust. The emphasis on learning has been replaced in recent years by concerns with information processing ("the cognitive revolution" in psychology). The enormous research literature on processes of attention, comprehension, cognitive heuristics, information storage, and memory systems signifies to the culture that the critical ingredients of human character are processes of thought.

Yet, to declare that the common suppositions about human nature are true is simply to assert that psychological accounts have been appropriately absorbed by the prevailing ethnopsychology. The psychologist would simply murmur assent to that which everyone knows and thus fail in the task of generating "insight." This leaves open the question of transcendence – how the profession secures voice by moving beyond the commonplace. In my view, where successful, this end is largely accomplished through *metonymic implication*. That is, elements of the common vernacular are used as token parts of more general but unarticulated wholes. By elaborating or filling out the images implied by the fragments, the scientific psychologist retains the commonsense conventions, but offers what is effectively a fresh body of insights. Thus, for example, to speak commonly of persons "knowing their way around" and having a "good sense of direction" is, by implication, to suggest a more general image of the individual as possessor of some form of map. Given the more general emphasis within modernist culture on processes of reasoning, the resulting theory is felicitously cast in terms of "cognitive mapping." Thus, researchers from Charles Tolman in the 1930s to ecological psychologists of the 1980s offer to the culture a corpus of theory (and supportive research) on the nature of cognitive maps (see, for example, Neisser's volume (1976), *Cognition and Reality*). Such theorizing is intelligible largely because it relies, at base, on the commonsense conventions. However, in its fuller elaboration of the image implied by these conventions, it carries the sense of an original scientific contribution.

There are two features of this process worthy of special attention, the first involving psychology's expansion of the culture's concept of the person and the second involving its constriction. In the former case, once the theorist has elaborated the general image suggested by various fragments of sedimented discourse, its implicature may be explored by a process of *propositional unpacking*. That is, given the psychologist's location of a guiding image or metaphor of the human being, he or she may then move on to develop deductively an array of corollary propositions. By unpacking the implicational network, the theorist advances a new array of propositions about human nature not directly contained in the common language. For example, one of the most rhetorically powerful images in the recent psychological literature is that of the mind as computational device, or form of computer. The metaphor is invited by numerous commonsense accounts of persons who "calculate," "carry information in their heads," "possess memories," and so on. However, once the metaphor is in place, the theorist can flesh out the picture of the human being in terms of discourse borrowed from the domain of computer technology. Current theories, for example, treat such topics as feature detection, information storage, storage capacity, working memory, information retrieval, semantic codes, sensory storage, and encoding processes – none of which were initially part of the commonsense idiom, but which may become so as the psychologist's constructions of the person gain status as "accepted knowledge."

At the same time as the elaboration of the dominant images leads to fresh conceptualizations of the person, there is also a way in which the profession circumscribes the cultural construction of character. In their natural habitat, that of informal communal life, the signifiers of personal being are subject to continuous catachresis. Fragments of person description are inserted into various and newly emerging contexts without risk of social sanction. Or, in Derridian terms, the signifiers enjoy a relatively high degree of freedom, and thus, the destiny and complexity of their traces are constantly expanding. However, once the scientific psychologist has appropriated the cultural argot, sealed it within the confines of a particular image, and disseminated the language to the culture in the form of "scientific knowledge," the cultural signifiers are thereby constrained. They are discounted or derogated as "mere folk talk." Thus, for example, as the profession increasingly defines human character in terms of the computer, common terms such as "calculate," "plan," and "think" lose their connotative richness. To "think about it," for example, is no longer a matter of "seeking inspiration from within" (one connotative trace for such a phrase), but of "accessing programs of propositional logic" – just as a properly programmed computer would do. Not only is linguistic flexibility lost in this definitional fixing, but as the computer metaphor is normalized, such terms as "spirit," "passion," "soul," "creativity," "mood," and "lust" become moribund. They are inconsistent with the dominant imagery of mind as computer and thus irrelevant to understanding human character.[5]

Constructing the Person in the Scientific Culture

Social scientists are not only members of the culture at large, but of particular guilds or "interpretive communities" within the academic domain. These communities possess histories of textual formulation, internal understandings of the nature of human character. And to the extent that the scientist is to be intelligible, he or she must construct the person within the constraints of these traditions. There are a number of stories to be told about such constraints and their violation. However, there is one of special relevance to what many take to be the breakdown of the empiricist tradition in recent decades, along with the associated deterioration of boundaries between science and art (fact and fiction, reality and myth, the literal and the metaphoric). It is again a story of equilibrating between convention and counter convention in the construction of the person. Its special interest lies in the irony of outcome. For in the very attempt to transcend the consensus view, psychologists have succeeded in subverting the foundational view of empirical science. In generating "pleasures of the text," they have undermined the very warrant of the scientific text as objective.

To begin the tale, scientific psychologists have shared with the scientific community at large a particular view of the character of the scientist. This view, largely constructed within logical empiricist philosophy, paints a heroic picture of the scientist. In dramatic terms, the scientist is one whose skills in observation and reason enable him (as feminist critics point out, the role is traditionally gendered) to step outside the vagaries of common opinion and political prejudice, to press beyond the frontiers of the unknown, and to carve truth from nature. (The similarity between this vision of the scientist-hero and Joseph Campbell's account of the heroic monomyth is hardly accidental.) In effect, by virtue of their training in the sciences, professional psychologists enter the research arena with a vision of the ideal person. And this intelligibility places significant constraints over the kind of portrayals that can be made of the human being within the research setting.

Given the close association between the empiricist construction of the scientist and twentieth-century modernism, the previous comments regarding the centrality of learning and cognition in psychology are apposite. Scientific psychology could not, in this sense, vindicate a romanticist view of human functioning, because such a view is contrary to the image of the heroic scientist. For the hero-scientist to prove through reason and observation that people's rationality and perceptions are governed by unconscious, irrational forces is to undo the very image that sustains the scientific endeavor. It was virtually incumbent upon scientific psychologists, then, to develop a picture of human functioning that celebrated reason and observation. The work of personality psychologist George Kelly nicely illustrates this attempt to harmonize the scientist's picture of himself with his accounts of human character more generally. In one passage of *A Theory of Personality*, Kelly attempts to replace the romantic view of the deeply driven being with a précis to his theory of personal cognition:

> Let us then . . . have a look at man-the-scientist. . . . When we speak of man-the-scientist we are speaking of all mankind and not merely a particular class of men who have publicly attained the stature of "scientists." . . . It is customary to say that the scientist's ultimate aim is to predict and control. This is a summary statement that psychologists frequently like to quote in characterizing their own aspirations. Yet, curiously enough, psychologists rarely credit the human subjects in their experiments with having similar aspirations. It is as though the psychologist were saying to himself, "I, being a psychologist, and therefore a scientist, am performing this experiment in order to improve the prediction and control of certain human phenomena; but my subject, being merely a human organism, is obviously propelled by inexorable drives welling up within him." . . . Now what would happen if we were to reopen the question of human motivation and use our long-range view of man to infer just what it is that sets the course of his endeavor? Would we see his centuried progress in terms of appetites, tissue needs or sex impulses? Or might he, in this perspective, show a massive drift of quite a different sort? Might not the individual man, each in his own personal way, assume more of the stature of a scientist, ever seeking to predict and control the course of events with which he is involved? Would he not have his theories, test his hypotheses, and weigh his experimental evidence? (Kelly, 1963: 4 – 5)

Kelly goes on to build his theory of human functioning on the basis of the latter assumption.

Yet, if the social scientist simply feeds back to the scientific community variations of its own image, he/she will ultimately be rendered invisible. Theoretical characterizations of the person would merely recycle "what all good scientists already know." The central problem for the theorist, then, is that of transcending the common intelligibility of the scientific community while simultaneously sustaining it. This problem is largely solved through the procedure of propositional unpacking described earlier. That is, the scientist dedicates himself to elucidating one or more of the ancillary propositions consistent with the dominant metaphor, but not a direct duplicate. Thus, for example, all of the above-cited topics central to the cognitive psychologist are consistent with the more general myth of the rational scientist at work. They are sufficiently fresh that they appear to carry new knowledge; at base, however, they sustain the myth of the heroic scientist.

It is at just this juncture that the seeds of subversion are inadvertently sown. For as the implicature is extended and new bodies of discourse are articulated, so do the boundaries of the dominant metaphor become fuzzy.

Its initial meanings become distorted, diffused, and eventually threatened by opposing images. Or, in the Derridian sense, as the traces of the initial signifier are extended, one reaches a point at which the signifier is deconstructed. It is precisely this unravelling of the prevailing metaphor that has helped to undermine the empiricist conception of the scientist (and thus the privilege of scientific discourse).

More specifically, as the metaphor of the individual as computational device has been progressively unpacked in various research settings, an increasing array of proactive attributes have been assigned to the individual. The individual has become one who *actively searches* for solutions, scans memory, formulates and carries out plans, processes information, and so on, all according to internal design. As it is commonly put, human beings are driven by "top down" processes (rationality operating on the world) as opposed to "bottom up" (the world determining what is rational) processes. However, as the individual *qua* computer becomes increasingly automaton or top-down in character, the impact of environmental inputs is suppressed. That is, it becomes difficult to speak of the individual as reacting to the stimulus of the real world because the character of the objective environment is determined by the internal operations of the computerlike individual. Reality within the machine is that which is allowed or determined by machine configuration. It is in this sense that Greenwald (1980) has characterized the cognitive system as "totalitarian." That is, it is closed to outside influence, seeking only to sustain its own position.

Yet, we find, to the extent that humans are portrayed as automaton-like computers, top-down in their determination of "what is the case," the traditional image of the scientist-hero cannot be sustained. For within the newly emerging story, scientists no longer search for and reveal the nature of the unknown; rather, they can only reveal in their writings the character of their machine operations. They do not record and reflect the world as it is, but as their own systemic processes require. Thus, in the very attempt to sustain and elaborate the image of the human being as rational agent, the traditional concept of rationality – with successful adaptation to existing circumstances at its core – is undone. The wholly rational individual proves irrational.

The Person in Laboratory Context

There is a third site of tension between the banal and the exotic, one that emerges in the context of empirical research in psychology. Traditional scientists claim warrant for their words largely on the basis of methodological procedures. In particular, it is the controlled experiment that enables the "behavior of organisms" (from single cells to entire societies) to be traced to their causal sources in an objectively rigorous way. As commonly proposed, by observing behavior in systematically varying conditions, the scientist can trace the causal connections between antecedents and consequents in a precise and replicable way. In whatever way human character is constructed within scientific psychology, its contours should be congenial (for the sake of logical consistency) with this central, justificatory text.

Indeed, one can trace the various ways in which this forestructure of methodological intelligibility interacts with the psychologist's portrayals of human nature. Thus, for example, the conception of the experiment is one in which "subjects" are exposed to "stimuli," which stimuli operate as "causal conditions." Actions of the subject in experimental conditions are viewed as "responses" caused by the stimuli. For many, the resulting characterization of the human proves morally problematic because this view of methodology virtually obliterates the discourse of voluntarism. Because "stimulus conditions cause responses," the scientist cannot conclude that subjects voluntarily choose their subsequent actions. A voluntary impulse would essentially operate as an uncaused cause and thus fall outside the ontological underpinnings of the method. It is in this respect that Hampden-Turner has written:

> It is not that . . . investigators themselves have a savage eye, but rather that their predicting and controlling tools demand the predictable and controllable man in order to consummate the Good Experiment. And what a misery the man turns out to be. The highly respected Dr. Jekyll discovers Mr. Hyde, the beast in man uncovered by inhuman instruments. (1970: 4)

In the same vein, Gigerenzer and Murray have demonstrated in their *Cognition as Intuitive Statistics* (1987) how prevailing concepts of statistical logic, inherent features of experimental procedure, ultimately serve as the basis for theories of human cognition. As they propose, the scientists' statistical tools, which "are considered to be indispensable and prestigious, lend themselves to transformation into metaphors of mind."[6] Methodology inscribes itself on human character.

In my view, however, methodology does far more than carry implications for psychology's conception of the person. In significant degree, forms of methodological writing also serve to answer the following question: If the science is to make an original contribution, which entails the novel construction of the person, how is it to be credible in terms of the common idioms through which the world is understood? I have offered a partial answer to this question above, but by focusing on methodological procedures, I will attempt to expand the horizons. Methodological procedures do provide the psychologist warrant for voice. However, they do not do so in terms of foundational rationality, rendering the scientific account superior in mimetic capacities. Rather, they do so in terms of rhetorical power. It is the rhetoric of experimental procedure that ultimately serves to vivify or render realistic the otherwise arcane argot of the theorist. Through methodological procedures, the language of the absurd is transformed into plausible understandings of human nature.

To illustrate the process by which this ontological transformation is accomplished, it is useful to consider a single text from the scientific annals. The text in this case is a standard research report (Bandura et al., 1988) appearing in one of the most prestigious journals in psychology, the *Journal of Personality and Social Psychology.* The research was conducted at Stanford University, and its funding provided by the National Institute for Mental Health and the National Science Foundation. At the outset, the title of the research report, "Perceived Self-Efficacy in Coping with Cognitive Stressors and Opioid Activation," informs the reader that its contents will reveal the secrets of an otherwise mysterious or unknown world. The terms rely very little on the commonsense vernacular, and their very impenetrability suggests that only the serious scientist will be able to appreciate their significance.

From the present perspective, it is the authors' major task to lend to the alien theoretical discourse a sense of palpable reality, that is, to secure the reader's assent that "yes, this language does describe events in the actual and commonly knowable world." The accomplishment is no small challenge in the present case, for in their abstract or decontextualized form, such theoretical terms as "perceived self-efficacy" and "cognitive stressors" are hopelessly ambiguous. "Perceived" by whom – a person, friends and acquaintances, the psychologist? And is "perception" to be understood in the sense of direct sensation, deductive categorization, interpretation, intuition, or something else? And is saying it is "perceived" to suggest that it is not truly known, as in "the perceived world" as opposed to "the actual world"? And what of the term "self-efficacy"? Is this the bodily self, the spiritual self, the unconscious self, the voluntary self, or something else? And is efficacy to be read as "achievement," "impact," "power," "result-producing," or in some other way? Similarly, the term "cognitive" suggests thinking, perceiving, remembering, intending, planning, and a variety of other possibilities: are they all intended; how are we to select among them? And are these cognitions conscious or unconscious, motivated or unmotivated, desirable or undesirable? Again the language proves opaque. Similarly, the term "stressor" succumbs to a variety of interpretations (physically straining, bending, shaping, rendering more flexible, and so on). And, of course, each of these translations bears the traces of other signifiers in an ever-expanding array of undecidable signification.

The introductory section of the research report provides the initial assurance that there is indeed an objective datum (a signified) to which the theoretical terms refer. Two rhetorical processes function in this capacity, the first *social corroboration* and the second *conceptual deferral.* The corroborative function is carried out largely through citations of other scientific reports that claim familiarity with the states in question. The most directly relevant studies are those carried out in the same laboratory, suggesting that this location is privileged in its access to the phenomenon in question. Yet to cite only the work of the single laboratory is to cast doubt on the existence of the phenomenon. A multiplicity of additional citations thus serves to assuage residual doubt. As the reader is told, for example "Findings of different lines of research underscore the influential role of perceived control in stress reactions (Averil, 1973; Lazarus and Folkman, 1984; Miller, 1980)." And so secure is the existence of the phenomenon, according to the report, that research has also succeeded in qualifying or extending know-ledge of its precise operations. As one learns, for example, "in some studies of controllability, merely the exercise of personal control over the occur-rence of aversive events without curtailing their intensity reduces stress reactions (Gunnar-von-Gnechten, 1978)." Yet, in the end, these many sup-porting documents prove inadequate, for in the authors' terms, "The fore-going studies have relied on plausible presumptive mediation inferred from the manipulations rather than on direct assessment. . . ." Or in terms of the scientist-hero metaphor, the other scientists did not really observe the mys-terious phenomenon; they were merely speculating from their results.

In addition to garnering social corroboration through citations (a tech-nique that has similarly served the cited authors), additional credibility is lent to the exotic language through conceptual deferral. By this I mean a process by which the ambiguous term is furnished a sense of meaning through paraphrase or deferring to other concepts. At times the deferral moves toward the common language. The reader learns, for example, that "Perceived self-efficacy" is concerned with "beliefs in one's capabilities to mobilize the motivation, cognitive resources, and courses of action needed to meet given situational demands." The fact that a definition is given in more or less comprehensible terms has the rhetorical effect of securing the existence of the phenomenon. If we are uncertain that X exists, it is forti-fying to learn that, in fact, X = a presumably existing Y. However, the precise identity of Y – other than its equivalence of the mysterious X is left unspecified – as if transparent. In the above, for example, what is it to "mobilize motivation"? Is this to consume more calories, give oneself pep talks, thrust oneself into adrenalin-producing situations, or something else? In other locations in the introductory section, the conceptual deferral of the sacred terminology is largely removed from the domain of daily language. For example, few outside the sacrosanct community of knowers would com-prehend the definition of cognitive stress: "Psychological stress is the result of a relational condition in which perceived environmental demands strain or exceed perceived coping capabilities in domains of personal import." The words are teeming with profundity – "stress," "demands," "strain," "exceed," "coping" – but do little to disambiguate the putative phenom-enon.

Far more significant in the achievement of ontological transformation is the second section of the report, "Method." Here scientists report on the pro-cedures used to carry out their investigations. These reports are written in plaintalk or literal language of the kind that would enable other scientists to replicate (and thus evaluate objectively) the featured research. Most impor-tant for present purposes, investigators report in everyday language the means by which the theoretically specified phenomenon is assessed or estab-lished. These definitional linkages (the "operational definitions") thus furnish a direct equation in which X (in the exotic language) = Y (in the every-day vernacular). In this way the reader is informed that the otherwise mysti-fying theoretical language is actually reducible to commonly known, wholly palpable matters of fact. It is thus in the present manuscript that we learn that the conditions necessary for producing "perceived self-efficacy" result from placing college students in a "mathematical problem-solving task" for 18 minutes. "High perceived self-efficacy" occurs when the students can work at their own speed at a set of arithmetic problems; "low perceived self-efficacy" takes place when the problems are presented to students more rapidly than normally required for completion. The state is measured by a questionnaire in which the students are asked to rate their certainty in completing the problems. Similarly, "cognitive stress" is assessed by a questionnaire in which students are asked how much "stress" and how much "mental strain from time pressure" they experienced. Thus the alien discourse becomes intimate – now a constituent of the comfortably ordinary surrounds.

Yet ontological transformation is not yet complete, for if the theoretical language remained tied to mundane operations, it could easily be rendered superfluous. Why, one might ask, is the theoretical language essential if all is intelligible in the common language? The third section of the manuscript, carrying the results of the investigation, serves as a hedge against such queries. In this section the operational or everyday language of the preceding section is progressively abandoned or suppressed. Increasingly the researchers slip back into the uncommon or exotic vernacular. We learn, for example, that "Perceived self-inefficacious subjects showed a heightened heart rate, whereas the perceived self-efficacious ones displayed a marked decline in heart rate." In the plaintalk idiom it might be said that the hearts of those faced with solving problems at a rapid rate pounded faster than those working at their own speed. However, this form of account never appears. It is, after all, the reality of the exotic language that must be established. This is accomplished, in important degree, by borrowing from the preceding equation of the exotic with the taken for granted. Once the equation is achieved, the latter must be silently shed.

The present research study is exceptional in its objectification of the mental terminology, for it goes on to demonstrate a causal link between the mental and the material world. Because the material world is commonly accepted as objective within modernist culture and the ontological status of psychological terminologies is suspect, then to demonstrate that psychological states act on physical states is to solidify the existence of psychological states. The possibly subjective (and thereby discreditable) becomes objective. This "causal connection" is established in the present instance by demonstrating that depending on their perceptions of self-efficacy (a psychological state), subjects are more or less susceptible to a chemical, naloxone, that blocks opiate or pain-reducing receptors (a physical state). This account treats perceived self-efficacy as an independent reality, not at this point reducible to work on mathematical tasks.

In the final section of the paper, the "Discussion," the ontological transformation is made complete. For here the commonplace intelligibilities are altogether suppressed. The reader has previously learned that the alien language refers to palpable events, reducible to the commonly known. Now that the linkage is established, it is possible to speak almost wholly within the novel ontology. The reader is confidently told, for example, that "The results of the present experiment provide evidence that perceived self-efficacy in coping with cognitive stressors activates endogenous opioid systems." The reality of the new ontology is further extended by relating it to other exotic but scientifically acceptable accounts. And finally, to inject the newly created reality with everyday significance, its implications for personal health are outlined: "A growing body of evidence reveals that the stress of coping inefficacy . . . impairs cellular components of the immune system." The newly molded person, replete with perceptions of self-efficacy, is now readied by the laboratory literature to venture forth and cope with cognitive stressors of the world.

In Conclusion

The psychologist no less than the writer of fiction is engaged in the literary process of rendering the human mind both interesting and intelligible. By focusing on the character of these problems and the means by which they are solved within the human sciences, the traditional privilege of objectivity accorded to the scientist is threatened. However, this is not to argue toward the end of psychological inquiry. Simply because psychological accounts are rhetorically fashioned, essentially creating their subject matter, is no reason for abandonment. As I have argued elsewhere (Gergen, 1994), psychological terms are essential constituents of cultural practices. Without the vocabulary of intention, emotion, reason, hope, and so on, cultural life would be radically altered; most of what we hold dear in our traditions would be lost. Further, psychology is that unique discipline in which deliberation on this vocabulary is focal. To add to the array of cultural conceptions of mind can add to the vitality and richness of cultural life. At the same time, to carry out such deliberations without regard to the process of reification, and without careful attention to the way in which psychological discourse may be used in the society more generally, is both myopic and dangerous. To appreciate the point we need simply ask whether the creation of several hundred categories of "mental disease" in the present century is a contribution to cultural life. The present offering is made in the hope of enhancing professional consciousness of existing shortcomings and future potentials.

Notes

An earlier version of this chapter appears in *Style* (1990, 24: 365–79).

1 For critical assessments of the effects of psychological discourse on cultural life see, for example, Sampson (1993) and Greenberg (1994).

2 The present paper thus extends my earlier incursions into the uses of narrative (Gergen and Gergen, 1988), metaphor (Gergen, 1990) and rhetoric (Gergen, 1992) in constructing objectively palpable persons.

3 For a more extended account of current assumptions of personhood and their historical origins, see Amelie Rorty's *Mind in Action* (1988). For discussion of psychological discourse in historical context see Graumann and Gergen (1996).

4 See, for example, Lyotard's (1984) account of the modernist narrative of progress.

5 For a more detailed account of how mental health language has diminished the common vocabulary of accounting, see Gergen (1994, ch. 5).

6 See Danziger (1990) for an illuminating discussion of the way in which the transformation in preferred methodology over the century has altered psychology's characterization of the person.

References

Bandura, A., Cioffi, D., Taylor, C.B., and Brouillard, M. (1988) "Perceived self-efficacy in coping with cognitive stressors and opioid activation," *Journal of Personality and Social Psychology*, 55: 479–88.

Brown, R.H. (1971) *Society as Text.* Chicago: University of Chicago Press.

Burton, R. (1977) *The Anatomy of Melancholy.* New York: Vintage.

Clifford, J. and Marcus, G. (eds) (1986) *Writing Culture.* Berkeley, CA: University of California Press.

Danziger, K. (1990) *Constructing the Subject.* Cambridge: Cambridge University Press.

Gergen, K.J. (1990) "Metaphors of the social world," in D. Leary (ed.), *Metaphors in the History of Psychology.* Cambridge: Cambridge University Press. pp. 267–99.

Gergen, K.J. (1991) *The Saturated Self.* New York: Basic Books.

Gergen, K.J. (1992) "The mechanical self and the rhetoric of reality," *Annals of Scholarship,* 9: 87–109.

Gergen, K.J. (1994) *Realities and Relationships.* Cambridge, MA: Harvard University Press.

Gergen, K.J. and Gergen, M.M. (1988) "Narrative and the self as relationship," in L. Berkowitz (ed.), *Advances in Experimental Social Psychology,* Vol. 21. New York: Academic Press. pp. 17–56.

Gigerenzer, G. and Murray, D. (1987) *Cognition as Intuitive Statistics.* Hillsdale, NJ: Erlbaum.

Graumann, K.F. and Gergen, K.J. (eds) (1996) *Historical Dimensions of Psychological Discourse.* New York: Cambridge University Press.

Green, B. (1988) *Literary Methods and Sociological Theory.* Chicago: University of Chicago Press.

Greenberg, J. (1994) *The Self on the Shelf.* Albany, NY: State University of New York Press.

Greenwald, A. (1980) "The totalitarian ego: fabrication and revision of personal history," *American Psychologist,* 35: 603–18.

Hampden-Turner, C. (1970) *Radical Man: The Process of Psycho-Social Development.* Cambridge: Schenkman.

Kelly, G. (1963) *A Theory of Personality.* New York: Norton.

Latour, B. (1987) *Science in Action.* Cambridge, MA: Harvard University Press.

Lyotard, J.F. (1984) *The Postmodern Condition.* Manchester: Manchester University Press.

Mahony, P. (1987) *Freud as a Writer.* New Haven, CT: Yale University Press.

McClosky, D. (1985) *The Rhetoric of Economics.* Madison, WI: University of Wisconsin Press.

Neisser, U. (1976) *Cognition and Reality.* San Francisco: Freeman.

Rorty, A. (1988) *Mind in Action.* Boston: Beacon Press.

Sampson, E.E. (1981) "Cognitive psychology as ideology," *American Psychologist,* 36: 730–43.

Sampson, E.E. (1993) *Celebrating the Other.* Boulder, CO: Westview Press.

Spence, D. (1982) *Narrative Truth and Historical Truth.* New York: Norton.

Stam, H.J. (1987) "The psychology of control: a textual critique," in H.J. Stam, T.B. Rogers and K.J. Gergen (eds), *The Analysis of Psychological Theory*. Washington, DC: Hemisphere. pp. 131–51.

Weston, C. and Knapp, J.V. (1989) "Profiles of the scientific personality: John Steinbeck's 'The Snake'," *Mosaic*, 22(1): 87–99.

White, H. (1978) *Tropics of Discourse*. Baltimore: Johns Hopkins University Press.

Whyte, L.L. (1960) *The Unconscious Before Freud*. New York: Basic Books.

7

Repopulating Social Psychology: A Revised Version of Events

Michael Billig

"Oh my God, what am I doing here?" Vanessa was thinking as she passed yet another name-plated door along the corridor. Please report to Dr Snitting's Room, Second Floor, Department of Psychology, two o'clock – the letter had said. Well, it had now passed two. And it wasn't her fault if Dr Snitting had the most out-of-the-way office imaginable. Another turning, another door, another labora-tory. Oh God, this is ridiculous. Yet another turn (how am I ever going to get out of this maze?) and what looked like a dead-end. Finally – past a door marked "Cleaners only," and opposite "Store Room Only" – was the door itself.

Vanessa glanced at her watch and knocked.

Scufflings inside. Then nothing. She knocked again. The door opened slightly. A beard, spectacles and frown popped round: "Yes?"

"I've come for the experiment."

"Oh, sorry, oh, two already?" The door opened fully. "Please. Dr Snitting."

Thus, the short, bald man introduced himself. He wiped his mouth on his right hand, which he held out to Vanessa. As he did so, his eyes shot downwards, to the floor, to her feet. Hand back and eyes up – oh God, thought Vanessa. Snitting bustled to a desk on the other side of the room. Wiping his mouth again, he bent over some computer paper: "Vanessa Jones, is it? Welcome." Vanessa noted a half-eaten sandwich on the desk.

"Sorry" he said again. "Please, come this way."

Vanessa followed him through a door at the back of the office into a tiny, win-dowless, cluttered room. He closed the door behind them. "Would you sit down, please?", he said, indicating a chair. This time, Snitting was looking her straight in the face. Vanessa did as she was told.

What the hell am I doing here? she was asking herself.

She was alone with a stranger in a room, hardly bigger than a broom cupboard, at the back of the most forsaken room in the whole department. And Dr Snitting was now standing right behind her, whispering: "This experiment involves judging patterns. I would like you to watch the screen. Soon I will turn off the light and . . ."

As Snitting spoke, Vanessa found herself thinking of his interrupted lunch. Oh God, it must have been an egg sandwich.

This sort of description is unlikely to be considered as appropriate for a standard journal of experimental psychology. The rhetorical conventions favored by editors, reviewers, and readers (not to mention the authors themselves) would normally prevent Ms Jones and Dr Snitting from enter-ing a journal's pages. Even in a critical article about the rhetoric of psy-chology, the account is problematic. An early version of the present paper was submitted to the *European Journal of Social Psychology*. An anonymous reviewer, whose critical report extended to seven pages, declared himself (and a presumption of gender is probably appropriate) "to be embarrassed by the Vanessa case study." Five times during the report, the reviewer mentioned his embarrassment. When the article was published in *Theory & Psychology*, it was accompanied by three commentaries, one by an experimentalist (Spears, 1994), one by a feminist (Ussher, 1994), and one urging greater reflexivity (Stringer, 1994). The last thought the intro-duction of Vanessa to be "bizarre" (1994: 353), adding "I think Vanessa is a mistake" (1994: 359).

It would be hard to exclude her at this late stage. But let her, together with Snitting, be reduced to devices. They appear in the exordium within a literary genre – the psychology article – which has coldly discarded exordia. Having performed their preliminary parts, Vanessa and Snitting shrink into metonymic devices for raising questions about rhetorical devices. The aca-demic journals of psychology tend not to examine the rhetoric which is rou-tinely reproduced in their pages. Even critics of experimental psychology tend to avoid discussing styles of writings, concentrating their critiques upon method and theory, as if psychology were constructed solely upon those twin pillars (but see Harré, 1981, and Gergen, 1990 and 1994, for analyses of psychology's rhetorical style). The presence of Vanessa and Snitting serves to announce that the routine rhetorics of psychology are to be inter-rupted, so that those routines can be called into question.

Rhetoric should not be lightly dismissed as "mere rhetoric." The propo-nents of the "Rhetoric of Inquiry Movement" have shown that academic writings, especially in the human and social sciences, have their own per-suasive rhetoric (Gusfield, 1976; McCloskey, 1986; Nelson et al., 1987; Shotter, 1993a, 1993b; Simons, 1989, 1990). Writing practices are not merely means to persuade readers of "facts," but those "facts," of which the readers are to be persuaded, are themselves constituted through writing. As Myers points out with respect to biology, "writing *produces* biology" (1991: xii; emphasis in original). To put the issue bluntly: without scientific texts there would be no science (Latour and Woolgar, 1979).

In the human and social sciences, conventional rhetoric bears wider mes-sages. For example, Bazerman (1987, 1988) has suggested that the rhetoric of experimental psychology expresses an underlying philosophy of behav-iorism. The theoretical implications of sociological rhetoric have been dis-cussed by Brown (1989, 1994) and Edmondson (1984). Some critics have argued that the power relations between the anthropologist and the objects of anthropological study have been echoed in the rhetorical conventions of anthropology (Clifford, 1988; Clifford and Marcus, 1986; Geertz, 1988; Rosaldo, 1989; Van Maanen, 1988). In order to escape from the theories and power relations of the past, such critics have been experimenting with new, reflexive writing practices (see also, Ashmore, 1990; Hicks and Potter, 1991; Mulkay, 1991; Pinch and Pinch, 1988).

It may be obvious that the account of Vanessa, Snitting, and the sandwich would be out of place in a standard psychology report. Why it is inappropriate is not so obvious. A detailed analysis could be undertaken, in order to differentiate the rhetorical structure of the Vanessa story from Dr Snitting's own report. One aspect bears particular attention: neither Vanessa Jones nor Snitting would appear as named characters in "Snitting (forthcoming)." The names would be replaced by anonymous descriptions. Other details, such as beard, mouth-wiping, and downward glance of the eyes would all disappear. So would all marks of Vanessa's and Snitting's respective individuality.

The journal texts of psychology tend to be "depopulated texts," devoid of individual characters (Billig, 1992; Danziger, 1994). When people appear in this psychology, they are stripped of what Foucault called the "ordinary individuality – the everyday individuality of everybody" (1979: 191). "Vanessa" and "Dr Snitting" are textual constructions designed to convey this ordinary individuality: they stand for individuals, who, while performing social roles, do so in their own individual way. Texts which include such named characters are populated. By contrast, "Experimenter (E)" and "Subjects (S)" are constructions which abolish this ordinary individuality. They serve to depopulate the writing, expelling individuals *qua* individuals beyond the textual margins.

Danziger (1994) has traced the historical origins of this depopulation. He argues that the rhetoric, by which experimental participants are described, is by no means a trivial matter. Epistemological and theoretical business is accomplished by the descriptions of "Experimenter" and "Subjects." In the early days of experimental psychology, introspectionist psychologists often used themselves as "subjects" – except that they did not use the term "subject," preferring to describe participants, including themselves, as "observers." The triumph of behaviorism, which saw the elimination of experience as a topic for psychology, brought about rhetorical changes, as well as theoretical and methodological ones. Textually, the "observers" disappeared from psychology journals, being replaced by "subjects." The latter term, as Danziger suggests, conveyed claims to objectivity and universality. The "subjects" were universal figures, with no personal autonomy or individual backgrounds. Thus, findings from one group of "subjects" could be universally generalized, or so the rhetoric routinely implied.

In a perceptive critique, Gigerenzer (1987) claims that the "elimination of the individual" in psychological writing is linked to the growth of conventional statistical procedures. It will be suggested that statistical practices on their own are not the prime cause, or indeed a necessary condition, for the depopulation. A rhetoric is involved, for statistics, in so far as they appear in scientific reports, are bound by rhetorical practices (Gephart, 1988). That being so, it might be possible to alter the conventional rhetoric for statistics in ways which make it possible to write individuals back into the text, while retaining the same statistical tests which are now conventionally reported. Thus, the means of reporting would be altered, even if the means of the statistics were held constant. Far from indicating the unimportance of rhetoric, this would indicate its importance. The changes of rhetoric would question the epistemological assumptions lying behind the rhetorical ascendency of the impersonal, universalized "subject."

The Project to Repopulate

At the outset, a basic question must be raised: why should the texts of psychology be repopulated? What gain would there be? In anticipation of later arguments, some brief words in support of repopulating psychological writing can be given.

First, the examples, which are to be discussed in this article, are drawn from social psychology. In common with other fields of experimental psychology, social psychology uses the rhetoric of realism, which denies that it is a rhetoric (Bazerman, 1988; Gergen, 1994; Gigerenzer, 1987; Lopes, 1991; Soyland, 1994). Psychological reports claim to present "facts," which contribute to the development of an unproblematically "real" discipline. As will be suggested, this sort of writing produces "unreal" descriptions of psychological processes. These descriptions depict psychological states which are not to be ascribed to ("real") ordinary individuals but to disembodied abstractions.

Second, the project to repopulate psychology raises issues that lie beyond the scope of standard theoretical and methodological critiques. There have been numerous critiques of the theoretical and methodological assumptions of experimental social psychology (Gergen, 1973; Harré and Secord, 1972; Henriques et al., 1984; Shotter, 1975), especially from those interested in creating discursive alternatives (e.g., Billig et al., 1988; Edwards and Potter, 1992; Parker, 1991; Parker and Shotter, 1990; Potter and Wetherell, 1987; Shotter, 1993a, 1993b, 1995). If rhetoric has an importance over and above what is conventionally called "theory" and "method," then it should be possible to put aside direct theoretical and methodological critique, and work *with* (not *against*) the methodologies and theoretical framings of the experimental reports. In so doing, the importance of rhetorical practices can be illustrated.

Third, there is a more general reason for repopulating psychology: critical writing should in general try to avoid reproducing depopulated practices. A number of feminist writers have articulated this position clearly, even if they have not used the term "depopulated." Harding (1989) and Keller (1985) argue that current ways of producing science and social science reflect masculine abstraction and impersonality (see also, Hawkins, 1989; Spitzack and Carter, 1989). Smith claims that current social scientific writing describes "people's activities, talk, relations, thinking, without the subjects who talk, act, relate, think" (1991: 163). Some feminist critics have argued that freeing psychology and other social sciences from masculine assumptions entails that more personal styles of writing are used (e.g., Smith, 1987, 1991; Squire, 1989, 1990, 1991). The editorial in the first issue of *Feminism and Psychology* specifically stated that the "question of subjectivity" would be a major issue in the new journal (Wilkinson et al., 1991: 14). Subsequent issues have regularly included articles involving a more personal style of reporting than is permissible in standard psychology journals, as, for example, in the contributions of the special issue on "Heterosexuality" (Wilkinson and Kitzinger, 1993).

The feminist point can be widened in order to cover critical writing in general. Radical social analyses, which are themselves depopulated, run the risk of subverting their own radicalism. The authors might claim that existing social arrangements and cultural forces are alienating. However, if critics use a dehumanized language to make such a claim, then, in certain respects, they are themselves reproducing a dehumanized culture through their texts. Marx and Engels (1971), in *The German Ideology*, claimed that, in contrast with "ideologists," they started from "real" men. More generally, one might claim that writers of ideology-critique should start from "real" women and men (or even a "Vanessa" or a "Snitting"), if they are to avoid producing dehumanized, depopulated writing.

The present article concentrates upon the depopulation of experimental social psychology, but this does not mean that writings in other disciplines fare better. Even fashionably critical writings are frequently, and disturbingly, depopulated (Billig, 1994a; van Dijk, 1995). A separate article would be needed to demonstrate this. For example, a story needs to be told how readers can wander through the pages of supposedly radical Lacanian psychology, without encountering a recognizable individual. That story will need to be told on another occasion.

The Subjects of Social Psychology

The first step is to document depopulation in social psychological journals (the textbooks, which are not generally taken seriously by academic readers, are often populated after their own fashion). The *European Journal of Social Psychology*, an internationally refereed journal, officially published by the European Association of Experimental Social Psychology, is to be taken as a case-study. It was also the journal to which the present paper was first submitted and from which it was decisively rejected. The case-study concentrates on the journal's first two issues of 1991, which contained 10 experimental reports and one theoretical paper (Galam and Moscovici, 1991). All together, these papers reported results gathered from 927 subjects. Over 900 of the subjects are identified as undergraduate students, but the precise number is impossible to ascertain from the reports. The subjects appear as shadowy, nameless figures. None of the 927 appears in person. All are presented merely as "subjects" (see Billig, 1994b, for more details about the conception of "subjects" in the Galam and Moscovici study).

To ask "who are the subjects of experimental texts?" is not to ask who they *really* were, as if seeking to recapture their lost individuality. It is to ask how they are presented within the texts. As Bazerman (1988) and Gigerenzer (1987) note, descriptions of subjects are conventionally brief in modern psychological reports. The descriptions in the *European Journal* sample are no exception. Three examples can be given, all taken from the start of "methods" sections or "subjects sub-sections" of the papers:

1 "53 students of the University of Oregon participated in 50-minute sessions in groups of four in exchange for credit in an introductory psychology course" (Krueger, 1991: 39).
2 "Subjects were seventy-one male and female undergraduate volunteers who received class credit for participation" (Wright and Gregorich, 1991: 78).
3 "Twenty male and female sophomores of a higher music-educational program (Lemmensinstitut, Leuven) answered an anonymous questionnaire during a course on psychology of music taught by the author" (Peeters, 1991: 140).

Each description specifies the number of subjects and briefly describes source of the subjects. The authors use a common impersonal style and do not identify themselves, or their assistants, in describing the recruitment of subjects. A small habit of wording can be noted. The examples do not talk of "*the* subjects." The participants are merely "subjects" without the definite article. Bellquist, in his *Guide to Grammar and Usage for Psychology*, criticizes this rhetorical habit. He identifies reasons in favor of the omission. These include the point that "the omission of the definite article creates a professional tone, which confers covert prestige on the writer as part of a scientific elite" (1993: 179). Against that, he comments that the omission "is depersonalizing and therefore demeaning to the subjects themselves, particularly human ones" (1993: 179). He also argues for the inclusion of "the" on stylistic and grammatical grounds.

The reports in the *European Journal* offer different information about the subjects. In the first example, the gender of the subjects is not mentioned. In 2 and 3, the authors mention that there were males and females, but not how many of each. There were other variations: "Twice as many female than male students participated in each cell," wrote Sachdev and Bourhis (1991: 7) without giving exact figures overall or within the cells. McAllister and Anderson (1991) are more exact, specifying that there were "12 males and 12 females." Kalma (1991) presents the numbers of males and females within different experimental groups, allowing the reader to sum the total numbers.

All the studies, except McAllister and Anderson (1991), used students as subjects. The descriptions varied. In 1 and 3, but not 2, the institution and the course taken by the subjects are specified. Example 3 mentioned that the author was teaching the course, but 2 provided no such information. Schaller states: "Participants were 141 introductory psychology students at a large North American university who participated in partial fulfilment of a course requirement" (1991: 28). The students' year (sophomores) is mentioned by Peeters, but not by other authors. McAllister and Anderson mention that some of their subjects were undergraduates, but not how many were (1991: 152). Wallbott (1991) gives some very specific details: the numbers of males and females; the course taken by the students; their age range, and mean age, calculated to one place of decimal. However, the institution, which these students attended, is not mentioned.

These descriptions possess what can be called "a variable vagueness." All are vague in some respects, but not in the same respects: what is precise and what is vague varies from one report to another. The authors do not justify their own individual patterns of precision and imprecision. Instead, the descriptions are presented as if routine. However, the routine routinely varies. The uncontroversial regularity of this practice suggests that variable vagueness might not be a methodological failing, but a rhetorical accomplishment.

Variable Vagueness as Rhetorical Solution

To understand the rhetorical meaning of discourse, it is often necessary to take into account what is left unsaid (Billig, 1987, 1991). The descriptions of subjects contain a routine omission: there is no "sampling discourse." Authors do not regularly include justifications of why the particular sample of subjects was selected. Nor do they routinely claim that care had been taken to select that particular sample (with the exception of Joule, 1991, whose design demanded that experimental subjects be regular smokers). Typically, authors present their samples, as if it is "natural" to use such subjects and as if justification is unnecessary. The descriptions tend to present the samples as if homogeneous: (the) subjects are described as coming from the same class/university/music institute, etc. The omission of the definite article in "subjects" also helps to create the impression of generality (Bellquist, 1993).

The conventional styles of reporting can be seen as accomplishments, but what they accomplish can be analysed at different levels. For example, one can see the accomplishment in broad historical and epistemological terms. Thus, Danziger (1994) examines the changes in the reporting of participants' "extraexperimental" and "intraexperimental" identities, in terms of the historical growth of positivism within psychology. The absence of sampling discourse fits the presumption that the experimental "subject" is a universal, substitutable figure. One can also inquire how the broader philosophical themes are instantiated in the details of experimental writings. Textually based analyses can aim to discover what the particular rhetorical devices are accomplishing *within* the texts. This involves taking rhetoric as a topic, and then analysing the rhetoric rhetorically, rather than historically or philosophically. This is the strategy of the present article.

In following this strategy, one can analyse what routine rhetorical devices accomplish textually by asking what would be rhetorically implied if the texts failed to use such devices. In the present case, the devices include the omission of detail. In consequence, one might inquire what would have been the rhetorical effect had the experimental reports failed to omit details about the participants. Two different sorts of detail can be distinguished.

The first sort concerns *within-sample characteristics*. Details about the various characteristics of subjects would undermine the image of homogeneity. Significantly, this includes details of socio-demographic background, which might be expected in the social sciences. For instance: "Out of 40 subjects, studying X at University Y, there were 24 males and 16 females; 12 from rural backgrounds and 28 from urban or suburban; 12 Catholics, 16 protestants, 1 Buddhist and 10 professing no religion . . . etc., etc." The description indicates more heterogeneity than, "subjects were 40 students, male and female, studying X at Y."

The inclusion of details might also convey the impression that such differences between subjects might be theoretically or methodologically relevant. It might suggest that the subjects might not be theoretically substitutable one for another: the socio-demographic differences might perhaps indicate psychological differences. As Danziger (1994) details, such implications run counter to the impression that the results of psychological experimentation are universally valid and that psychology is a natural, rather than social, science.

According to the logic of experimentation, individual variation is overcome by the practice of randomly assigning subjects to treatment conditions (Gigerenzer, 1987). In all the experimental reports except McAllister and Anderson (1991), subjects are described as being randomly assigned to different experimental conditions. The brief descriptions do not say how randomization was accomplished in practice. Had details of "major demographic characteristics" been given, the expectation would be created that equal numbers of subjects of different religions, geographical backgrounds, ethnic membership, and gender be placed in the various cells. Given the comparatively large numbers of cells of the standard experimental design, this would mean increasing the numbers of subjects. Also, the details might raise doubts that variations between the subjects might be "contaminating" the results.

There are indications that more detailed descriptions of subjects carry this rhetorical implication. Along with McAllister and Anderson (1991), Kalma (1991) was the only study which used both males and females and which indicated, albeit obliquely, how many of each participated. Having given the numbers of males and females, Kalma stated in the next sentence "we will not report on sex differences." A justification is offered: a study by another author did not find sex differences on this sort of task. By following the information about the numbers of males and females immediately with a justification for not analysing gender differences, the author tacitly indicates that readers might expect information about gender to be followed later by analyses of sex differences. Without such an assumed expectancy, the proximity of Kalma's two statements would be strange. Thus, the information about the differences between subjects is accompanied by a "safety-warrant," assuring readers that the differences do not affect the results.

In most cases, experimental authors do not want to create a sense of heterogeneous subjects, for they are writing about their attempts to place "identical," or substitutable, subjects in different experimental conditions. The rhetoric of variable vagueness can be seen as a rhetorical solution to a problem. Mentioning differences between subjects in a casual way indicates, but does not assert, that the differences are unimportant. There were "males and females" – the casualness about numbers dismisses their potential relevance. Crucially, an author presents the numbers, when the theoretical implications of this presentation could be specifically dismissed by quoting past studies which had failed to find differences.

The second sort of detail concerns *characteristics of the sample*. Authors do not routinely justify their samples. Why the music college? Why the large North American University? Why females? The authors do not claim their samples to be representative of any wider population. To do so would rhetorically have the reverse effect: it would draw attention to the limitations of the sample. It would indicate that "subjects" were merely "*the* subjects," who happened to participate. As Gergen (1973, 1994) has pointed out, social psychologists implicitly claim that their studies have a universal validity. However, the claim is not asserted directly: that might invite challenge. Instead, it is built into the routine rhetoric of the report.

The unstated, and unstatable, imputation of universality is most markedly conveyed by the abstracts, which accompanied each article. These summaries, which are reproduced in other publications such as *Psychological Abstracts*, can be crucial for transmitting the claims of articles to academics who are not regular readers of the journal in question. None of the abstracts specified who the subjects were. "Subjects," unaccompanied by the definite article, were presented as an unproblematic, unqualified category: "subjects were initially assigned to be members of a minority group" (Schaller, 1991: 25); "97 subjects were observed during free discussions in same sex triads and dyads" (Kalma, 1991: 165). The absence of description implies an absence of limitation. An amorphous category – "subjects" – is indicated, as if the subjects of one experiment could be exchanged for those of another without the results being affected.

Variable vagueness can be seen as a rhetorical solution to a dilemma. Too much information about the subjects cannot be given, for risk of raising questions about generalizability and lack of homogeneity. On the other hand, a complete lack of information would indicate casually unscientific procedures. If variable vagueness offers a rhetorical solution, it cannot be justified as such. Imagine an openly declared editorial policy: "Authors cannot be expected to check for the effects of all major demographic variables on their data, and so they are advised to mix precise and imprecise descriptions of their subjects." As soon as the solution is stated, it is undermined. It needs to be practiced, as a "natural," or unconsidered, routine of writing.

The upshot of this practice is that ordinary individuality is written out. Subjects are presented as a homogeneous group, any one of whom could be substituted for any other. Residual individuality is tacitly claimed to have been conquered by a randomization, whose practices need not be specified. If individuality makes an appearance in the reports, it is as a reason for exclusion from the faceless anonymity of "subjects." Wright and Gregorich mention an individual who underwent their experimental procedures, but whose data was excluded from the analysis: "One subject admitted in debriefing that he was intoxicated" (1991: 79). He was not interchangeable for the others, who were all interchangeable for each other and for everybody else. Their sobriety, along with much else, was not specifically indicated. His drunkenness was.

The Results of Subjects

The ways in which the experimental results are presented maintain the textual depopulation. The sections devoted to the results report statistical operations. In these sections, authors tend to present averaged group scores, rather than the data of individual subjects, thereby adding to the elimination of the individual (Danziger, 1994; Gigerenzer, 1987). In the 10 experimental reports, there were 30 tables of data, 27 of which presented mean scores in one form or another, yielding 404 tabled means. The papers varied in the number of statistical tests described. Kalma (1991), who included two tables of correlations, only described four such tests. Sachdev and Bourhis (1991) described over 70 tests. In contrast to this detail about averaged scores, there were no data scores of individual subjects. Standard deviations were often included. However, information about standard deviations, together with group means, do not permit the reader to reconstruct scattergrams of individual scores.

The routine conventions for presenting quantified material serve rhetorical purposes, for authors use their statistics to tell an "action story-line" (Yearley, 1984; see also Gephart, 1988; Gusfield, 1976; Potter et al., 1991; Potter and Wetherell, 1994). Even authors in journals of theoretical mathematics use persuasive rhetorical devices to make their mathematical points (Davis and Hersh, 1986, 1987). In experimental psychology journals, the "action story-lines" of the results sections tend to tell a simple tale. In compliance with editorial policy, papers narrate the disproving of null hypotheses and the discovery of differences between experimental groups (Gigerenzer, 1987). The story is that subjects, within an experimental group all differ from other subjects, who were placed in a different situation. This story-line is part of the wider philosophical project of experimental psychology, which presents itself as developing a universal science, based upon experimentally validated facts (Danziger, 1994).

In line with the present strategy of rhetorical analysis, the attention here is on the textual details and how these convey the action story-line, rather than on the philosophical implications *per se*. Again, this means examining rhetorical omissions. The results sections may be filled with precise information – such as *F* values, mean scores, decimal points, and so on – but they also contain routine areas of imprecision. They avoid data, which might enable readers to reconstruct the scores of individual subjects, particularly to see whether individuals actually responded in messier ways than the smooth averages that the action story-line suggests. The reports do not present data in ways which might indicate overlap between spreads of scores from different experimental groups. For instance, there are no frequency tables, which list the numbers of subjects within each experimental group scoring above and below the median point of the whole sample. The omission of such frequency data, as well as that of scattergrams, is interesting. Such ways of presenting data would permit readers to see overlap between experimental groups, by noting that, for example, some individuals in Group X did not score above many individuals in Group Y, despite differences between group means. By contrast, the presentation of the group means, together with the claim that analysis of variance shows the group scores to be significantly different, draws attention away from overlap.

Verbal imprecision follows statistical precision, to create the impression of between-group differences and within-group similarities. Wright and Gregorich (1991) asked their subjects in one experimental condition to memorize two nonsense "words" of three letters, and other subjects to memorize five such "words." The subjects were also asked to rate how difficult they considered their task to be. The authors, in their results section, compute the relevant statistics, presenting *p* and *F* values:

4 "As expected, subjects in the 5-trigram conditions had higher difficulty scores than did subjects in the 2-trigram conditions" (Wright and Gregorich, 1991: 80).

The report does not specify how many of (the) subjects in the 5-trigram condition had higher difficulty scores than those in the 2-trigram condition. The authors do not claim that "*all* the 5-trigram subjects had higher difficulty scores than *all* the 2-trigram scores;" nor that "*most* had higher scores than *all* the 2-trigram scores;" nor "*all* had higher scores than *most*," etc., etc. Words such as "most" or "many" or "some" seem imprecise, but they are not replaced by the precision of numbers.

The linguistic imprecision achieves a rhetorical effect. "Most" or "many" imply exceptions: if "most" subjects in condition X have higher scores than subjects in condition Y, then this implies that some did not. The general term "subjects" suggests no exceptions:

5 "Subjects were seventy-one male and female undergraduate volunteers who received class credit for participation" (Wright and Gregorich, 1991: 78).

"Most subjects were undergraduate volunteers" would imply that some were not. If the unmarked "subjects" indicates "all" in this context, then in the results section it presents the same rhetorical nudge. It cannot affirm uniformity directly – but it does not deny it. The precision about aggregate differences is accompanied by a rhetorically directed imprecision about the performance of individuals who constitute the groups. This imprecision helps the action story-line on its way.

McAllister and Anderson (1991) used an a posteriori allocation of subjects, as did Moscovici and Personnaz (1991) for some statistical purposes. McAllister and Anderson were interested in the differences between the cognitive styles of conservatives and non-conservatives. Subjects were categorized as being "conservatives" or "non-conservatives" on the basis of their scores on a scale of Conservatism (Wilson and Patterson, 1968). The cut-off point was the median. The analyses of results concentrate on the differences between the two groups. In all likelihood, a scattergram would have shown the similarity between the higher "non-conservatives" and the lower "conservatives," who would probably resemble each other to a greater extent than either would have resembled the extreme respondents in their respective groups. The differentiating criterion was relative (based on the median), rather than absolute, so that the more "moderate" subjects might have been categorized differently had different samples of subjects been selected. Nevertheless, the labels assigned to the groups ("conservatives" and "non-conservatives") rhetorically convey absolute differences between the members (see Gergen, 1990, for a discussion of the implicit claims for "ontological validity," which psychological concepts make).

McAllister and Anderson describe their results thus:

6 "As expected, conservatives preferred plausible over implausible texts to a significantly greater extent than did non-conservatives" (1991: 161–2).

Quantitative markers are absent: "conservatives" and "non-conservatives" implies, without asserting, homogeneity within the groups. On one occasion, McAllister and Anderson introduce the marker "some." As so often happens, the "deviant case" reveals the assumptions of the more conventional, discursive routines (Heritage, 1988). In this instance, "some" makes its appearance when the results are statistically non-significant:

7 "Data from the present study indicate that some conservatives do recall slightly but not significantly more than non-conservatives" (1991: 160).

This statement seems to elide differences between the statistical and everyday conceptions of "significance" (McCloskey, 1986). Statistical significance refers to the data from all the subjects, not to "some" of them. However, the main point is the presence of "some" in the reporting of the non-significant result. The inclusion of "some," when reporting the non-significant result, highlights its absence in the routine reporting of statistically significant results. Unless the spread of scores from the two groups did not overlap at all in 6, there is no more, nor less, statistical justification for omitting "some" from 6, or other descriptions of significant results, than for adding it to 7.

Even if the pattern of description does not have strict statistical justification, it has a rhetorical one. The addition of "some" to 6, or to any instance where statistically significant differences had been found, would indicate that the subjects within the experimental group were not homogeneous in their responses. It would suggest overlaps between different groups. In short, "some" would interrupt the story's action-line.

Reconstructing a Generalized Psychology

Typically the presentation of results is followed by interpretations. Here authors frequently, but not invariably, attempt to depict the mentality of the subjects, so that the pattern of reported responses is made psychologically understandable. These reconstructions of the subjects do not return the social psychological texts to descriptions of individuals. Instead, they remain at a general, aggregate level, producing a disembodied, unpopulated psychology.

McAllister and Anderson reconstruct the ways "conservatives" and "non-conservatives" treated ambiguous texts:

8 "Conservatives, it seems, felt impelled to simplify their disrupted causal and intentional framework by drawing inferences to resolve ambiguities to a greater extent than did their non-conservative counterparts" (1991: 161).

This psychological reconstruction contains a marker – "it seems" – to indicate that the authors are speculating (or reconstructing), rather than claiming to present objective data. The authors can provide no direct evidence to suggest that subjects, especially the conservatives, had feelings of being impelled. The reconstruction uses a quantitatively unmarked descriptor – "conservatives." Not *all* conservatives are said to experience the impulsion: that would be an unwarranted overstatement. Not *many* or *most*: that would imply exceptions. But "conservatives" experience the impulsion.

Moscovici and Personnaz discuss the laboratory finding that subjects' judgments can be indirectly affected by the judgments of consistent minorities, even though the subjects appear outwardly unaffected:

9 "It is as though the subjects' mental activity, by being focussed on the stimulus, became more intensive and uninterrupted in this situation" (1991: 110).

Again, there is a marker of reconstruction: "as though." There also is quantitative imprecision. The authors write of "the subjects' mental activity," as if all *the* subjects could be included. The use of quantitatively unmarked terms ensures that the reconstructions of thoughts, or of feelings, are ascribed to groups of subjects in general, rather than to particular individuals. The data to be brought to psychological life is aggregated data, which does not represent the responses of any actual individual.

The reconstructions, although seeking to make sense of central findings, are brief. Readers are not invited to imagine in detail what it must have felt like to be a subject participating in the particular experiment and to have produced the effects, which are the main claims of the particular papers. It could be argued that the brevity of the reconstructions reflects the conventions of empiricism, which encourage scientific writers to "stick to the data," rather than to tell stories. However, as can be seen, the data itself does not stick to the data – it too tells a story.

There is a further consideration. In order to reconstruct the thinking of "subjects," psychologists would need to attempt to describe the thinking and feeling as it was actually experienced by the subjects. This would typically involve framing the reconstructions in the language of those subjects, for it is ordinary language which typically constitutes ordinary thinking (Billig, 1991; Edwards and Potter, 1992; Gilligan, 1982; Potter and Wetherell, 1987). However, social psychologists often retain their specialist language when formulating their psychological explanations. If they cling too firmly to this language in their reconstructions, the results can carry an air of unreality. An illustration, not taken from the *European Journal of Social Psychology*, can be briefly cited: "if . . . subjects were aware of the possible self-esteem depressing consequences of discrimination-contingent norm violation, why did they discriminate?" (Hogg and Abrams, 1990: 34). This is not the language to be spoken by subjects themselves: their inner voices would not report being aware of "discrimination-contingent norm violation" and other such technical matters. In this respect, the psychologists speak for their subjects, as if the latter could not know themselves. A hierarchy of expertise and knowledge is expressed.

Furthermore, the psychologists' reconstructions can be left hovering above, and beyond, the mentality of those they seek to understand. The bearers of the reconstructed mental states are not only fictions, but shadowy, disembodied fictions. They are "averaged" individuals who do not, and cannot, exist as ordinary, everyday individuals (see Danziger, 1994 for a discussion of the historical "triumph of the aggregate" within psychology). Any detailed examination, or imaginative reconstruction, of a mental state needs to consider the particular bearer of the mental state. A similar point was well expressed by Bakhtin with respect to language. In his essay "The Problem of Speech Genres," Bakhtin wrote that speech only exists in the form of concrete utterances: "Speech is always cast in the form of an utterance belonging to a particular subject, and outside this form it cannot exist" (1986: 71).

By the same token, mental activity is always cast in the form of thinking or feeling belonging to a particular subject. In this respect, each instantiation of a generally described psychological state will typically contain untypical, unique aspects. Thus, "Vanessa" is a typical experimental subject *because* she possesses unique, but ordinary, individuality. To ascribe thoughts to "subjects in general" is to reconstruct particular patterns of thinking in the absence of thinkers.

This presents a problem for the standard psychological report, whose rhetorical conventions exclude the textual creation of individuals. The reconstructions are the end-point of the particular investigation (and, perhaps, the start of the next one). Yet, these end-points are brief and unelaborated. The experimental reports, despite their rhetoric of scientific realism, result in fictions: they describe thinking/feeling in forms in which, as Bakhtin realized, it cannot exist. In consequence, the crucial reconstructions, which should be the report's culmination, are textually and intellectually stunted.

Particular Reconstructions

Experimental reports typically exemplify a movement from the particular to the general. The experimenter greets a subject, who possesses the ordinary individuality of everybody and who may even be known to the experimenter. This much is always implied, even if typically excluded from the likes of "Snitting (forthcoming)." Particularity is shed, as the subject is transformed into an anonymous member of homogeneous "subjects." The report conventionally remains on this level of generality. Even the reconstructions do not permit a dialectical move back from generality to a particularity, which reconstructs individual subjects in their inevitable individuality. However, the repopulation of social psychology's texts could be accomplished by such a move back to particularity.

The move would involve producing case-studies of particular subject's thoughts/feelings/reactions in the experimental situation. To retain only the details which could be generalized to all subjects would be to produce a portrait, which, in depicting everybody, would depict none. The "typical" case-study must retain typically untypical features. This is illustrated by the use of case-studies in one of the classic studies of social psychology. In *The Authoritarian Personality*, Adorno et al. (1950) presented detailed descriptions of "Larry" and "Mack" as "typical" authoritarian and non-authoritarian respondents. Each was described as coming from particular families, and having lived unique lives. It was assumed that others would exemplify the general patterns of authoritarianism and non-authoritarianism in analogous, but not identical, ways. As such, case-studies are metonymic tropes, as opposed to metaphorical ones (Squire, 1989).

If reports are to reconstruct case-studies, then the status of the case-studies in psychological writing will need to be raised from its present lowly position. "Larry" and "Mack" appear in the early part of *The Authoritarian Personality*, as illustrative guides before the serious details of the *F* scale are introduced. By contrast, "Amy" and "Jack" in Gilligan's *In a Different Voice* (1982), do not perform the warm-up act required of "Larry" and "Mack." They are presented as ends not means. Their lives are described and the aim of theory is to understand such lives, rather than the lives serving the interests of theory. Gilligan recognizes that this reversal, together with the discovery of woman's different voice, necessitates a change in psychology's own voice (see her prologue of Gilligan et al., 1988; see also the aims of narrative psychology, as described by Murray, 1995). In a repopulated psychology, "Amy" and "Jack" (or even "Vanessa" and "Snitting") would not be textual devices, humbly serving the grander purposes of theory; the theory would serve to present "Amy" and "Jack" to the readers.

A detailed, particular reconstruction would have the merit of enabling a rigorous testing of the psychologist's theoretical hunches. It would be the rhetorical equivalent of a computer model, which "runs" theoretical constructions in practice. If a psychological account is valid, it should be able to be instantiated as a plausible account. The stories of Larry and Mack "hang together" as recognizable persons. If social psychologists regularly produced detailed particular reconstructions, rather than brief generalized accounts, then some implausibilities might be avoided. No-one, except another social psychologist, could be convincingly reconstructed as worrying about the "possible self-esteem depressing consequences of discrimination-contingent norm violation."

The conventional patterns of psychological writing are paradoxical. The self-conscious language of scientific realism creates its own unacknowledged fictions. The language describes generalities, which cannot exist as generalities. To produce reconstructions a change of rhetorical practice would be necessary. The psychologist-as-author would need to use different literary practices than are required at present, including those used to construct characters in fictional realism (Jameson, 1986). For example, psychologists-as-authors might need to pay greater attention to devices of narrative and *mise-en-scène*, which portray the individual character through the unfolding of action (Booth, 1961). Metonymic details (a beard, a mumbling) would play their parts. It would not be enough to include as many details as possible, for details have to carry a narrative weight. Over 50 years ago, Ernst Bloch expressed the dilemma faced by those attempting to write history: "To have everything that is past without a prevailing voice as [if] it were infinitely many-voiced is merely historicism; to apply typically identical, or at least formally identical 'laws' or 'shapes' to everything that is past is merely sociologism" (1991: 114).

As Bloch implied, the issue is to find an appropriate voice, to replace the voice of the apparently voiceless experimental report. This involves finding a way to describe a "Vanessa," an "Amy" or a "Mack." It also means creating ways to describe a "Snitting," even within the pages of "Snitting (forthcoming)." As critical anthropologists have stressed, ethnographers can never be fully absent from their texts (Clifford, 1988; Clifford and Marcus, 1986). The problem is how to write the self into the text.

Perhaps "I" might make an appearance as an all-seeing eye – the wise psychologist who understands the foibles of others (this "I" is no stranger to the anecdotal sections of the textbooks); or perhaps, in a voice currently favored by critical anthropologists, there will be a confessional "I," absorbed with the self's own embarrassment as privileged researcher and author. Perhaps the "I" will confess past failures of rhetorical nerve, when the author has cravenly – or worse, unwittingly – followed the rhetorical conventions which downgrade the case-study. Note an author's apologetic tone in one of the few case-studies published by the *European Journal of Social Psychology*: "At an early stage in an area's theoretical development, single case studies can be especially useful, for the detailed analysis of a particular phenomenon can enable the identification of basic features" (Billig, 1989: 204). The author implies that once an area is established, case-studies are less useful; thus, the case-study accepts its own low status. Billig (1989) may have written the words; it is now appropriate that I regret.

The experimental psychologist's confessional "I" might be self-consciously aware of the power to order experimental instructions and to close the door behind each solitary subject. Maybe, the experimenter will be recreated in the third person as a figure of fun (balding and messy – distanced and ambiguous) – a character whom readers appear to be invited to mock. This is a figure who seems unaware of his power, even as he is exercising it. At any rate, the "I" will be a rhetorical creation, not a guarantee that an unmediated experience of truth has found its way into the text.

One point needs to be emphasized. The recommendation to move back from the general to the particular is not a recommendation for individualism, as if the social sciences should only speak of individuals. The recommendation is not to replace nomothetic social science by idiographic inquiry, as if the search for generality is to be abandoned. Quite the contrary: the reconstructed individuals would contain, in their literary construction, traces of the former move to generality. The recommendation can work with the methodology of experimentalism. As such, the case-studies can be introduced as metonymic representations of the general.

Spears, in his perceptive and open-minded critique of the original version of this (my) article, argued that the recommendation is a form of individual reductionism. He points to the irony of my present position, given Billig's past "role in developing social identity theory and the powerful critique of individualism this entailed (Billig, 1976)" (1994: 340). But it is not simply a case of youthful radicalism being replaced by an ageing (and, yes, bald) conservatism, which trusts only the experience of the individual and brackets off the social structure. As much feminist writing has shown, the reconstructions of individuals can express social analysis.

Spears, in arguing against reconstructions, states that "behaviour may be guided by forces beyond the immediate grasp of the individual consciousness," adding that this point has been "a consistent feature of disciplines as diverse as psychology, psychoanalysis, social theory and ideology-critique" (1994: 341). If Spears's point about behavior being guided by forces beyond the consciousness of the individual is valid, then it too can be illustrated by examples. Indeed, the behavior, which is under question, cannot take place without persons to do the behaving. Examples of such behavior should be described in ways which illustrate the forces beyond the limitations of the individual consciousness, just as Freud's case studies were the instantiation, justification, and metonymic representation of general psychoanalytic processes. The reconstructions are not merely descriptions of individualized consciousness, but there is a *mise-en-scène*, so that readers might notice more than the individual so described. Is not Snitting represented as understanding less about the situation, which he inflicts upon Vanessa, than does either the latter or the reader? Vanessa hardly notices the traces of the cleaners. Might not the author hint at those class relations, which still keep the working classes below the textual stairs, invisibly cleaning the scenes in preparation for the grand appearances of the middle-class actors?

Much will depend on the writing of the reconstructions. These should have a very different texture than standard experimental reports. To write an individual's journey through the experimental laboratory, the psychologist-as-author would need to notice those details of place, procedure, and person which are omitted in the variable vagueness of the standard report. The reconstructions will be texts of resuscitation, using words to breathe life into subjects, presently condemned to a common experimental cell.

Median Case Reconstruction

The version of this present paper which was published in *Theory & Psychology* contained the recommendation that every experimental report should contain at least one reconstructed case-study. It also proposed a mechanism for choosing which experimental subjects should be reconstructed. "Why Vanessa Jones? And why not the spotty young man, who entered Dr Snitting's room later that afternoon?", the paper had asked (Billig, 1994b: 327). Cases for reconstruction could not be selected merely because they illustrated the author's chosen theoretical point. That would permit the authors too much license to select tendentiously. The traditional experimentalist would wish for a method, or routine procedure, which would eliminate the temptations of bias. A proper method must have a name, preferably a capitalized noun phrase without prepositions and articles. Serious labels, with their upper-case beginnings, reassure readers of the scientific nature of the business. Thus, the procedure of Median Case Reconstruction was proposed.

The selection of cases would be determined statistically, for it would be based upon the median instance. If the report tells a story of two experimental groups, then the experimenter could select, from each experimental group, the median scorer on the key dependent variable. In consequence, the "typical" instance would not be the most extreme, but would be the median. To produce a Median Case Reconstruction, the experimenter would need to take extensive notes about the conduct of each experimental session. These notes will have to be collected in advance, for, until results are computed, the researcher will be unaware which subject will be the Median Case. The notes would focus upon the particularities of the occasion and of the participants. Experimenters would also have to present information about themselves, noting their own behavior during the conduct of the experiment. When reconstructing the scene, they might wish to imagine themselves as seen by subjects. These median cases, having been statistically selected, would then be reconstructed. To say how the reconstruction could be accomplished would take the researcher dangerously beyond the province of "methodology."

The recommendation seemed to find little favor with early readers. The *European Journal's* reviewer, whose review comprised seven pages of crushing criticism, was most put out, not to say "embarrassed," by the recommendation. The journal's editor, in his polite letter of rejection, mentioned that the procedure would result in longer, and thus fewer, published articles. He was unconvinced that this would be a benefit. Both Spears (1994) and Ussher (1994), in their commentaries on the finally published version, also criticized the procedure, but for very different reasons. Ussher thought that the recommendation did not go far enough: it was merely dealing with the surface of psychology's ills. Spears, by contrast, thought that the recommendation, if applied, would go too far. However, not all the reaction has been critical. Already, the recommendation is being cited as a justification for particular qualitative methodologies (Kidder et al., 1994).

The original recommendation was ambiguous. How could an article, which was arguing for the priority of rhetoric over methodology, itself make a methodological recommendation? Just how serious was the proposal? If the proposal were ironic, should it now be cited as a methodological justification? Perhaps, the original proposal should now appear as if it were an experiment – a rhetorical experiment. Like any experiment, it tested questions. In this case, the questions concerned its own text. Could it be published in an experimental journal, whose rhetoric was being questioned? If it were published, what would be the results? Would it be ignored, or might there be ripples of rhetorical change? Hypotheses could be made; but the matter had to be tested by the experiment of writing and submitting for publication.

The proposal, as presented, contained a further ambiguity. Even if readers accepted the methodological principle of Median Case Reconstruction, it was unclear how the principle should be rhetorically accomplished. The recommendation did not come with stylistic guidance. Many different genres of writing could be applied to the task with differing rhetorical, theoretical, and philosophical effects. Perhaps, the Median Case Reconstruction could be built with heavy blocks of scientistic rhetoric, in which the individual case remains trapped as a cipher of general theory. On the other hand, the literary conventions of fiction could be recruited for the task, as they are in the scene of Vanessa and Snitting. Perhaps, today's psychologists could imitate Freud, imitating the nineteenth-century short-story writer: "In the summer vacation of the year 189 – I made an excursion into the Hohe Tauern so that for a while I might forget medicine" began Freud's tale of Katherina and her neuroses, as if starting a Victorian tale of ghosts or adventure (Freud, 1995: 79; for discussion of Freud's style of writing case-histories, see Marcus, 1986). There are limitless literary possibilities for the Median Case, each reconstructing peoples and their relationships in its own way.

The ambiguity of the proposal lies at the heart of the different reactions expressed by Spears and Ussher, who might be seen respectively to represent the voices of experimentalism and radical feminism. According to the former, the article represented a strategy of "entryism." It was working with accepted practices, but doing so in a way which threatened to subvert them. The article was seeking "to challenge the mainstream on its home ground so to speak" (Spears, 1994: 338). Spears sounded a note of warning: "It is not clear whether experimentalists should regard this as a reassuring general vindication of their modus operandi or as a sort of 'entryist' thin end of the wedge" (1994: 338).

On the other hand, the strategy of entryism carries dangers for the entryist. The radicalism becomes co-opted, absorbed safely into the old structures. The original proposal ironically depicted such a rhetorical co-option. The operation of the Median Case Reconstruction was imagined:

> Perhaps, experimenters might wish to interview again the median subjects, or Within-Cell Median Subjects (W-CMSs), as they might come to be known officially, if the procedure becomes popular. Some experimenters might recommend showing the returning Within-Cell Median Subjects the reconstructions, which they have already begun to reconstruct: this might be the Within-Cell Median Subject Preliminary Reconstruction Feedback Interview. (Billig, 1994b: 328–9)

The helpful suggestions seem to indicate how the procedure could be successfully implemented. Ironically, successful implementation would involve self-destruction. The procedure would be established as a method. The prevailing rhetoric would welcome it, easing its passage into the journal pages. Lengthy noun phrases and "W-CMSs" would act as textual police, ensuring the ideas were confined to the realms of methodology. In this way, the prevailing rhetoric would assert itself. The potentially subversive rhetoric would itself be sublimated into the safety of methodology.

Rhetoric is seldom "mere rhetoric." Spears, generously regretting the treatment of the original version by the *European Journal*, commented that the success of the project to repopulate social psychology "may not depend just on the power of argument, however, but also on the power of prevailing institutional forces" (1994: 338). He doubted whether the institutional forces would permit the changes required by the project. This consideration lay at the heart of Ussher's critique. My analysis and proposals were, to her mind, merely playing with words. Current psychological practices are not haphazard, but reflect the operation of power – and gender power in particular. Mainstream psychological thinking, she argued, is malestream power. Unless the conditions of this power are tackled, then introducing a new methodological procedure – a Median Case Reconstruction – is fruitless.

Ussher's basic argument is surely correct. She went on to comment that "there is little point tinkering with the surface of the text which Billig suggests" (1994: 348). Of course, if the tinkering involves establishing a new aspect of methodology as a routine practice, surrounded by the old rhetorical practices, then that would, indeed, be tinkering. Similarly, some radical feminists have criticized feminist experimentalists, for only making minimal changes in rhetoric while carrying on with business as usual, without recognizing that the feminist project demands much more radical upheaval of accepted practices (see, for instance, the criticisms by Kitzinger, 1991; Wilkinson and Kitzinger, 1995). However, the entryist tactic, noted by Spears, suggests another possibility. Under the guise of methodology, a new way of writing is introduced. Once the text is changed, so is the nature of what is to be called psychology, and, in consequence, what is to be done in the name of psychology. Ussher, too, recognizes this. She uses the same "thin wedge" metaphor as Spears: "Even the Median Case Reconstruction could be the thin end of a dangerous wedge and . . . its implications are far more wide-reaching than Billig appears (however ironically) to allow" (1994: 350).

The word "appears" is a saving grace. The entryist cannot appear as an entryist. Humbly, he or she seeks an invitation to the party, bearing the gift of a new methodology and, perhaps, an ironic smile. If entryism is suspected, the door will be closed. However, the "methodology," which the original article seemed to recommend, is more than a methodology, just as rhetoric is more than rhetoric. Ussher argues that institutional forces, operating by rule of masculinity, would not permit the changes, which would undermine their own institutional powers. The gate-keepers of the journals will preserve their positions. If challenged, they will assert their power.

The little experiment of the original paper illustrates Ussher's general point. A seven-page, single-spaced hostile review ensured that pages of the *European Journal* were kept free from thoughts, which, if pursued seriously, would demand changes in the patterns of publication and which, in any case, criticized present rhetorical practices. The reviewer asserted that the purpose of the *European Journal* was to provide an outlet "for a nomothetic approach to psychological topics." An occasional case study might be possible: "One might grant that case studies are often quite useful and may be acceptable as an anecdote within experimental articles and that occasionally a case study could constitute a whole article, even in *EJSP*." In short, the challenge prompted an articulated defence that the journal must maintain its original purpose and rhetoric. Commenting on the original version of this article, the reviewer declared: "I think the paper should not be accepted by the *EJSP* and that its publication anywhere else would be ill-advised as likely to hurt the reputation of the author."

Ussher makes the point that those who challenge the dominant hegemonies of thinking in psychology must seek their own outlets. Most notably, feminists have established their own feminist journals and book series. As Ussher states, "the rebirth of the author is only taking place in specific contexts" (1994: 348). The fate of this article illustrates Ussher's argument. It was published in a journal specializing in theoretical critiques, addressing those who specifically want to read such material. And now, in its present revised form, it is to be reproduced in a book, alongside other critical pieces, in a series which has its own specialist market. If the piece is to make (or unmake) a reputation, it must do so in non-experimental circles, before a restricted audience. The eyes of experimentalists need not be troubled.

Ussher's point is not that there are separate fields of academic specialization, each with their own journal, intellectual traditions, and adherents. It is that the separate fields are not equal. Feminists must operate on the disciplinary margins. The center still maintains its institutional power. As Bourdieu (1993) has remarked, the intellectual capital produced by academic institutions is maintained by discourses of censorship. One might add that the academic institutions themselves are situated within a wider political economy. Fundings from governmental and business sources ensure that the market of ideas is no free market. Powers of dominance maintain the dominance of particular rhetorics.

Concluding with a Prediction

Even so, the ambivalence remains. The call to populate social psychological writing might now be a message addressed to a selected, sympathetic audience. Any changes in rhetoric might be confined within a delimited academic space. Perhaps if the message were to wander further afield, and to find sympathetic ears, then the proposed changes might be safely transmuted into methodology: the entryist would be incorporated into the entered structures of intellectual practice. On the other hand, nothing is fixed. The movement of ideas is unpredictable; language is never still. Maybe, a repopulated psychology, mirroring other changes in political economy, might emerge from the margins as part of a wider cultural current which is sweeping aside unquestioned masculine assumptions. It would not be possible to guess in advance the precise characteristics of this repopulated psychology, just as it is not possible to describe the stylistic features of the future's unwritten novels.

It would be arrogant to make wide claims for a repopulated psychology, as if the turning of the world depended on the rhetoric of psychology, or the capture of experimental journals. Instead, two parochial, small-scale benefits might result from a turn towards repopulation. The consequences of such benefits might not be predictable in advance. That, surely, is reason enough to run the rhetorical experiment in practice.

First, a repopulated psychology should bring an increased attention to language (unless, of course, the rhetoric gets bogged down in the methodology of Median Case Reconstruction or the uncritical boastings of "I"). Social psychological theories are verbal constructions, yet the discipline does not encourage verbal sensitivity. If its texts are to be repopulated, then social psychologists would need to take the same care with language as they currently do with statistics. At present, psychologists tend to accept uncritically the conventions of experimental writing, absorbing without reflection the rhetoric contained therein. The routine repetition of unacknowledged rhetoric cannot be conducive to intellectual advance. Worse still, students are taught this rhetoric. And, how often do teachers of psychology condone (or fail to recognize) infelicities of language, while vigorously policing infelicities of methodology or statistics? It is as if language is seen as merely the tool by which more important things – data, truths, theories – are conveyed from mind to mind. If rhetoric is fundamental to producing the discipline of psychology, then the consequences of a rhetorical change could be profound. An end to the tyranny of the noun phrase might signal the decline of other tyrannies.

There might be another advantage of repopulating psychology. This refers to a delicate matter which those seeking to publish in the pages of the psychology journals might hesitate to mention. Academics occasionally whisper about the journals, as if in guilty confession. Students complain more loudly and frequently: the standard journals are immensely boring to read. Tables of ANOVA values and heavy-syllabled concepts of interpretation slip easily from the memory, as the eye slides from the text. Again, psychology journals are by no means the sole, nor necessarily the worst, culprits in the social sciences. Rosaldo (1989) asks why the classic texts of anthropology are so tedious to read. He notes that the question rarely finds its way into academic print. And as for the heavy worded, big texts of deconstructionism. . . .

Commercial publishers are aware that anecdotes and characters can enliven popular books. In *The Saturated Self*, Gergen (1991) recounts the story of an American professor, a mysterious woman, and an unscheduled air-line stop in Iceland. It remains in the mind, as few *F* values do. Perhaps, repopulation might awaken the reader, as individuals are to be met across the page. Repopulated journals could even provide occasional textual pleasures, of the sort which Barthes (1975) has described – perhaps a *jouissance* of recognition.

It is all very well to speculate idly, but such pleasures demand metonymic instantiation. A hypothetical reader needs to be modeled, and then run upon the program of the textual imagination.

Imagine Vanessa Jones, now a postgraduate student, having graduated with honors two years ago. She is more confident than she was: less likely to take shit, as she often now says. Anyway, she is in the library, reading a psychology journal, forcing her attention upon the text. It's a quiet, orderly, early evening scene – the studious postgraduate, the empty desks, and librarians going about their hushed business. Suddenly, the peace is shattered. Vanessa, despite herself, and despite the stare she now gives undergraduates who giggle at the library desks, turns a page and exclaims out loud: "My God, it's me; yes, it is." Librarians stare. Vanessa's voice comes even louder: "And that's him, the funny little man with the bad breath."

Finally, a prediction: Ms Jones will not be the only reader to smile.

Note

An earlier version of this chapter appeared in *Theory & Psychology* (1994, 4(3): 307–55).

References

Adorno, T.W., Frenkel-Brunswik, E., Levinson, D.J., and Sanford, R.N. (1950) *The Authoritarian Personality*. New York: Harper and Row.

Ashmore, M. (1990) *The Reflexivity Thesis*. Chicago: University of Chicago Press.

Bakhtin, M.M. (1986) *Speech Genres and Other Late Essays*. Austin, TX: University of Texas Press.

Barthes, R. (1975) *The Pleasure of the Text*. New York: Farar, Straus and Giroux.

Bazerman, C. (1987) "Codifying the social scientific style: the APA *Publication Manual* as a behaviorist rhetoric," in J.S. Nelson, A. Megill, and D.N. McCloskey (eds), *The Rhetoric of the Human Sciences*. Madison, WI: University of Wisconsin.

Bazerman, C. (1988) *Shaping Written Knowledge*. Madison, WI: University of Wisconsin.

Bellquist, J.E. (1993) *A Guide to Grammar and Usage for Psychology and Related Fields*. Hillsdale, NJ: Erlbaum.

Billig, M. (1976) *Social Psychology and Intergroup Relations*. London: Academic Press.

Billig, M. (1987) *Arguing and Thinking*. Cambridge: Cambridge University Press.

Billig, M. (1989) "The argumentative nature of holding strong views: a case study," *European Journal of Social Psychology*, 19: 203–22.

Billig, M. (1991) *Ideology and Opinions*. London: Sage.

Billig, M. (1992) *Talking of the Royal Family*. London: Routledge.

Billig, M. (1994a) "Sod Baudrillard! Or ideology-critique in Disneyworld," in H.W. Simons and M. Billig (eds), *Ideological Analysis in Postmodern Times*. London: Sage.

Billig, M. (1994b) "Repopulating the depopulated pages of social psychology," *Theory & Psychology*, 4: 307–35.

Billig, M., Condor, S., Edwards, D., Gane, M., Middleton, D., and Radley, A.R. (1988) *Ideological Dilemmas*. London: Sage.

Bloch, E. (1991) *Heritage of Our Times*. Cambridge: Polity Press.

Booth, W.C. (1961) *The Rhetoric of Fiction*. Chicago: University of Chicago Press.

Bourdieu, P. (1993) *Sociology in Question*. London: Sage.

Brown, R.H. (1989) *A Poetic for Sociology*. Chicago: University of Chicago Press.

Brown, R.H. (1994) "Reconstructing social theory after the postmodern critique," in H.W. Simons and M. Billig (eds), *After Postmodernism*. London: Sage.

Clifford, J. (1988) *The Predicament of Culture*. Cambridge, MA: Harvard University Press.

Clifford, J. and Marcus, G.E. (eds) (1986) *Writing Culture*. Berkeley, CA: University of California Press.

Danziger, K. (1994) *Constructing the Subject*. Cambridge: Cambridge University Press.

Davis, P.J. and Hersh, R. (1986) *Descartes' Dream*. Sussex: Harvester Press.

Davis, P.J. and Hersh, R. (1987) "Rhetoric and mathematics," in J.S. Nelson, A. Megill, and D.N. McCloskey (eds), *The Rhetoric of the Human Sciences*. Madison, WI: University of Wisconsin.

Dijk, T.A. van (1995) Editorial: "Esoteric discourse analysis," *Discourse and Society*, 6: 5–6.

Edmondson, R. (1984) *Rhetoric in Sociology*. London: Macmillan.

Edwards, D. and Potter, J. (1992) *Discursive Psychology*. London: Sage.

Foucault, M. (1979) *Discipline and Punish*. London: Allen Lane.

Freud, S. (1995) "Katherina," in P. Gay (ed.), *The Freud Reader*. London: Vintage.

Galam, S. and Moscovici, S. (1991) "Towards a theory of collective phenomena: consensus and attitude changes in groups," *European Journal of Social Psychology*, 21: 49–74.

Geertz, C. (1988) *Works and Lives: The Anthropologist as Author*. Stanford, CA: Stanford University Press.

Gephart, R.P. (1988) *Ethnostatistics: Qualitative Foundations for Quantitative Research.* Newbury Park, CA: Sage.

Gergen, K.J. (1973) "Social psychology as history," *Journal of Personality and Social Psychology*, 26: 309–20.

Gergen, K.J. (1990) "Textual considerations in the scientific construction of human character," *Style*, 24: 365–79.

Gergen, K.J. (1994) *Realities and Relationships: Soundings in Social Construction.* Cambridge, MA: Harvard University Press.

Gigerenzer, G. (1987) "Probabilistic thinking and the fight against subjectivity," in L. Kruger, G. Gigerenzer, and M.S. Morgan (eds), *The Probabilistic Revolution* (vol. 2). Cambridge, MA: MIT Press.

Gilligan, C. (1982) *In a Different Voice.* Cambridge, MA: Harvard University Press.

Gilligan, C., Ward, J.V., Taylor, J.M., and Bardige, B. (1988) *Mapping the Moral Domain.* Cambridge, MA: Harvard University Press.

Gusfield, J. (1976) "The literary rhetoric of science: comedy and pathos in drinking driver research," *American Sociological Review*, 41: 16–34.

Harding, S. (1989) "Feminist justificatory strategies," in A. Gary and M. Pearsall (eds), *Women, Knowledge and Reality.* Boston: Unwin Hyman.

Harré, R. (1981) "Rituals, rhetoric and social cognitions," in J.P. Forgas (ed.), *Social Cognition.* London: Academic Press.

Harré, R. and Secord, P.F. (1972) *The Explanation of Social Behaviour.* Oxford: Blackwell.

Hawkins, K. (1989) "Exposing masculine science: an alternative feminist approach to the study of women's communication," in K. Carter and C. Spitzack (eds), *Doing Research on Women's Communication.* Norwood, NJ: Ablex.

Henriques, J., Hollway, W., Urwin, C., Venn, C., and Walkerdine, V. (1984) *Changing the Subject.* London: Methuen.

Heritage, J. (1988) "Explanations as accounts: a conversation analytic perspective," in C. Antaki (ed.), *Analysing Everyday Explanation.* London: Sage.

Hicks, D. and Potter, J. (1991) "Sociology of scientific knowledge: a reflexive citation analysis *or* science disciplines and disciplining science," *Social Studies of Science*, 21: 459–501.

Hogg, M.A. and Abrams, D. (1990) "Social motivation, self-esteem and social identity," in D. Abrams and M.A. Hogg (eds), *Social Identity Theory.* New York: Springer-Verlag.

Jameson, F. (1986) "The realist floor-plan," in M. Blonsky (ed.), *On Signs.* Oxford: Blackwell.

Joule, R.-V. (1991) "Practicing and arguing for abstinence from smoking: a test of the double forced compliance paradigm," *European Journal of Social Psychology*, 21: 119–130.

Kalma, A. (1991) "Hierarchisation and dominance at first glance," *European Journal of Social Psychology*, 21: 165–81.

Keller, E.F. (1985) *Reflections on Gender and Science.* New Haven, CT: Yale University Press.

Kidder, L.H., Lafleur, R.A., and Wells, C.V. (1994) "Re-membering harassment". Unpublished paper, Temple University, Philadelphia.

Kitzinger, C. (1991) "Feminism, psychology and the paradox of power," *Feminism and Psychology*, 1: 111–29.

Krueger, J. (1991) "Accentuation effects and illusory change in exemplar-based category learning," *European Journal of Social Psychology*, 21: 37–48.

Latour, B. and Woolgar, S. (1979) *Laboratory Life.* Princeton, NJ: Princeton University Press.

Lopes, L.M. (1991) "The rhetoric of irrationality," *Theory & Psychology*, 1: 65–82.

Marcus, S. (1986) "Freud and Dora: story, history, case-history," in C. Bernheimer and C. Kahane (eds), *In Dora's Case.* London: Virago.

Marx, K. and Engels, F. (1971) *The German Ideology.* London: Lawrence and Wishart.

McAllister, P.O. and Anderson, A. (1991) "Conservatism and the comprehension of implausible text," *European Journal of Social Psychology*, 21: 147–64.

McCloskey, D. (1986) *The Rhetoric of Economics.* Sussex: Harvester.

Moscovici, S. and Personnaz, B. (1991) "Studies in social influence VI: is Lenin orange or red? Imagery and social influence," *European Journal of Social Psychology*, 21: 101–18.

Mulkay, M. (1991) *Sociology of Science: A Sociological Pilgrimage*. Milton Keynes: Open University Press.

Murray, K.D. (1995) "Narratology," in J.A. Smith, R. Harré, and L. van Langenhove (eds), *Rethinking Psychology*. London: Sage.

Myers, G. (1991) *Writing Biology*. Madison, WI: University of Wisconsin Press.

Nelson, J.S., Megill, A., and McCloskey, D.N. (eds) (1987) *The Rhetoric of the Human Sciences*. Madison, WI: University of Wisconsin Press.

Parker, I. (1991) *Discourse Dynamics*. London: Routledge.

Parker, I. and Shotter, J. (eds) (1990) *Deconstructing Social Psychology*. London: Routledge.

Peeters, G. (1991) "Evaluative inference in social cognition: the roles of direct versus indirect evaluation and positive-negative asymmetry," *European Journal of Social Psychology*, 21: 131–46.

Pinch, T. and Pinch, T. (1988) "Reservations about reflexivity and new literary forms: or why let the devil have all the good tunes," in S. Woolgar (ed.), *Knowledge and Reflexivity*. Chicago: University of Chicago Press.

Potter, J. and Wetherell, M. (1987) *Discourse and Social Psychology*. London: Sage.

Potter, J. and Wetherell, M. (1994) "Analyzing discourse," in A. Bryman and R. Burgess (eds), *Analyzing Qualitative Data*. London: Routledge.

Potter, J., Wetherell, M., and Chitty, A. (1991) "Quantification rhetoric – cancer on television," *Discourse and Society*, 2: 333–65.

Rosaldo, R. (1989) *Culture and Truth*. Boston: Beacon Press.

Sachdev, I. and Bourhis, R.Y. (1991) "Power and status differentials in minority and majority group relations," *European Journal of Social Psychology*, 21: 1–24.

Schaller, M. (1991) "Social categorization and the formation of group stereotypes: further evidence for biased information processing in the perception of group-behaviour correlations," *European Journal of Social Psychology*, 21: 25–36.

Shotter, J. (1975) *Images of Man in Psychological Research*. London: Methuen.

Shotter, J. (1993a) *Conversational Realities*. London: Sage.

Shotter, J. (1993b) *Cultural Politics of Everyday Life*. Milton Keynes: Open University Press.

Shotter, J. (1995) "Dialogical psychology," in J.A. Smith, R. Harré, and L. van Langenhove (eds), *Rethinking Psychology*. London: Sage.

Simons, H.W. (ed.) (1989) *Rhetoric in the Human Sciences*. London: Sage.

Simons, H.W. (ed.) (1990) *The Rhetorical Turn*. Chicago: University of Chicago Press.

Smith, D.E. (1987) *The Everyday World as Problematic*. Milton Keynes: Open University Press.

Smith, D.E. (1991) "Writing women's experience into social science," *Feminism and Psychology*, 1: 155–69.

Soyland, A.J. (1994) *Psychology as Metaphor*. London: Sage.

Spears, R. (1994) "Why 'depopulation' should not (necessarily) be taken personally: a commentary on 'Repopulating the depopulated pages of social psychology'," *Theory & Psychology*, 4: 337–44.

Spitzack, C. and Carter, K. (1989) "Research on women's communication: the politics of theory and method," in K. Carter and C. Spitzack (eds), *Doing Research on Women's Communication*. Norwood, NJ: Ablex.

Squire, C. (1989) *Significant Differences: Feminism in Psychology*. London: Routledge.

Squire, C. (1990) "Crisis what crisis? Discourses and narratives of the 'social' in social psychology," in I. Parker and J. Shotter (eds), *Deconstructing Social Psychology*. London: Routledge.

Squire, C. (1991) "Science fictions," *Feminism and Psychology*, 1: 181–99.

Stringer, P. (1994) "A letter to Michael Billig," *Theory & Psychology*, 4: 353–62.

Ussher, J. (1994) "Sexing the phallocentric pages of psychology: repopulation is not enough," *Theory & Psychology*, 4: 345–52.

Van Maanen, J. (1988) *Tales of the Field: On Writing Ethnography*. Chicago: Chicago University Press.

Wallbott, H.G. (1991) "The robustness of communication of emotion via facial expression:

emotion recognition from photographs with deteriorated pictorial quality," *European Journal of Social Psychology*, 21: 89–98.

Wilkinson, S. and Kitzinger, C. (eds) (1993) *Heterosexuality: A Feminism and Psychology Reader*. London: Sage.

Wilkinson, S. and Kitzinger, C. (eds) (1995) *Feminism and Discourse*. London: Sage.

Wilkinson, S., Condor, S., Griffin, C., Wetherell, M. and Williams, J. (1991) "*Feminism and Psychology*: from critique to reconstruction," *Feminism and Psychology*, 1: 5–18.

Wilson, G.D. and Patterson, J.R. (1968) "A new measure of Conservatism," *British Journal of Social and Clinical Psychology*, 7: 264–9.

Wright, R.A. and Gregorich, S.E. (1991) "Difficulty and instrumentality of imminent behaviour as determinants of goal attractiveness," *European Journal of Social Psychology*, 21: 75–88.

Yearley, S. (1984) *Science and Sociological Practice*. Milton Keynes: Open University Press.

8

Repopulating Social Psychology Texts: Disembodied "Subjects" and Embodied Subjectivity

Henderikus J. Stam, Ian Lubek, and H. Lorraine Radtke

Having quoted Billig's title in our own, we seek in another way to expand on his claim that social psychology constitutes an argument against common sense (1990, 1994, also see Billig, this volume). The form of knowledge that is social psychology competes with common sense for an understanding of everyday, garden-variety topics. In generating social psychological knowledge, elaborate arrangements must be made. We want to revisit the rhetorical construction of the experiments, and the bodies of the participants, actors, and experimenters that pass through this ritual of scientific data production. In doing so we will try to see how the argument for social psychology comes from the bodies of its "subjects." In order to make this salient we will reconstruct the depopulated version of one of the controversies in the history of social psychology by seeking to find the bodies that populated Milgram's studies on obedience and what these bodies can tell us about authority, destructive obedience, and the enterprise of experimental social psychology. In short, we wish to repopulate the obedience research with its oblique narrator, Milgram himself, and secondly, repopulate textbook versions of this research that are designed for today's students.

The version of social psychology that is dominant in North America is notoriously individualistic. This complaint has been aired so often that it almost bears no repeating were it not for the fact that it has had very little impact on the discipline, nor is it always clear what individualism means (Stam, 1993). In this paper we wish to examine a version of this thesis by examining the construction of bodies in social psychology and its textbooks. This is because social psychology is individualistic in a peculiar way: it is a disembodied individualism that seeks not to find the experience of social life in the concrete details of individual activity but, instead, extrapolates back to an abstract individual from the aggregate statistics obtained from normative questionnaire or experimental data (cf. Danziger, 1990). The individualism of social psychology characterizes individuals who do not exist but come into being only at the conclusion of a complicated set of methodological practices; practices that extract bits of "data" from individual "subjects" in such a way as to obliterate the identity and experience of any *one* of those "subjects" as persons.

This began early in social psychology's history as behaviorism was imported from general psychology. Floyd Allport characterized *psychological* social psychology in 1924 as an individualist enterprise precisely at a time of increased institutional signs of (sub-)disciplinary growth in teaching, publishing and textbook writing.[1] Laying down the rhetorical foundations for the discipline, he argued that "social behavior comprises the stimulations and reactions arising between an individual and the *social* portion of his environment; that is, between the individual and his fellows.... Social psychology ... *is a part of the psychology of the individual*" (1924: 3–4; italics in original).[2] Under the influence of a behavioral language, and fighting to distinguish itself clearly from the evolving "social psychology" formulations in sociology, this individualistic social psychology was grafted onto a physiological body. The second chapter of Allport's book was devoted to descriptions of the neuron, the brain, and the physiology of the autonomic nervous system. To what end? All of this physiology was presumed to be important for such research topics as how individuals rank order important facial expressions. Yet the presentation of the physiology of the central nervous system was neither necessary nor relevant to the social psychological research that followed although it provided rhetorical support for conventional empiricist claims sprinkled throughout Allport's book, such as the notion that pleasure and pain underlay all emotional states and their expression.

For those who suggest that since its late-nineteenth-century beginnings, psychology itself emerged as a hybrid combination of philosophy and physiology, this understanding of the body in Allport is familiar – it is the body bequeathed by the established sciences and adopted by psychology as the basis for first, consciousness, later behavior, and more recently cognition (Stam and Mathieson, 1995). With various movements towards "objectivity" in twentieth-century psychology (e.g., behaviorism, operationism), this body was flattened; that is, it became one object among many in the world in which our sense experience was devalued as *merely* subjective. Deleule (1992) reminds us that such a world of objects can not act as the "horizon of our experience," as Merleau-Ponty had it, but instead naturalizes psychic life. Having been devalued, the psychic object could now be subjected to scientific analysis which, in turn, would invest it with a kind of objectivity. For Deleule, "in order to purify the body and present it in a more manageable form, [psychologists] replaced its messy, invasive subjectivity with a marvelously intelligible and finely tuned machine whose working parts could easily be interchanged" (1992: 204). In psychology the body is not *just* machine but the machine becomes a metaphor for living processes.[3]

Social psychology is a latecomer to this process and claims for itself the stultified nature of social life that is bequeathed by this body. Social processes that are wholly the outcome of intrapsychic, natural processes make the "other" unknowable. By reducing social life to individual variables, a notion of "social" as anything more than intrapsychic processes was lost. What was gained was the understanding that those processes are readily amenable to investigation, manipulation, and to understanding a productive body, a body whose parts are themselves fit into larger processes of production and reproduction. The biological body becomes incorporated into the social body.

There is a second sense in which bodies are productive in their manifestations in the work of psychologists. Bodies must operate and be operated on by machinery. The relationship between machines and bodies was explored in multiple ways by psychologists in the early- to mid-twentieth century. The body is not just a natural machine but, in a continued form of Taylorism, it is always positioned in some relation to machinery. In demonstrating its machine-like properties, psychology also inserts the body into the mechanization and routinization of productivity. A prototypical example is Skinner's paper in the *Harvard Educational Review* (1961/1972) entitled "Why we need teaching machines." In it he argued for a "true technology of education" in which reinforcements to build discriminative behavior are systematically applied. Since the number of reinforcements required are "far beyond the capacity of teachers . . . *relatively simple machines will suffice*" (1961/1972: 175–6; italics in original). The position of the human body relative to the machine is, as Skinner rightly notes, not unlike the arrangement of the laboratory animal to the machine (see Figure 8.1). The child in the figure is oriented to and responsive to not just learning "a good sense of rhythm," which is what this machine "teaches," but has

Figure 8.1 *An illustration of a "machine to teach 'a good sense of rhythm' " from Skinner (1961/1972).* © *B.F. Skinner Foundation. Photo Credit: Will Rapport. Reprinted with permission from J.S. Vargas and the B.F. Skinner Foundation.*

become integrated into the production of rhythm as both biological and machinelike. Where does the machine end and the child begin? Where does the psycho-biological organism end and the productive body begin? Nowhere, for here the productive body as machine/body is perfectly integrated. The body will be productive as the machine does its work to integrate its functions into the machine/body.

In order to follow the unfolding of social psychology's body we turn to a story in psychology that begins a year before Skinner's publication. It concerns the relations between a group of volunteer "subjects" and another piece of machinery – the shock machine used in the obedience research of Stanley Milgram. As if to emphasize the technological innovation of his research program, Milgram (1976) was to say later, "I think this machine was quite important for psychology." In particular we trace this story through to its presentation in textbooks as the narrative gradually unfolds to incorporate today's students of social psychology in the story itself.[4] In the section that follows we want to locate this research within the tradition of experimental social psychology. This matters because social psychology came to experimentation relatively late compared with most other areas of psychology, and insecurity about the use of experimentation only made the controversies surrounding Milgram's work more searching and ultimately more damaging. In the following section we examine Milgram's research and his own conception of it, the "standard view" that emerged about it, and the textbook presentations of his studies. We then reconsider the criticisms leveled at this research (both methodological and ethical) and how these are dismissed on the standard view. Finally, from the standpoint of the productive body we engage the standard view to articulate what is hidden by its continual reproduction and in the last section of the paper examine how the transition of the Milgram research to the classroom presentation positions today's students of social psychology.

Textbooks, Handbooks, and Methods

One of our tasks is to examine the Milgram obedience studies as they have been transmitted to several generations of undergraduates through their textbooks. We do not come to this task without investments; one of us has already suggested that textbooks should, like cigarettes, carry a warning label about their potential hazards (Lubek, 1993b). Lubek argued that social psychology textbooks serve a knowledge-conserving function for the discipline in both its psychological and sociological manifestations. Indeed, there is a great deal of temporal consistency, a shared core of material and authors to be discussed, and the adoption of a homogeneous, conservative perspective. On the basis of his analysis of 64 social psychology textbooks, Lubek concluded that "with few exceptions, neither the writers nor publishers are making the textbook marketplace a forum for critical, innovative conceptualizations or radical reconstructions of social psychology' (1993b:

373). The transmission of Milgram's obedience experiments will be no exception.

In earlier papers we (Lubek and Stam, 1995; Stam and Lubek, 1992) examined the rhetoric of experimentation in social psychology as manifested in its methodology textbooks and handbooks after the Second World War. These texts were chosen because they recapitulate the methodologies of the discipline for novice researchers and graduate students. They contain idealizations and replies to the implied and stated problems of experimentation that were not appropriate for journals but too technical and complex for junior level textbooks. The use of experimentation, and the justificatory rhetoric surrounding it, have allowed psychological social psychologists to gradually but clearly demarcate their area of expertise from sociological social psychology. There is something unique, however, to the emergence of experimentation in social psychology, especially when contrasted with the description of experimentation by experimental psychologists working in other areas of psychology. Social psychologists did not share, in their writings, the same methodological confidence exuded by their experimental colleagues outside social psychology. From the very beginning of the codification of experimentation in social psychology, its adherents have shown a marked degree of defensiveness about, and ambivalence towards, their self-proclaimed "powerful tool."[5]

The *Handbook of Social Psychology*, published in 1954 and revised in 1968 and 1985 (Lindzey, 1954; Lindzey and Aronson, 1968, 1985), has gradually come to be the "expert" source for matters methodological in social psychology.[6] The handbook came to represent most clearly (and came to be relied on as the authority for) the notion that psychological social psychology was an experimental science. This was due in part to the late institutionalization of research practices in this discipline. In 1953 Newcomb still lamented that "strictly speaking, there are probably no social-psychological methods as such" (1953: 9) at a time when experimentation had been solidly institutionalized in almost all corners of psychology. The tensions which developed in methodological prescriptions for social psychology reflected (a) the problem that there were no logical, a priori reasons for adopting experimentation, (b) if experiments became too "artificial" they would lose their applicability to "real-life situations," and (c) experiments must derive their problems from those same "real-life situations" (this argument is fully developed in Stam and Lubek, 1992).

More important for us is the problem raised in almost all methodological writing in social psychology from the early 1950s forward: what to do with the research volunteers? The researchers wanted "strong effects," and in order to obtain these effects the psychologist must use "deception, prevarication, misdirection of subject, and the like" (Festinger, 1953: 170). The "subject" is no longer a true participant, observer, or equal (cf. Danziger's, 1990, discussion of the early egalitarian, reciprocating, and interchangeable Wundtian subject) but a technical problem that requires the careful insertion of the body into a scenario. Festinger creates a picture of the smart experimenter who must wrest the appropriate effects from docile "subjects." Social psychologists will be able to develop their own brand of experimentation by being clever and outwitting "subjects" at every turn. This in turn will not be a technology handed down to future generations in an unproblematic manner but becomes the accumulated wisdom and experience of the artful experimenter.[7]

The clever experimenter and the docile "subject" take on their clearest form in the 1968 handbook chapter on experimentation by Aronson and Carlsmith. Perhaps this is not surprising since they had to defend experimentation against real critics, although the definitive epistemological critiques were yet to appear. Ethical concerns had by then been raised along with those of demand characteristics and experimenter expectancy effects. At 79 pages, the chapter is filled with redundancies – a strategy itself designed to bring home the chapter's message that good experimentation is largely an intuitive affair, and that the experiment itself is inviolate as the source of knowledge. In their opening statement Aronson and Carlsmith target the more mundane and less explicit aspects of the experimental process in social psychology ". . . many of which are essential ingredients in the social psychology experiment but are difficult to specify in research reports or in methodological discussions because of their relatively 'artistic,' intuitive, ephemeral nature" (1968: 1).

Too much intuition, however, belies the technical and logical nature of the scientific experiment. Thus, at the same time Aronson and Carlsmith play out the tension by noting that "there are as many ways of building and conducting an experiment as there are experimenters. As experimenters, we do not believe that all of these are equally effective or fruitful . . . for ultimately, the question of how to conduct an experiment is, in itself, an empirical one" (1968: 3). There are criteria, then, by which to judge an experiment, except they are not logical, they must be found. The circularity feeds back into the expertise of the experimenter. On this account, theoretical concerns are minimal in learning the art of experimentation: "where the idea [for an experiment] comes from is not terribly important . . . ideas are cheap in social psychology" (1968: 37). Although this strident position would be tempered in the 1985 handbook, there too ideas are minimized for the intuitive scientist – one simply *has* ideas. The phenomena of social psychology exist in the arrangements of an experimental situation.

In 1968 Aronson and Carlsmith could not avoid the problems raised in discussions on the ethics of experimentation. Their moral exhortations confirm the image of the conscientious, caring, ethical, intuitive experimenter.[8] At the same time, the work of the intuitive and caring experimenter lives in tension with the expectation that such work will eventually lead to a formalized technology. This tension is very difficult to maintain, for as Aronson and Carlsmith point out, they do not wish to "sacrifice the advantages of the 'personal touch' of the breathing experimenter who, in our opinion, has not been and should not become another victim of automation" (1968: 53). Yet the rhetorical power of a technology of experimentation demands precisely the capacity to develop automated, cook-book approaches to research.

Maintaining the special authority of the experimenter is one way to guard against threats to professional autonomy. When faced with legitimation crises, professions no longer defend their technical abilities as formalized, transferable, and controllable but instead rely on their important "clinical expertise," "intuition," and so on. This is the indeterminate non-transferable charisma based on principles at odds with the claims for technical expertise made by professionals, the technical expertise that is normally transferable via training, textbooks, journals, and so on (de Swaan, 1991).

The second point of tension noticeable here is that the body of the experimenter is above automation, remains essentially human, whereas that of the "subject" is not. Because "the docility and cooperativeness of subjects can be a serious impediment to research" (Aronson and Carlsmith, 1968: 65), it is the "subject's" body that requires automation. "Subjects" are the dangerous "other;" they are the unknowing and uncaring raw material of the scientific enterprise in social psychology. They cannot be trusted – all manner of manipulations, deception, and checks must be built into an experiment to guard against this other. From 1953 to 1968 such safeguards on behalf of the integrity of the scientific enterprise become an ever greater concern at the same time as this concern is also a response to the critics. Together with the "subject," the critic represents an attack on the enterprise of the intuitive scientist.

These tensions that play themselves out in the handbooks and methodology chapters over a period of 30 years are gradually transmitted to the level of the textbook for the neophyte social psychologist. By the time they reach this level there is no longer any intimation that the methodology should be other than experimental and there is no hint of disagreement about the nature of this method. Due in part to the mass-marketing of texts and the requirement by publishers that textbooks have overlapping content, social psychology texts from the 1960s onward have increasingly favored a single, sanitized, "scientific" version of the discipline (Cherry, 1995; Lubek, 1993b). Frances Cherry's historical account of social psychology texts notes that textbooks also changed with the rise in enrollment in post secondary education and the increasing pressure to popularize these books for mass consumption. "The current concern over textbooks is not that they have a point of view but the uncritical way in which their point of view prevails" (1995: 88). And Milgram's obedience research is an icon in the introductory social psychology textbook. To understand how it has come to be so venerated in the annals of the discipline, we must engage in both iconoclasm and iconography: first, remove the icon from its frame to see the discipline that has shaped it and, second, restore the images in the likeness of human bodies.

Milgram and the Standard View

Our entrance to Milgram's research is Radley's claim that textbook reports of Milgram's studies are merely descriptions of what "subjects heard and saw" in the actual experimental situation and what they "said and did." This in turn is of interest only in so far as something is revealed about the differences in manipulations between the varying experimental contexts (Radley, 1991: 6). Because social psychology has "no way of comprehending the body in pain, and particularly the structure of torture" (1991: 7), the experiments have become, in their textbook descriptions, either simplified reiterations of the details of the studies which emphasize the problem of obedience or a discussion of the problems of deception and the need to revise methods in social psychology. For Radley, the problem remains that "pain was *effectively* inflicted upon the victim" (1991: 8; original emphasis). It was the application of pain and suffering, whatever the real status of the "victim," that makes these studies poignant and renders them problematic for social psychology. We wish to expand this claim by noting how the victim's body is figured in the Milgram studies, with important consequences for how we "read" this body.

Milgram's Conceptions of Obedience

Before we turn to the discussions of these experiments in social psychology textbooks we need to ask what Milgram himself took these experiments to signify. This is crucial to understanding our claims that they served a far different purpose in the iconography of social psychology. As a recent graduate from Asch's laboratory in the early 1960s, Milgram placed himself in the tradition of research on obedience in social psychology by noting the connection to the work of Sidis in 1898 and the traditions of Asch, Lewin, and others. Much of this work, however, was on "conformity," the concern of social psychologists in the inter-war period with the developments of "mass society." It was not until the horrors of the Second World War, specifically the Nazi extermination camps, became more widely known in 1945 that social psychologists conceptualized *obedience* as a form of conformity. In his 1974 book Milgram cites three works in particular that "have especially interested me." Each of these was written after the war (Bierstedt, 1954; Comfort, 1950; Koestler, 1967).

The problem of obedience was formulated around the concern frequently expressed that the actions of the Third Reich required accomplices, bystanders, and perpetrators. In Milgram's words,

> The Nazi extermination of European Jews is the most extreme instance of abhorrent immoral acts carried out by thousands of people in the name of obedience. Yet in lesser degree this type of thing is constantly recurring: ordinary citizens are ordered to destroy other people, and they do so because they consider it their duty to obey orders. Thus obedience to authority, long praised as a virtue, takes on a new aspect when it serves a malevolent cause; far from appearing as a virtue, it is transformed into a heinous sin. Or is it? (1974: 2)

The question at the end of that paragraph was a deliberate opening for Milgram to imply further relevance for his work. For while he began his research specifically with the Nazi extermination camps and the "banality of evil" in mind, by the time he wrote his book in 1974 there were multiple references to Vietnam and the nuclear arms race in his conceptions of obedience to authority: "in wartime, a soldier does not ask whether it is good or bad to bomb a hamlet," (1974: 8) and ". . . the types of justification experienced by the person are essentially similar whether they occur in a psychological laboratory or the control room of an ICBM site"[9] (1974: xii). What justified the experiments in Milgram's eyes was their universal applicability and their demonstration of the phenomenon of obedience ("a common psychological process") within the context of obeying an authoritative figure. In this respect his analysis is typical of social psychology: his references to "society" are superficial and undifferentiated and his notion of democracy is implicit. He condemns "malevolent systems of authority" without social or historical analysis, repeating only the conclusions of his experiments, namely, that a "substantial proportion of people do what they are told to do, irrespective of the content of the act and without limitations of conscience, so long as they perceive that the command comes from a legitimate authority" (1974: 189). The bodies that performed the tasks in his experiments are no more than symbolic entities whose lives are representative of larger social forces. They become an object lesson in obedience – as if denouncing Nazi extermination camps and My Lai could not have been done without the evidence of social psychology experiments.[10] The "social" that is represented here is a caricature that serves as a homogeneous backdrop to bolster the theory. "Subjects'" bodies are first abstracted from their social context and then recontextualized in a way that denies their social constitution (Stam, 1987). The setting of the experiment, a "teaching" and "learning" exercise, is natural to an educational context but not to the historical examples of obedience Milgram wishes the experiment to address. Social relations, then, are unproblematic and they enter the structure of the theory in a natural, ahistorical way. Milgram was himself employed by large, hierarchical, bureaucratic organizations (universities). Many of his "subjects" were as well, yet his description of their backgrounds made their negotiation of institutional structures in their everyday lives irrelevant to the fact of their one act of obedience or disobedience in the experimental context. It had to be this way if Milgram was going to make the experiments do the theoretical work they were required to do.

The Standard View

In recent years there has come to be a standard view of the obedience experiments. This view is circulated not only through textbooks but also through the commentaries that the research has received in the broader literature (e.g., Blass, 1991; Miller, 1986). Miller's (1986) review and summary of this literature provides the clearest and most extensive example of this view. Many of the commentaries raise questions that cannot be answered by either Milgram's research or that conducted by other social psychologists. Although ostensibly focused on ethics and methodology (e.g.,

Baumrind, 1964/1972; Orne and Holland, 1968), what is at stake is the very *epistemology* of social psychological research. How do we know that these studies tell us anything about obedience? How do we know what any social psychological research studies tell us? What justifies their continued use as knowledge-producing devices? Such issues remain a subtext, buried by a host of details addressing the finer points of the experiments or their ethical impact. Like many commentators from within social psychology, Miller falls back on a standard defense of the research. He considers the critiques as problems to be solved by either empirical means or institutional arrangements. The criticisms are not considered central to understanding the nature of social psychological research, and indeed, Miller's book can be read as an *apologia* for experimental social psychology in general. The ethical questions are questions that, in part, can be treated empirically to determine individual differences in ethical preferences. The ethical response to Milgram's research can be determined by one's "point of view." When Milgram is accused of being "preachy" and "moralistic" by Marcus (1974), Miller retorts that Milgram's aim was merely to emphasize an "empirical" orientation to obedience rather than a "theological" or "philosophical" one (1986: 121). In concluding his discussion of the ethical issues raised by the obedience studies, Miller quotes McGuire, who argued that "we must also be concerned about an equally questionable ethical position epitomized by the words, 'I have *not* run any subjects today' . . . go on with our work we must, or else we must change our field" (1967: 131). Miller cites, favorably, comments by Roger Brown and Philip Zimbardo who both lament the lack of influence that research psychologists exert over the lessons of other, more influential people in our lives. Finally, he draws the conclusion that Milgram's "singularly most impressive achievement" was the

> . . . development of the experimental paradigm itself. . . . While anyone could have an opinion about what an individual would or should do when given destructive orders from an authority, Milgram went beyond speculation. A choice point was created in his laboratory – a moral "fork in the road." He constructed a telling moment of truth. (1986: 258)

Miller's accounts of the experiments and his rebuttals to the critics are revealing for the continuing work that is required to quell the damage done by Milgram's studies *at the same time* as they serve as paradigmatic case studies of the power of experimentation. The obedience research continued (and continues) to be a point of debate around questions of ethics and experimentation. While Miller's book is thus an insider's defense of experimental social psychology, in particular through the avoidance of epistemological questions, the real enemy is not named. The obedience research is no longer a case study of the importance of obedience to authority but *an important promoter of the importance and necessity of experimental social psychological research*. The visibility of the research has become a token: by its critics, a token of the vulnerability of the discipline; by proponents a token of its strengths. Within the discipline, Milgram is valorized for his contributions but the recurring appearance of discussions of methodology and ethics indicate that, in order to valorize Milgram's studies, social psychologists must continually engage in damage control. It is this combined valorization/defensiveness that we take to be the standard view of the obedience experiments. Let us now turn to the promulgation of that discourse to the student.[11]

Textbooks of Social Psychology

Because of the textbook's role in the delivery of *the* way of doing social psychology, the standard view of the obedience research has become a key case study to promote an understanding of the difficulties with the ethics and methodology of experimentation. This, of course, makes the standard view crucial for textbooks of social psychology which, after all, must pass the message on to generations of undergraduates, some of whom will continue in the discipline. In order to render these studies harmless, to invoke a social psychology whose aims are indeed benign and humanitarian, they are reinterpreted within the confines of a discussion which emphasizes their importance as a demonstration of obedience to authority and their usefulness in helping an earlier generation of social psychologists solve important ethical and methodological problems. Without denying the moral purposes of such rhetoric for colleagues who would genuinely wish to transform society into a kinder, more just society in which to practice their *métier*, we nonetheless feel it important to ask what is obscured by such moves in reconstitution, and to indicate what such reinterpretations might mean to today's generation of students partaking of these discussions in digestible format. In particular, these accounts must treat the subjection of the body as normal and acceptable within the confines of limits in ethics and experimentation.[12] In addition, it must seduce the student into believing that all of this is normal as well as giving the student the experience of having acquired specialist "knowledge." The student must be drawn into the process.

To follow the discussions about the obedience studies over the years, we read 33 textbook accounts (see Table 8.1). Twenty-seven of the books were introductions to social psychology and six were general introductions to psychology. Our texts dated from 1965 to 1995 and our search was representative, not comprehensive. It included books that had actually been used or were in use by members of our departments as well as several volumes available in our libraries. These included popular texts, Canadian editions of American texts, one sociological social psychology text, two texts written by critical voices in social psychology (whose references to Milgram were remarkably indistinct from those of their colleagues), as well as some lesser known works. We included six representative introductory textbooks because students are frequently introduced to Milgram's work on obedience in their very first psychology course. The table outlines the texts and the extent of the discussion of Milgram's research on obedience.[13] The only

Table 8.1   *Textbooks in psychology and social psychology examined and*
number of pages devoted to Milgram's obedience studies

Authors of Text	Type	Edition	Year	No. of Pages
Alcock, J.E., Carment, D.W., and Sadava, S.W.	soc	3rd	1994	5
Allen, L. and Santrock, J.W.	intro		1993	2
Aronson, E.	soc	1st	1972	5.5
Aronson, E.	soc	2nd	1975	5.5
Aronson, E.	soc	3rd	1980	6.5
Aronson, E.	soc	4th	1984	7
Aronson, E.	soc	5th	1988	9.5
Aronson, E., Wilson, T.D., and Akert, R.M.	soc		1994	8
Baron, R.A. and Byrne, D.E.	soc	2nd	1977	17.5
Baron, R.A. and Byrne, D.E.	soc	3rd	1981	8
Baron, R.A. and Byrne, D.E.	soc	7th	1994	7
Baron, R. A., Byrne, D.E., and Griffitt, W.	soc	1st	1974	10.75
Baron, R.A., Earhard, B., and Ozier, M.	intro	Can[1]	1995	2.5
Baron, R.A., Byrne, D.E., and Watson, G.	soc	Can	1995	2.3
Baron, R.M., Graziano, W.G., and Stangor, C.	soc		1991	4.5
Baum, A., Fisher, J.D., and Singer, J.E.	soc		1985	1.3
Benjamin, L.T., Hopkins, J.R., and Nation, J.R.	intro		1994	2
Brown, R.	social	1st	1965	0
Brown, R.	soc	2nd	1986	15.5
Cvetkovich, G., Baumgardner, S.R., and Trimble, J.E.	soc		1984	4
Deaux, K. and Wrightsman, L.S.	soc		1988	3
Feldman, R.S.	soc		1995	4.4
Gergen, K.J. and Gergen, M.M.	soc	2nd	1986	3.5
Lauer, R.H. and Handel, W.H.	soc[2]	2nd	1983	0
Matlin, M.W.	intro		1992	1.5
Michener, H.A. and DeLamater, J.D.	soc	3rd	1994	5
Myers, D.G.	soc	2nd	1987	9
Myers, D.G.	soc	4th	1993	6
Penner, L.A.	soc		1978	2
Plotnik, R.	intro		1993	3
Sampson, E.	soc		1991	4
Smith, E.R. and Mackie, D.M.	soc		1995	9.2
Wade, C. and Tavris, C.	intro		1987	2.5

[1] Can refers to the Canadian edition of an American textbook.

[2] *Sociological* social psychology textbook.

Note: Only those textbooks explicitly cited in the text are listed in the reference list at the conclusion of this chapter.

two books that make no mention of Milgram's studies are Brown (1965), published just as the studies and the controversy broke, and Lauer and Handel (1983), the one *sociological* social psychology text and a textbook that does not concern itself with obedience. Interestingly, some of our colleagues in sociology do not share psychologists' enthusiasm for this research.

Despite the time that has passed since the original research (1960–63), the discussions about the research have not abated. What *has* occurred is that the discussions have become stereotypical – they are predictably embedded in text that begins with some depiction of the Nazis, Eichmann, and My Lai (with Jonestown sometimes added in the 1980s). Then follows a description of the experiment with some textbooks giving more or less detail of the replications and the varying conditions in those replications. The dramatic nature of the results is frequently highlighted by some reference to the findings reported by Milgram himself that neither psychiatrists, college students, nor middle-class adults could predict that up to 65 percent of "subjects" would go to the highest levels of shock (in what Milgram called his "Remote-Feedback" variation).[14]

Methodology: High-impact versus Methodological Wrinkles

Almost all of the texts slide into a discussion of the controversies surrounding the studies, particularly those dealing with the generalizability of the findings and the ethics of experimentation and deception. This is frequently an implicit or explicit recognition of the controversies engendered by the studies. For example, Aronson (1972, 1975, 1980, 1984) warns against an "overinterpretation" of the studies. In earlier editions of his text he simply notes the differences between a laboratory experiment and "situations encountered by Eichmann [and] by Calley" (1972: 36). In later editions this concern focuses on the study itself, "it should be emphasized that there are, in fact, some important factors in the situation encountered by Milgram's subjects that tend to maximize obedience" (1980: 37). These discussions, however, disappear in Aronson et al. (1994), and the entire research program is here described as one that demonstrates that it is difficult to switch social norms once people realize that they are following the wrong one. Participants found it difficult to "abandon the obey authority norm" (1994: 280).

Questions about the "realism" of the studies are uniformly defended by reference to Milgram's own replies to the critics. For example, Aronson quotes Milgram who "observed a mature and initially poised businessman enter the laboratory smiling and confident. Within 20 minutes he was reduced to a twitching, stuttering wreck, who was rapidly approaching a point of nervous collapse" (1972: 281). Deaux and Wrightsman note that "evidence of stress testifies to the impact of the procedures and the reality of the subjects' experience" (1988: 225). Most are explicit in repeating Milgram's own justifications. For example, Myers claims that although we

are not often asked to administer shock to others, the "psychological processes engaged in the laboratory" are similar to those in everyday life just
as "combustion is similar for a burning match and a forest fire" (1987:
272–3). Milgram used this analogy of the match and the forest fire in his
book-length description of the research program (1974).

There are two aspects to the concern over generalizability in the textbooks. The first consists of the question, is this setting sufficiently similar to
others that require obedience under authority so that the results are gener-
alizable? Some authors then discuss the differences between a laboratory
setting with a scientist and those of the historically relevant cases such as
the genocide committed by Nazi Germany against so many millions and
caution against "overinterpretation" (e.g., Aronson, 1972, 1975, 1980). A
second aspect, however, bypasses this concern by asking the question a
different way: is this setting sufficiently robust so that most people would
do the same if they were to take part in this experiment? This allows authors
to argue from replications that have been conducted elsewhere (e.g., Australia, Spain, West Germany) that the studies are sufficiently general regardless of the artificial nature of the laboratory. As Aronson claims, "this
behavior is not limited to American men living in Connecticut" (1984: 40).

On the whole, such concerns over realism and generalizability have
declined over time or they are dealt with summarily. Baum et al. simply say
that the extent of the applicability of the obedience studies to real-life situations has been questioned "but parallels to real-life incidents of extreme
obedience, such as the massacre of civilians at My Lai . . . the unquestioning acceptance of poison by members of Jim Jones's cult . . . are unmistakable" (1985: 310). In fact, they are so unmistakable that they no longer need
to be accounted for, articulated, or otherwise demonstrated. The connections between Eichmann, My Lai, and in the 1980s, Jonestown, on the one
hand and the Milgram research on the other hand, have been repeated so
often that the formulaic response by textbook authors has gradually become
"unmistakable." This is one indication that the research has reached the
status of a "paradigmatic" experiment. This "high-impact" experiment has
come to define experimental social psychology in a way few other experiments have matched. The methodological questions have gradually faded
from the discussions, to be dealt with quickly (if considered at all).[15] Instead
authors now resort to descriptions such as "It is important to understand
that social psychological knowledge is much richer because of the Milgram
research" (Alcock et al. 1994), "one of the best-known studies in psychology" (Smith and Mackie, 1995), "Milgram's research . . . is one of the most
famous studies in psychology" (Matlin, 1992), and numerous other references to the "classic" studies on obedience. It is in no small measure due to
these repetitions in textbooks that this research remains a "classic." We will
return to the question of what gives this research such staying power when
other studies conducted in the same period have long been forgotten. First,
however, let us turn to the second point of criticism raised by textbook
authors – the problem of ethics.

Ethics

Unlike the methodological issues of generalizability and realism, ethical concerns have not only been consistently raised but have remained a constant feature of the descriptions of the Milgram research over the years. Interestingly, however, our survey led us to the conclusion that such discussions have tended, in recent years, to be more, not less, supportive of experimental social psychology research.

Discussions of the ethics of the obedience studies were varied and confusing. Most textbook authors were actually unclear about questions of ethics since these were often reduced to questions of method. Is it ethical to use deception? Must an investigator protect the privacy of participants? A certain resentment was sometimes articulated, although this is stronger in professional publications than in textbooks.[16] The confusion is perhaps inevitable in that the discipline takes its subject matter (and its "subject") to be functional entities and abstracted individuals to whom the investigator has no moral relationship but only a contractual "ethical" obligation. Indeed, in a statement the irony of which was lost on its authors, Mirvis and Seashore argued that researchers were personally responsible for the ethics of the research effort as demonstrated by Milgram's studies that "showed vividly how people can behave unethically because of their role in a social setting" (1982: 101). If Milgram's studies had not "shown" this, would we need to be concerned about ethics?

Before proceeding, it is also important to note what is *never* found in the textbooks. Milgram's research on obedience has been reported as one of three sets of research programs in the history of twentieth-century science that led to the clarification of voluntary informed consent (Sieber, 1982). The other two were the Nazi concentration camp "medical experiments" (which led to the Nuremberg Code), and the Tuskegee study in which semi-literate, syphilitic black men in Alabama were left untreated, even after the introduction of penicillin, to study the effects of untreated syphilis. Sieber acknowledges that the latter two cases do not approach the Milgram studies in severity of abuse, but their inclusion in the process leading to the regulation of research on human beings by governments, universities, and professional associations indicates that the public view of the Milgram studies differed radically from the benign picture created by Milgram and social psychologists themselves.[17] And yet there is no acknowledgment of this in any of the textbook accounts: the ethical issues are presented as the results of questions raised by insiders – by social psychologists themselves. This failure to acknowledge the extent of the ethical questions and the changes that were one outcome of these discussions is part of the overall implied defense of social psychology research practices. Let us turn then to the texts themselves.

The original research program was almost immediately subjected to ethical criticism (e.g., Baumrind, 1964/1972; Kelman, 1967) and Milgram responded to such critiques on a number of occasions (e.g., Milgram, 1964,

1974). He even responded to a critical dramatic presentation of the experiments in a London play in 1971 (contained in the 1974 text). The original criticisms focused extensively on the potential harm to the participants in the studies, their levels of stress, and the requirement that they hurt another human being under the guise of a scientific experiment. The "classic" defense carried by textbooks against the ethical charges was again laid down by Milgram himself. According to the texts, the participants in his research reported no ill effects after the experiment, and when 40 of those who took part were interviewed by a psychiatrist a year later, no lasting harm was found. Indeed, Milgram argues and textbooks report that many of his participants were grateful because they had learned something important about themselves as participants and that they should endeavor to work harder to avoid unjust authority. On a follow-up survey Milgram reported that "84% of the subjects stated they were glad to have been in the experiment" (1974: 195). This figure, which actually collapses over several categories in Milgram's questionnaire, is frequently cited in textbooks.

In almost all cases the texts strive to give a "balanced" approach. Authors raise the issues and give the standard defense with little comment, making it appear that the reader should decide for herself. Very few authors make the forthright statement that Deaux and Wrightsman made for example, "One can probably argue that such self-education [of the participants] might be beneficial, but it is probably not within the province of the experimental social psychologist to force such education on anyone" (1988: 224–5). More typical was the response by Myers:

> [obedience experiments] all demonstrate how compliance can take precedence over one's moral sense. . . . They all do more than teach us an academic lesson; they sensitize us to analogous conflicts in our own lives. And they illustrate and affirm certain social psychological principles discussed in earlier chapters. (1987: 250)

Sometimes the defense is implicitly drawn by contrasting the criticisms with the honors bestowed on Milgram and his research:

> Milgram's experiment is one of the best-known studies in psychology. . . . Many studies conducted a decade or two ago probably could not be done today. Milgram's study, which won the American Association for the Advancement of Science award for social-psychological research in 1964, is one of them. (Wade and Tavris, 1987: 71)

Another way in which the ethical questions are deflected is through the abstraction of these questions from the context of the results. For example, Feldman alerts the student to the ethical problems by noting that "the ethical issues cannot be dismissed. It remains an important, if ultimately unresolvable, footnote to Milgram's work" (1995: 405). As if to underscore the notion that this is merely a footnote, the text proceeds with ". . . independent of ethical issues, Milgram's studies reveal an important fact: Authority figures can induce people to perform antisocial acts with relative ease" (1995: 406). This separation of the "ethical" from the "factual" is a rhetorical accomplishment reproduced in most texts. They are different domains and hence do not affect each other; that is, the scientific conclusions obtained from the participants' bodies are not to be confused with what was done to them.

It is important to note that the original ethical critiques were *not* focused on the use of deception. For example, Baumrind's concern was with the experienced loss of dignity, self-esteem, trust, and so on, *"from the subject's point of view"* (1964/1972: 111; emphasis added). Over the years, however, textbook discussions have tended to eclipse the original ethical questions with a discussion of deception even though questions of deception were raised later and then only in a general way about all social psychology experiments, Milgram's included. Milgram's research became a useful way of introducing the question of deception since these studies could obviously not have been carried out without the deception (but see note 22). As Aronson argued, ". . . unless Milgram had used deception, he would have come out with results that simply do not reflect the way people behave when they are led to believe they are in real situations" (1984: 374). Baron et al. entwine Milgram's work with the problem of deception in the 1974 edition of their text. Over subsequent editions, however, Baron and Byrne dissociate the two topics, and Milgram's research becomes unproblematically discussed in a chapter on "Social Influence" while the ethical issues are separately mentioned in a first chapter. Deception in.this and most texts appears useful as a point of discussion because it inevitably turns around the question of necessity. The results of Milgram's obedience research would not have been obtained without deception. By tying deception to the original ethical questions raised about Milgram's research, the latter become reduced to a methodological problem. The authors of several texts repeat Mixon's (1974) argument that it is simply impossible to find out who will or will not obey without the deception.

A similar point is consistently made by numerous authors who contrast the results of the actual experiments to the expectations of psychiatrists, college students, and middle-class adults reported by Milgram himself. People will present themselves as moral beings, hence the studies had to be carried out. Moreover, given the very influential nature of the outcomes, who could be against deception? Of course, the "right, well-being, and privacy of research participants must be protected" (Baron et al., 1974: 20) but the "continued use of deception is both necessary and justified" (1974: 20).[18] The "docile subject" is to blame for this turn of events. People are simply not honest; experimenters express regret that they have to use deception; it is the "subject's" fault that, to obtain the truth, the experimenter must resort to methods that are sometimes unpleasant. We note that extracting the "truth" from a "subject" bears some resemblance to the topos of torturers who express regret for having to deal with the victim's obstinacy and apply their methods as unwilling agents of the state (DuBois, 1994).

What is peculiar about these presentations is the structure of the ethical talk. It has gradually become a justification for social psychological research methods. Textbook authors find it difficult to avoid the ethical questions (partly due to the publication practices of textbook publishers that have dictated a percentage of standard content for introductory texts). At the same time they seem so easy to dismiss, if only implicitly. The standard model of experimental research is often touted as the only legitimate way to develop social psychological knowledge. It is not surprising then that methodological considerations must, in the end, take precedence over the ethical questions. Adjustments have been made and acknowledgment is duly given, but the research process remains sacrosanct. Given the construction of social psychology as a scientific enterprise, social psychologists would undermine their own legitimacy if they did not find a way to contain and limit the ethical questions. Ironically, for a discipline that prides itself on having discovered the ubiquitous and dangerous effects of conformity, our case study of the description of obedience research reinforces the belief that those who write textbooks construct highly conformist stories (cf. Cherry, 1995; Lubek, 1993b).

This failure to address ethical questions results from the failure to understand that ethics are not simply the application of universal and foundationalist rules to work in the laboratory. The experimenter, moving bodies through the elaborate staging of a social psychology high-impact scenario, has no relationship with a participant (who does not "participate" in any process resembling conditions mutually agreed upon) but *subjects* that body to a series of techniques. Since there is no longer a moral ground, a conversation among persons, between investigator and participant who share common ground, the scientist–subject relationship must be worked out according to some fixed rules derived from legislatures and professional associations. The very need for rules and their application already confirms that the relationship between scientist and participant has been radically altered to one that is instrumentalist and deceptive in its surface features.

Reseachers' Bodies and Participants' Bodies

Participants' bodies in the obedience research are not only opaque (as Radley noted), so are the confederates' and the researchers' bodies. The experimenter, John Williams, was a 31-year-old high school biology teacher, and the "victim," James McDonough, was a 47-year-old accountant of "Irish-American descent" who was "trained for the role" and "most observers found him mild-mannered and likable" (Milgram, 1974: 16). Milgram appears not to have taken part in the actual experiments. The roles are articulated in such a fashion that the participants' activity can be precisely triggered. The bodies of the "experimenter," "victim," and "subjects" are not the bodies of humans whose capacity for obedience was to be determined.[19] The setting requires no explanation or elaboration; the body of the participant is no more than that of the single element in the entire operation requiring a single set of responses. The experiment is thoroughly depopulated of anything but staged and set responses. In this sense the participant is an appendage to the experiment-as-machine. This appendage acts in complete ignorance, so as a productive body it must have a kind of consciousness restored to it, a remote consciousness, a folkloric one (Deleule, 1992). This is what is theorized in the notion of "obedience" and the "agentic state" that Milgram (1974) posits in his theoretical account; an account that is largely a restatement of the results of the experiments in abstract, functional yet recognizable ordinary language categories.

What is obliterated in this account is not that the participant might be obedient but that the obedience measured is only one *kind* of obedience required of the "subject." The other obedience, thoroughly hidden from the reports of the experiments, is the obedience required by the entire apparatus which limits individual responses to those required by the apparatus in a context thoroughly artificial and staffed by actors. For not only are the participants obedient but the "experimenter" and the "victim" too participate in the sham of a scientific experiment. None of these bodies matters more than the responses given in predetermined fashion. Milgram, who authorizes/authors the entire arrangement is fulfilling his part in the machinery of constructing social psychological knowledge.[20]

Therapeutic Bodies

The role of obedience studies in social psychology texts is one that strengthens and dramatizes the enterprise of experimental social psychology. The methodological and ethical issues raised by the research have over time become justifications for the studies themselves. Moreover, many textbooks, after having discussed the negative consequences of obedience to authority, turn to some of Milgram's replications to show how influence can be resisted. Here the obedience research takes on a *therapeutic* place in the annals of the discipline. Now the studies are not only ethical but the bodies of participants and actors alike create a paradigmatic therapeutic context. For example, exposure to disobedient models reduced obedience in one of the replications (Milgram, 1965b). More important, however, is the advantage derived from the knowledge of the power of authority figures as demonstrated by this research. This advantage is beyond that which Milgram argued accrued to his participants, namely, the therapeutic advantage of knowing how you have responded in a setting requiring obedience. It is in fact more general:

> Growing evidence . . . suggests that when individuals learn about the findings of social psychological research, they may change their behavior to take account of this knowledge. With respect to destructive obedience, there is some hope that knowing about this process can enhance individuals' ability to resist. To the extent this is the case, then even exposure to findings as disturbing as those reported by Milgram can have positive social value. As they become widely known, they may produce desirable shifts within society. (Baron and Byrne, 1994: 384)

Milgram's research becomes an inoculation against false authority. But what authorities? Certainly, there is no call for resistance to the imposition upon students of the authority of their professors, who are armed with text-book accounts of Milgram's work (and other subject matter), examinations, and grading schemes that determine postgraduation career outcomes.[21] There is no replay of Mario Savio's calling upon Berkeley students in 1965 to rise up against the misuse of authority in their own midst and to throw their bodies onto the cogs of the machine to stop it. There are other struc-tures to dismantle, as is made clear in the next paragraph of Baron and Byrne's text. They conclude stridently that the power of authority figures is "not irresistible" and can be "countered and reduced" (1994: 384). That statement is immediately followed by a reference to a photograph, on the same page, of "German students dismantling the Berlin Wall in 1989" with the caption "Resisting sources of authority: The potential benefits are great." The text continues,

> As in many other spheres of life, there *is* a choice. Deciding to resist the dictates of authority can, of course, be dangerous. . . . Yet, as recent events in Eastern Europe, the former Soviet Union, and elsewhere demonstrate, the outcome is by no means certain when committed groups of citizens choose to resist. Ultimately, victory may go to those on the side of freedom and decency rather than to those who possess the guns, tanks, and planes. The human spirit, in short, is not so easily controlled or extinguished as many dictators would like to believe. (1994: 385)

What is most striking about this conflation of the obedience research with the dismantling of the Berlin Wall is the juxtaposition of "choice," "victory," "freedom," "decency," and the "human spirit" against the example (semi-otically and textually) of the Soviet Union and Eastern Europe: obedience research as therapy against "evil empires."

The absence of discussions of the moral basis of authority, the nature of authority and its exercise in modern nations, especially highly industrialized nations, makes this research entirely transparent as an object lesson for social psychologists. The docile, mechanical, scripted bodies of up to 1,000 Connecticut men and 40 women are available as a bulwark against Nazism, My Lai, Jonestown, the Soviet Union, and dictators everywhere. That these bodies are themselves the subject of a different kind of bureaucratic and technical authority escapes the grasp of social psychologists, indeed would make the social psychologists suspect as scientific advisors on the nature of human social life. The obedience research then serves not only as a justifi-cation for social psychological research itself but duplicates a standard line of thought in Western industrial democracies. As Crawford had it, "From the series of obedience studies, we have learned a great deal about the relationship between destructive obedience and factors such as authori-tarianism, education, proximity of the victim, surveillance by the authority figure, conflicting authority demands, and the liberating effects of group pressure. . . . We can hardly read the study without becoming more sensi-tized to analogous conflicts in our own lives" (1972: 183). Crawford's argu-ment is that we should identify less with the "teacher" who is familiar to us through our own position as "middle-class American social scientists" and identify more with the "victim," which would lead to a more positive evaluation of the Milgram studies. The research, however, was designed precisely to *prevent* us from identifying with the victim. Every discussion of Milgram's studies keeps the reader from empathizing with the victim; it is made clear from the very outset that the "victim" did not receive any shocks and was a confederate of the experimenter. Rather than sensitizing us to "conflicts in our own lives," of which, after all, we are usually aware without the help of social psychology, obedience studies become refracted through the lens of expert evidence. The evidence then becomes a reason for accepting the authority of social psychology as knowledge about the conflicts in our lives. The Milgram studies *show* the correctness of the American position as a nation, as a middle class, and as people on the "side of freedom and decency." Any attempt to examine the nature of authority as it plays itself out in a bureaucratized world of transnational corporations, and governments and their academic advisors, would require that social psychologists reflexively examine their own role in the processes of justification, exclusion, and obedience to authorities that are both complex and more than just "free" and "decent." In this sense the studies are not simply reported in modern-day textbooks; they become a form of raw material on which to project current socio-historical events.

As the academy is restructured, psychologists are joining the ranks of millions of other knowledge workers, and their output is no less scrutinized than that of other academics for the most useful "bits" of information. Thus at a time when ownership of "knowledge" itself is contested, Milgram's obedience research supplies a continuing stream of textbook commentators with the right material for justifying both the enterprise of social psychology and the context within which it is carried out – the marketplace of ideas in industrialized democracies.

Tortured Bodies

Milgram's research has become a tool for the inscription of other bodies. We agree with Radley that what is lost in commentaries on Milgram is the special nature of the relationship between "subject" and "learner." The "subject" does effectively inflict pain upon the "learner."

> The importance of the body of the victim . . . is that it specifies, concentrates, and ultimately displays for us a form of experience that we know enough about to want to repudiate. Interpreted in this way, Milgram's experiment becomes a statement about people who do not just judge, perceive, and attribute meaning, but are committed together in the pursuit of pain and suffering. (Radley, 1991: 8)

What is alarming then is not only the actions of the "naive subjects" as Milgram calls them, but the overall context of a psychologist and his confederates engaged in a seeming exercise of power, most of it "on the grounds of Yale University in the elegant interaction laboratory" (Milgram, 1963: 372). Not the power to demonstrate nor the power to demonstrate *experimentally*, but the demonstration of power itself. The engagement leaves us convinced, but of what? Years of critique have made many doubt that what has been demonstrated is in fact "destructive obedience." The research has been used to convince generations of students about the power of experiments to tell a story but never the power behind those experiments.

Radley's point is that the relationship between "learner" and "victim" is one of torturer and victim. The illusory nature of the pain, so clearly emphasized by both Milgram and his commentators, fails to cover over this dimension effectively. Torture is the organized production of pain and, in Foucault's words, "in the 'excesses' of torture, a whole economy of power is invested" (1979: 35). Torture was the eighteenth-century expression of marking victims and codifying relations of power. Theweleit's (1989) examination of torture under German fascism, particularly in the *Freikorps*, however, maintains that punishment and interrogation are secondary to the torturer's search for physical or embodied omnipotence at the expense of the negation, or disappearance of the subject. His account of the male body's destructive power, of torture as an attempt by men to maintain their own bodies, in a sense joins Milgram in agreement that German fascism was not irrational nor unthinkable. Implied, however, in psychology's instrumental account of the Holocaust and other horrors of the twentieth century is an organization and productivity that is itself at the root of the problem. What we need most to know, and what Milgram's research cannot give us, is a way to approach the spectacle of mass murder. In the obedience studies, as in other forms of instrumental research, fascism, obedience, and authority become representational and symbolic. They are still elsewhere, not in the experimenter or the victim – who are actors – nor in the "subject," who becomes for Milgram a "representation" of what we are all capable of doing. By construing obedience in this instrumental, artifactual manner with the "subject's" body as an appendage to the experiment-as-machine, it leaves fascism as an "irrational" other, the bodies of the participants in the entire experimental setup are not "really" the anti-erotic, hierarchically trained, expressionless fascists. The bodies of the participants are relevant only in so far as the instrumental establishment of their relations can be demonstrated.[22] In these relations we see a hierarchical arrangement which is the foundation of obedience itself.

In our view Milgram has invoked the very thing he wished to repudiate. The discourse of obedience to authority exists no less within the corporate structures of the modern academy as in other institutions. In purportedly demonstrating the effects of destructive obedience in the citizens of Connecticut, he must cover up the effects of the obedience of the social psychologist by invoking the abstract nature of science and the requirements of objectivity. As a consequence, Milgram and his supporters protest too much: the work of covering the entrails of this study under a blanket of scientific respectability raises questions about the authority of social psychology, of experimentation, and of the academy and its role as arbiter of right and wrong. Eventually it also raises the question of knowledge itself. It is the relationship between the "subject's" body and the "victim's" body, or what it is "to inflict pain on another's body" which forces this question on us. It is the experimental arrangement, established in the tradition of an instrumental social psychology, supported by the *accoutrements* of science, that has created the possibilities of these arrangements.

Milgram reminds us of the destructive nature of authority. In fact, his discursive framing of the obedience studies is presented in such a way that this point cannot escape the reader – it is the motivation for the original studies and the way in which he expects us to understand them. He wants us to question the unproblematic way in which we categorize the very common experience of obedience. As he argues at the close of his 1965 film and again in the 1974 book, ". . . human nature, or – more specifically – the kind of character produced in American democratic society, cannot be counted on to insulate its citizens from brutality and inhumane treatment at the direction of malevolent authority" (1974: 189). This is a moral enterprise (note the reference not to personality but to "character") directed at Milgram's own nation state. To add force to the conclusion he added in the film (1965a), "If in this study an anonymous experimenter could successfully command adults to subdue a 50 year old man, and force on him painful electric shocks against his protests, one can only wonder what government, with its vastly greater authority and prestige, can command of its subjects."

Milgram is a member of a scientific community that has relegated questions of morality to a discourse of "values." He must maintain this distinction yet still find a way to create space for the "moral" of the story to emerge. Milgram maintains this distinction, arguing elsewhere that perhaps it was the results of the studies that led to so much criticism. It was the "shockingly immoral" performance of his participants that made the studies so unpleasant. Hence this lack of foreknowledge is a factor in all research and "understanding grows because we examine situations in which the end is unknown. An investigator unwilling to accept this degree of risk must give up the idea of scientific inquiry" (1964/1972a: 113). But what was unknown? After the very first investigation it was clear what Milgram would find and he proceeded to conduct a further 17 variations on the same experiment. As Milgram himself reported:

> after a reasonable number of subjects had been exposed to the procedures, it became evident that some would go to the end of the shock board, and some would experience stress. That point, it seems to me, is the first legitimate juncture at which one could even start to wonder whether or not to abandon the study. But momentary excitement is not the same as harm. As the experiment progressed there was no indication of injurious effects in the subjects; and as the subjects themselves strongly endorsed the experiment, the judgment I made was to continue the investigation. (1964/1972a: 113–14)

How unexpected were the findings? Milgram had spent considerable time doing research on conformity under Asch. He also described a pilot study conducted in the winter of 1960 in which the "victim" gave no vocal feedback to the participant. In these sessions "virtually all subjects, once commanded, went blithely to the end of the board, seemingly indifferent to the verbal designations. . . . This deprived us of an adequate basis for scaling obedient tendencies. A force had to be introduced that would strengthen the subject's resistance . . . and reveal individual differences in terms of a distribution of break-off points" (1965b: 61). In other words, the pilot studies had already indicated almost complete compliance.[23] But without variance, there was little that could be said within the experimental tradition of social psychology. So Milgram began introducing his many manipulations to vary the level of compliance. The aim was therefore to obtain a reasonable and *varying* facsimile of obedience; its demonstration alone was insufficient.

Milgram was a master in designing "high-impact experiments." Not only in the case of obedience but elsewhere (e.g., the "lost-letter" technique) he created engaging situations that would idealize some property of social relations. His research continues to be widely cited and his relationship to social psychology remains central. He remains identified as a representative of what constitutes a pre-eminent researcher in the field, precisely because he successfully cloaked a strong moral message in the language of experimentation. Yet when we examine a complex and topical question like "obedience" and it remains an abstract entity to be theorized, and this theorization can only be effectively legitimized when it is clearly represented in a laboratory context, then we have lost the capacity to be morally indignant about any of our claims and "findings." We have already, from the outset, subjected the analysis to an instrumental language far from the bodies of those who are either victims or perpetrators in the realm of the ordinary nightmares of the world. Whatever moral can be drawn from such research then removes it from those settings where real bodies are tortured and killed. It becomes a sanitized message: "we must not obey destructive authority" without ever naming that authority or pointing to the effects of that authority in our world other than through distant historical analogy. In doing so, it simultaneously fails as analogy and as history. It folds back onto itself, proclaiming its own cleverness in its very inability to account for anything beyond itself.

Student Bodies

Our interrogation of the Milgram research eventually brings us back to the problem of repopulation, but this time, the repopulation of the text. By this we want to know how the text is populated in its rhetorical context in the classroom. What happens in the transition to university text, the demonstration of Milgram's research that has been transposed into several film versions, the lectures that describe in detail the nature of the deception and the manner in which the "subject" was entrapped, and so on? It is not only that the true nature of the relationship between "subject" and "learner" has become obscured by an emphasis on who did or did not follow instructions, on methodology, on ethics, and so on. The psychologists' message to students is that not only is "destructive obedience" to be deplored but social psychology legitimately manipulates authority to demonstrate this to the world.

Students share in the power between "subject" and "learner." They discover that social psychologists created a context of widely divergent power relations to represent an abhorrent act. This is the power of the *experiment*, it is the power of the psychologist over the "subject" who appears to be willing to inflict unlimited pain over the "learner." What makes the demonstration so compelling for generations of textbook writers is its ability to convince students of the profound quality and legitimate technical skills which social psychologists wield over their subject matter. As students they share in the "inside" story, they are let in on the secret immediately. In sharing this insider's view, they become insiders to the ways of social psychology; in repeating the standard view on their exams and essays they conform to the individualist, ahistorical, asocial understanding of the nature of conformity and obedience. And they discover the power of the experiment and the nature of social life proposed in such experiments in the form of the productive body of the docile "subject." Do students themselves not become docile "subjects" in this process? Who shines a reflexive light on these students as they take notes about the Milgram studies, prepare "Milgram" for their examinations, and learn about the nature of resisting students embodied as "subjects"? Only some, they are taught, rebel, and it is only against malevolent authorities inflicting pain. The coercive power of instructors or the authority of texts need not be questioned or resisted.

One of the most common representations of the Milgram experiment occurs in the form of the filmed version he produced in 1965 (1965a) that is still widely shown to undergraduate classes on many campuses. Most of this film contains scenes from his "Experiment 5" in which the learner has a "heart problem" that becomes the occasion for his complaints after several trials. Milgram produced a subsequent movie called *Conformity and Independence* in 1975 that consisted of a general discussion of conformity research and included only brief dramatic reconstructions of obedience experiments conducted with "groups." These groups consist of several confederates who together with the "subject" must decide on the shock level. In this film Milgram's narrative focuses on the ability of the "subject" to resist the group. The same reconstructed sequence is used in a 1976 film by Milgram to explain "aggression." David Rosenhan likewise uses dramatic reconstructions of the obedience experiments to illustrate Kohlberg's levels of moral development in a 1973 film.[24]

But of particular interest to our concerns is how the original film (most of it apparently filmed by using a hidden camera – cf. Meyer, 1970/1994) shows several "subjects" laughing when they first hear yells of "Ouch" from the "learner" (see Figure 8.2).

Milgram's voice-over offers this explanation:

> One puzzling sign of tension was the regular occurrence of nervous laughing fits. Fourteen of 40 subjects showed definite signs of nervous laughter and smiling. In a post-experimental interview subjects took pains to point out that they were not sadistic types and the laughter did not mean they enjoyed attacking the learner. (Milgram, 1965a)

Figure 8.2 *Two participants from Milgram's (1965) film* Obedience, *who are shown laughing during the administration of shocks. The only woman "subject" in Milgram's 45-minute film is this smiling woman who appears in a very brief clip of three stills. © 1965 Stanley Milgram. Distributed by Penn State Media Sales. Permission granted by Alexandra Milgram.*

Just prior to this voice-over Milgram interviews one of his "subjects," a middle-aged male:

Milgram: I'd like to ask you something. At one point, were you (.) you were doing something a little (.) unusual (.) Were you laughing (a little) at one point?

Man: [laughs] Yes, I was. At first I was laughing at him then I heard him (.) yell ouch.

Milgram: Why do you think you were laughing?

Man: I don't know (.) I thought it was funny I suppose (.) and then I got to thinking when he said "no that's enough" he had enough so (.) it wasn't funny to me then.

Only two written reports contain any mention of the laughter, the first is the original 1963 paper. Here Milgram mentions the same "14 of 40 subjects." He continues,

The laughter seemed entirely out of place, even bizarre. Full-blown, uncontrollable seizures were observed for 3 subjects. On one occasion we observed a seizure so violently convulsive that it was necessary to call a halt to the experiment. The subject, a 46-year-old encyclopedia salesman, was seriously embarrassed by his untoward and uncontrollable behavior. In the post-experimental interviews subjects took pains to point out that they were not sadistic types, and that the laughter did not mean they enjoyed shocking the victim. (1963: 375)

The only other mention of the laughter occurs in one of the descriptions of individual "subjects" in the 1974 book-length discussion of the research. Milgram never attempts a formal account of this "unexpected sign of tension – yet to be explained" (1963: 371). No commentary that we have read makes explicit reference to the laughter nor is it seen in any of the filmed dramatic reconstructions of the experiments.[25] Milgram argued that it was simply a sign of tension and nervousness. It could also be a way for "subjects" to account for their action – they continue to give shocks because it is funny. If it were not they would stop. Yet the laughter remains ambiguous perhaps because, as the 1965 movie version makes clear in a way that the written reports do not, the "subjects" found the situation itself ambiguous. Despite the assurance of the post-experimental interviews that indicated that participants generally believed they were indeed shocking the "learner," the participants in the original film make statements such as "I don't know what this is all about" or, as one participant states after the experiment has been called off, "I should have known better, I mean, you wouldn't take any chances with a human life you know, [in] these experiments. . . ." Likewise, Milgram's 1974 description of the one participant who laughs includes the participant's claim that he felt the experiment may have been designed to "test the effects on the teacher of being in an essentially sadistic role" (1974: 53).

Although this might indicate that Orne and Holland (1968) were right to suspect something like "demand characteristics" could account for the results, this is not our concern. When the 1965 film is shown to undergraduate classes today, one of the first reactions among students is giggling and laughter. This too seems decidedly ambiguous laughter. Do students laugh because the situation looks amusing and dated – an early 1960s period piece? Do they laugh because they already know the ending – the shocks are not real and "subjects" are being fooled making the students the equivalent of a Candid Camera audience? Perhaps in the classroom students simply replicate similar collective audience experiences, such as the laughter they might display in their local cinemas, always packed with the interminable sequels of their favorite "slasher" films, in which a masked machete-wielding serial killer brutally murders innocent victims. Are the student viewers in the classroom and the cinema, who seemingly laugh at suffering, saying "this isn't real, but it is troubling"? Or are they, like the experimenter, participant-witnesses in the staging of a high-impact situation which will "fool" people into showing their true selves? Have they laughed because they have immediately seen through the contradictions of the playfulness of scientists in their white coats, seemingly tackling serious moral questions through deceptive play acting? In their own "naive" way, have they picked up the notion that certain forms of knowledge generation within scientific social psychology are a "joke"? And is that spontaneous laughter an all-too-fleeting insight, soon to be replaced in graduate school with an acceptance of Milgram's work according to the standard view, such that it becomes one of the classic foundation stones of social psychology? Whatever the reasons for their laughter, students commit themselves to the scenario with their laughter; they are positioned by the classroom setting as privileged spectators and give their bodies over to science no less than the participants in the research. Do their bodies become part of the productive machine, the machine that is the productive body/living machine? Milgram illustrates that complex moral worlds, even that of torturer and victim, can be reduced to the productive body/machine. The subjectivity of obedience is displaced onto the mechanics of the experimental setup only to be returned to the body-subject in the form of a technically clean "explanation." Or, perhaps, as the "subjects" laugh, so students laugh: the process is not clean. Is laughter the last form of resistance to obedience?

Acknowledgments

We thank Nancy Johnson-Smith for her help in analysing the contents of undergraduate textbooks. H.J. Stam thanks the Calgary Institute for the Humanities for a Fellowship which enabled the original research for this paper; Ian Lubek thanks SSHRC for facilitating this collaboration and the GEDISST, IRESCO, CNRS in Paris, France for research facilities; H.L. Radtke thanks the Faculty of Social Sciences, University of Calgary for financial support of this research.

Notes

1 For ease of expression, hereafter we refer to social psychology as a discipline rather than "sub-discipline" or "specialty." See Lubek (1993a) for a discussion of social psychology as a

sub-discipline, and the question of whether social psychology should be referred to as singular or plural.

2 An even more important role in institutionalizing such an individualist conception was made by his brother, Gordon Allport, in his chapters on social psychology's history in the *Handbook of Social Psychology* (1954, 1968, 1985). It is Gordon Allport's definition of social psychology that often appears, without citation, in social psychology's textbooks (Lubek, 1993b).

3 On Deleule's account, this is because our conception of life in the scientific view following the Galilean revolution is essentially *conquest*. Vital energy occupies a central place in this conquest and mastery. Science (and psychology) create the body as organic machine. "The organic machine is destined to be productive, not because the machine is more productive than the body, but because the life process itself must be presented as a productive force in keeping with its mission to conquer; and the machine is an extension of that life activity" (1992: 206–7). See also the important work of Bayer in this respect (Bayer and Malone, 1996).

4 Lubek (1995) has traced the evolution of social psychological "shock-box" research, particularly for the social psychological study of aggression.

5 This was true from the very beginnings of attempts to experimentalize social psychology. Festinger's (1953) chapter on laboratory experimentation in the volume *Research Methods in the Behavioral Sciences*, was written long before any "crisis" was declared or public criticism was aired on the problems of experimentation. Yet Festinger devoted considerable space in his chapter to defending himself against an implied charge of "artificiality." He noted that there were often difficulties in interpreting the results of experiments – a discussion that later became one of "validity" – and he argued for the importance of laboratory studies in the testing of theories. In addition he noted the responsibilities of the researcher towards "subjects" and the importance of ethical research. This kind of concern was never a part of the discussions in general experimental psychology texts such as Stevens's (1951) *Handbook of Experimental Psychology*.

6 Sociologist Kimball Young's *Handbook of Social Psychology* (1946, 1957), a revision of an earlier social psychology text, was largely ignored in the psychological book by the same name. The Young handbook's reliance on sociological theories, especially those of George Herbert Mead, along with its lack of methodological certitude may have contributed to its invisibility within the psychological community.

7 At almost the same time as the Festinger (1953) chapter appeared for social psychology students, Edwards (1954) contributed a chapter to the *Handbook of Social Psychology* in which it is difficult to tell whether the subjects he described are in fact humans.

8 The public, sober image contrasts sharply with another theme which recurs in methodology texts and handbooks: the tension between doing science for the sake of science and the fun and playful aspects involved in experimentation and the manipulation of settings to fool participants. We discuss the darker side of "ludicro-experimentation" in Lubek and Stam (1995).

9 ICBM = Intercontinental Ballistic Missile, extensively deployed in the USA between 1962 and 1973.

10 Milgram is not the only social psychologist to use Nazi Germany and Vietnam to support a particular set of findings. Lefcourt (1982) discusses these very same historical cases as an example of the failure to maintain an internal locus of control which can be a bulwark against unquestioning submission to authority (see Stam, 1987).

11 After this paper was written an entire issue of the *Journal of Social Issues* (vol. 51, no. 3) was devoted to the Milgram obedience studies (Miller et al., 1995); its actual publication date was April/May, 1996. Although some of the papers in the special issue attempt minor reconstructions of the obedience studies, the entire issue is remarkable for its adherence to the standard view – 30 years after the original studies were published. Indeed, the authors attempt in various ways to show how the controversies can now be put behind us as we celebrate the "towering impact" of the research.

12 We deliberately use the phrase "subjection of the body" as the embodied subjectivity of the participants is denied, both in the original research and its retelling in textbooks.

13 We have restricted ourselves solely to discussions of the obedience research conducted

by Milgram himself and replications of his work, ignoring the broader discussions of conformity and obedience. The Milgram discussions take up, on average, 5.4 pages of text and have a range of from 0.3 percent to 2.5 percent of these texts' content.

14 Coincidentally, Arthur Miller (1995; as part of the *JSI* special issue on Milgram that was published after this paper was written) also reviews social psychology textbooks to see what has become of the Milgram research. He looks at 50 *recent* texts, however, and is primarily interested in the question of how these texts treat the ecological validity of these experiments. Miller concludes that "there is no controversy about the ecological validity of the obedience experiments" (1995: 40). We do not know which texts Miller examined (there is no list in his paper) but we are surprised by his conclusions. Texts generally try to explain the context of the obedience studies as an attempt to explain historical accounts of "destructive obedience." Many authors make note, however, that there is a controversy about whether Milgram's studies actually tell us anything about the historical cases. We do not agree therefore with Miller's claim that "there is no controversy." Miller appears to take the mere mention of a historical analogy in the context of the obedience research in the texts as support for its ecological validity and argues, against the thesis that other factors are at work in the citation of the research, that the research remains "virtually unchallenged in the sheer amount of space given to it in contemporary textbooks" (1995: 40). Our point is that this serves an important function in legitimating experimental social psychology and is not an indication of the "ecological validity" of anything.

15 Again, Milgram set the stage for this kind of reception by the manner in which he dealt with criticisms, in particular in his debate with Orne and Holland (1968). In his response, Milgram carefully sets the tone by placing his research on the side of "fact" and "logic" and dismisses the Orne and Holland critique as one that posits that "there is no substance in things, only methodological wrinkles" (1972b: 151). Indeed, Milgram credits Orne with cultivating a "school of social psychology" which consists of "rigid presuppositions" animated by "ideology." We have only given a partial indication here of the invective that characterized Milgram's response to a position that was to become a part of the "crisis" in social psychology.

16 For example, while Mirvis and Seashore claimed in a volume on ethics that "becoming fixated on ethics itself has ethical consequences" and takes "precious time and energy away from research" (1982: 100), their sentiment, but not similar words, appears in the textbooks. As for the obedience studies, it is not uncommon to find statements such as this one by Miller that "Milgram's research has seemingly become a scapegoat for moral criticism" (1972: 157).

17 It was, of course, critics outside psychology who were most vociferous, such as Bruno Bettelheim, who objected that these experiments "were in line with the human experiments of the Nazis" (in Miller, 1986: 124).

18 Outside of the textbooks the defense of the experiments took place on many levels, with various psychologists claiming that the "public outcry" was a response to the fact that these experiments reminded us of "how fragile our ethical independence and integrity really are" (Helmreich et al., 1973: 343); that is, the outcry was a response to the *findings*. These authors also used Milgram's experiments to defend the experimental method in general; ". . . another part of their power lies precisely in their demonstration of how strong situational determinants are in shaping behavior. No resort to a correlation between 'those' people who do 'evil' things is allowed: the subjects were randomly assigned. It is the experimental method, not a fascination with the artificial that convinces" (1973: 343).

19 Harré cogently noted that the "most morally obnoxious feature" of the research was the "failure of any of Milgram's assistants to protest against the treatment that they were meting out to the subjects" (1979: 106).

20 The various methodology texts and handbook chapters previously surveyed (Lubek and Stam, 1995; Stam and Lubek, 1992) idealize the tightly controlled experiment. Here, no body moves or varies. Independent variables are experimentally manipulated preferably by standardized notes, tape, or video-recordings, and are deliberately repeated so as to remove the need for questions. As for dependent variables, body movements or reactions are constrained and minimalized; subjects may only push a button, commit a predetermined behavior or make a pencil mark, and these responses in turn are often "untouched by human hands," being

directly processed by a mechanical device or counter, computer, or optical reader. Almost all other human activities in the experimental context constitute noise or "error variance," which must be reduced or avoided. Failure to do so is grounds for an epistemological termination as the corporeal presence is made invisible to science, its "data" is buried or discarded, the "subject's" actions are obliterated and all that remains of their passage is a common footnote marker in a scientific report cataloguing subject rejection rate.

21 Textbook authors who provide the standard view of the Milgram studies also supply pre-packaged multiple-choice examination kits, with one correct answer for each question, where student resistance may have heavy costs in terms of grades. Although Milgram notes the various sources of authority at work in his studies (scientific authority; Yale as an "institution of unimpeachable reputation," 1963: 377), he never suggests that the authority of the social psychological experiment might demand resistance.

22 The masculinized style of the obedience research is itself a question seemingly irrelevant to the secondary literature. Not only are women largely absent from the studies themselves, but the very manner of conducting research by "teaching" through "punishment" suggests a style of investigation that we have associated with clever male experimentation (see Lubek and Stam, 1995, for a discussion of the misogynistic elements in social psychological experimentation of the period).

23 The "unanticipated effects" argument was questioned when various investigators reported that they had obtained similar results as Milgram using role-playing as an alternative to deception (Geller, 1978; Mixon, 1972; O'Leary et al., 1970).

24 Rosenhan's film relies on the obedience research as dramatic foreground only since the actions of the "subjects" do not in any clear way illustrate Kohlberg's stages. For example, Rosenhan argues that 25 percent of those at Stage 6 delivered the full 450 volts. Milgram's account of the research is entirely missing from the film. All of these films attest to the rhetorical power of the experiments and the way in which they can be incorporated into multiple social psychological explanations.

25 What is most peculiar about the dramatic reconstructions in subsequent films (Milgram, 1975, 1976; Rosenhan, 1973) is that they do not contain any laughter whatsoever whereas the 1965 film shows several of the "real" participants distinctly smiling, giggling, and laughing. Were the dramatic reconstructions designed to eliminate the embarrassment of laughing "subjects"? Was the laughter, so enigmatic, difficult to explain or theorize, edited out of subsequent versions?

References

Alcock, J.E., Carment, D.W., and Sadava, S.W. (1994) *A Textbook of Social Psychology* (3rd edn). Scarborough, ON: Prentice-Hall Canada.

Allport, F.H. (1924) *Social Psychology*. Boston: Houghton Mifflin.

Allport, G. (1954) "The historical background of modern social psychology," in G. Lindzey (ed.), *Handbook of Social Psychology* (vol. 1). Reading, MA: Addison-Wesley. pp. 3–55.

Allport, G. (1968) "The historical background of modern social psychology," in G. Lindzey and E. Aronson (eds), *Handbook of Social Psychology* (vol. 1, 2nd edn). Reading, MA: Addison-Wesley. pp. 1–79.

Allport, G. (1985) "The historical background of modern social psychology," in G. Lindzey and E. Aronson (eds), *Handbook of Social Psychology* (vol. 1, 3rd edn). New York: Random House/Erlbaum. pp. 1–46.

Aronson, E. (1972) *The Social Animal*. New York: W.H. Freeman.

Aronson, E. (1975) *The Social Animal* (2nd edn). New York: W.H. Freeman.

Aronson, E. (1980) *The Social Animal* (3rd edn). New York: W.H. Freeman.

Aronson, E. (1984) *The Social Animal* (4th edn). New York: W.H. Freeman.

Aronson, E. and Carlsmith, J.M. (1968) "Experimentation in social psychology," in G. Lindzey and E. Aronson (eds), *Handbook of Social Psychology* (vol. 2, 2nd edn). Reading, MA: Addison-Wesley. pp. 1–79.

Aronson, E., Wilson, T.D., and Akert, R.M. (1994) *Social Psychology: The Heart and the Mind*. New York: Harper Collins.

Baron, R.A. and Byrne, D. (1994) *Social Psychology: Understanding Human Interaction* (7th edn). Boston: Allyn and Bacon.

Baron, R.A., Byrne, D., and Griffitt, W. (1974) *Social Psychology: Understanding Human Interaction*. Boston: Allyn and Bacon.

Baum, A., Fisher, J.D., and Singer, J.E. (1985) *Social Psychology*. New York: Random House.

Baumrind, D. (1972) "Some thoughts on ethics of research: after reading Milgram's 'Behavioral study of obedience'," in A.G. Miller (ed.), *The Social Psychology of Psychological Research*. New York: Free Press. pp. 106–11. (Originally published 1964.)

Bayer, B.M. and Malone, K.R. (1996) "Feminism, psychology and matters of the body," *Theory & Psychology*, 6: 667–92.

Bierstedt, R. (1954) *Freedom and Control in Modern Society*. New York: Van Nostrand.

Billig, M. (1990) "Rhetoric of social psychology," in I. Parker and J. Shotter (eds), *Deconstructing Social Psychology*. London: Routledge. pp. 47–60.

Billig, M. (1994) "Re-populating the depopulated pages of social psychology," *Theory & Psychology*, 4: 307–35.

Blass, T. (1991) "Understanding behavior in the Milgram obedience experiment: the role of personality, situations, and their interactions," *Journal of Personality and Social Psychology*, 60: 398–413.

Brown, R. (1965) *Social Psychology*. New York: Free Press.

Cherry, F. (1995) *The "Stubborn Particulars" of Social Psychology: Essays on the Research Process*. London: Routledge.

Comfort, A. (1950) *Authority and Delinquency in the Modern State: A Criminological Approach to the Problem of Power*. London: Routledge and Kegan Paul.

Crawford, T.J. (1972) "In defense of obedience research: an extension of the Kelman ethic," in A.G. Miller (ed.), *The Social Psychology of Psychological Research*. New York: Free Press. pp. 179–86.

Danziger, K. (1990) *Constructing the Subject: Historical Origins of Psychological Research*. Cambridge, MA: Cambridge University Press.

Deaux, K. and Wrightsman, L.S. (1988) *Social Psychology* (5th edn). Pacific Grove, CA: Brooks/Cole.

Deleule, D. (1992) "The living machine: psychology as organology," in J. Crary and S. Kwinter (eds), *Incorporations: Zone*. New York: Zone. pp. 203–33.

de Swaan, A. (1991) "Kwaliteit is klasse" (Quality is class), in A. de Swaan, *Perron Nederland*. Amsterdam: Meulenhoff. pp. 59–92.

DuBois, P. (1994) "Subjected bodies, science, and the state: Francis Bacon, torturer," in M. Ryan and A. Gordon (eds), *Body Politics: Disease, Desire, and the Family*. Boulder, CO: Westview. pp. 175–91.

Edwards, A.L. (1954) "Experiments: their planning and execution," in G. Lindzey (ed.), *Handbook of Social Psychology* (vol. 1). Cambridge, MA: Addison-Wesley. pp. 259–88.

Feldman, R.S. (1995) *Social Psychology*. Englewood Cliffs, NJ: Prentice-Hall.

Festinger, L. (1953) "Laboratory experiments," in L. Festinger and D. Katz (eds), *Research Methods in the Behavioral Sciences*. New York: Holt, Rinehart and Winston. pp. 136–72.

Foucault, M. (1979) *Discipline and Punish: The Birth of the Prison*. New York: Vintage Books.

Geller, D.M. (1978) "Involvement in role-playing simulations: a demonstration with studies on obedience," *Journal of Personality and Social Psychology*, 36: 219–35.

Harré, R. (1979) *Social Being: A Theory for Social Psychology*. Oxford: Basil Blackwell.

Helmreich, R., Bakeman, R., and Scherwitz, L. (1973) "The study of small groups," in P.H. Mussen and M.R. Rosenzweig (eds), *Annual Review of Psychology*. Palo Alto, CA: Annual Reviews. pp. 337–54.

Kelman, H.C. (1967) "Human use of human subjects: the problem of deception in social psychological experiments," *Psychological Bulletin*, 67: 1–11.

Koestler, A. (1967) *The Ghost in the Machine*. New York: Macmillan.

Lauer, R.H. and Handel, R.H. (1983) *Social Psychology* (2nd edn). Englewood Cliffs, NJ: Prentice-Hall.

Lefcourt, H.M. (1982) *Locus of Control: Current Trends in Theory and Research*. Hillsdale, NJ: Erlbaum.

Lindzey, G. (ed.) (1954) *Handbook of Social Psychology* (2 vols). Reading, MA: Addison-Wesley.

Lindzey, G. and Aronson, E. (eds) (1968) *Handbook of Social Psychology* (2 vols, 2nd edn). Reading, MA: Addison-Wesley.

Lindzey, G. and Aronson, E. (eds) (1985) *Handbook of Social Psychology* (2 vols, 3rd edn). New York: Random House.

Lubek, I. (1993a) "Some reflections on various social psychologies, their histories and historiographies," *Sociétés Contemporaines*, 13: 33–68.

Lubek, I. (1993b) "Social psychology textbooks: an historical and social psychological analysis of conceptual filtering, consensus formation, career gatekeeping and conservatism in science," in H.J. Stam, L.P. Mos, W. Thorngate, and B. Kaplan (eds), *Recent Trends in Theoretical Psychology* (vol. III). New York: Springer-Verlag. pp. 359–78.

Lubek, I. (1995) "Aggression research: a critical-historical, multi-level approach," *Theory & Psychology*, 5: 99–129.

Lubek, I. and Stam, H.J. (1995) "Ludicro-experimentation in social psychology: sober scientific versus playful prescriptions," in I. Lubek, R. van Hezewijk, G. Pheterson, and C. Tolman (eds), *Trends and Issues in Theoretical Psychology*. New York: Springer. pp. 171–80.

Marcus, S. (1974) "Obedience to authority," *The New York Times Book Review*, 13 January: 1–3.

Matlin, M.W. (1992) *Psychology*. Fort Worth, TX: Harcourt Brace Jovanovich.

McGuire, W.J. (1967) "Some impending reorientations in social psychology: some thoughts provoked by Kenneth Ring," *Journal of Experimental Social Psychology*, 3: 124–39.

Meyer, P. (1994) "If Hitler asked you to electrocute a stranger, would you?," in E. Krupat (ed.), *Psychology is Social: Readings and Conversations in Social Psychology*. New York: HarperCollins. pp. 99–111. (Originally published 1970.)

Milgram, S. (1963) "Behavioral study of obedience," *Journal of Abnormal and Social Psychology*, 67: 371–8.

Milgram, S. (1964) "Issues in the study of obedience: a reply to Baumrind," *American Psychologist*, 19: 848–52.

Milgram, S. (1965a) *Obedience* [Film]. Distributed by New York University Film Library.

Milgram, S. (1965b) "Some conditions of obedience and disobedience to authority," *Human Relations*, 18: 57–76.

Milgram, S. (1972a) "Issues in the study of obedience: a reply to Baumrind," in A.G. Miller (ed.), *The Social Psychology of Psychological Research*. New York: Free Press. pp. 112–21. (Originally published 1964.)

Milgram, S. (1972b) "Interpreting obedience: error and evidence – a reply to Orne and Holland," in A.G. Miller (ed.), *The Social Psychology of Psychological Research*. New York: Free Press. pp. 138–54.

Milgram, S. (1974) *Obedience to Authority: An Experimental View*. New York: Harper and Row.

Milgram, S. (1975) *Conformity and Independence* [Film]. Harper and Row.

Milgram, S. (1976) *Human Aggression* [Film]. Harper and Row.

Miller, A.G. (1972) "The deception and debriefing dilemma," in A.G. Miller, (ed.), *The Social Psychology of Psychological Research*. New York: Free Press. pp. 155–62.

Miller, A.G. (1986) *The Obedience Experiments: A Case Study of Controversy in Social Science*. New York: Praeger.

Miller, A.G. (1995) "Constructions of the obedience experiments: a focus upon domains of relevance," *Journal of Social Issues*, 51 (3): 33–53.

Miller, A.G., Collins, B.E., and Brief, D.E. (1995) "Perspectives on obedience to authority: the legacy of the Milgram experiments" (special issue), *Journal of Social Issues*, 51 (3).

Mirvis, P.H. and Seashore, S.E. (1982) "Creating ethical relationships in organizational research," in J.E. Sieber (ed.), *The Ethics of Social Research: Surveys and Experiments*. New York: Springer-Verlag. pp. 79–104.

Mixon, D. (1972) "Instead of deception," *Journal for the Theory of Social Behavior*, 2: 145–74.

Mixon, D. (1974) "If you won't deceive, what can you do?" in N. Armistead (ed.), *Reconstructing Social Psychology*. Harmondsworth: Penguin. pp. 72–85.

Myers, D.G. (1987) *Social Psychology* (2nd edn). New York: McGraw-Hill.

Newcomb, T.M. (1953) "The interdependence of social-psychological theory and methods: a brief overview," in L. Festinger and D. Katz (eds), *Research Methods in the Behavioral Sciences*. New York: Holt, Rinehart and Winston. pp. 1–12.

O'Leary, C.J., Willis, F.N., and Tomich, E. (1970) "Conformity under deceptive and non-deceptive techniques," *Sociological Quarterly*, 11: 87–93.

Orne, M.T. and Holland, C.C. (1968) "On the ecological validity of laboratory deceptions," *International Journal of Psychiatry*, 6: 282–93.

Radley, A. (1991) *The Body and Social Psychology*. New York: Springer-Verlag.

Rosenhan, D. (1973) *Moral Development* [Film]. CRM Educational Films.

Sidis, B. (1898) *The Psychology of Suggestion*. New York: Appleton.

Sieber, J.E. (1982) "Ethical dilemmas in social research," in J.E. Sieber (ed.), *The Ethics of Social Research: Surveys and Experiments*. New York: Springer-Verlag. pp. 1–29.

Skinner, B.F. (1972) "Why we need teaching machines," in B.F. Skinner, *Cumulative Record* (3rd edn). New York: Appleton-Century-Crofts. (Original work published 1961.)

Smith, E.R. and Mackie, D.M. (1995) *Social Psychology*. New York: Worth.

Stam, H.J. (1987) "The psychology of control: a textual critique," in H.J. Stam, T.B. Rogers, and K.J. Gergen (eds), *The Analysis of Psychological Theory: Metapsychological Perspectives*. Washington: Hemisphere. pp. 131–56.

Stam, H.J. (1993) "Is there anything beyond the ideological critique of individualism?", in H.J. Stam, L.P. Mos, W. Thorngate, and B. Kaplan (eds), *Recent Trends in Theoretical Psychology* (vol. III). New York: Springer-Verlag.

Stam., H.J. and Lubek, I. (1992) "A textual analysis of the development of experimentation in social psychology." Paper presented at the annual meeting of the Cheiron Society, Windsor, 21 June.

Stam, H.J. and Mathieson, C.M. (1995) "Psychological perspectives on the body," in I. Lubek, R. van Hezewijk, G. Pheterson, and C. Tolman (eds), *Trends and Issues in Theoretical Psychology*. New York: Springer-Verlag. pp. 119–25.

Stevens, S.S. (ed.) (1951) *Handbook of Experimental Psychology*. New York: Wiley.

Theweleit, K. (1989) *Male Fantasies* (vol. 2). Cambridge: Polity Press.

Wade, C. and Tavris, C. (1987) *Psychology*. New York: Harper and Row.

Young, K. (1946) *Handbook of Social Psychology*. London: Kegan Paul, Trench, Trubner.

Young, K. (1957) *Handbook of Social Psychology* (2nd edn). London: Routledge and Kegan Paul. (Reprinted 1969.)

9

Between Apparatuses and Apparitions: Phantoms of the Laboratory

Betty M. Bayer

> The crucial question is not "What does the phantom signify?" but "How is the very space constituted where entities like the phantom can emerge?"
>
> (Slavoj Zizek (1991), "Grimaces of the Real, or When the Phallus Appears")

Phantoms would seem to represent the very antithesis of the scientific order. After all, is it not science that is to separate fact from fiction, the authentic from the phantasmal? And is it not in the service of securing an objective way of knowing individual, cultural, and social psychological life that scientific psychology has deployed its vast assemblage of tools, instruments, and apparatuses? In psychology's world of mainstream positivism, social relations and scientific practices are governed by a discourse of restraint and by a clear set of boundaries drawn around subjects and objects, subjectivity and objectivity. Likewise, investigative technologies (apparatuses and discourses) are regarded as neutral tools, and, moreover, as divorced from subjects and objects of knowledge. Knowers and knowledge are to be free of the traces of the process of knowledge production and to be beyond or outside of history, time, and location. What place could phantoms, those wily figures of illusion, immateriality, and things imagined, possibly have in this scientifically ordered universe of rationality, restraint, and regulation?

Yet, however much science presumes its domain to be otherwise, this "other" world of phantoms and the phantasmal is coterminous with science itself. By "other" worlds I mean those things which trouble the mind of scientists and haunt the house of science – subjective desires, epistemological uncertainty or doubt, the encumbrance of the body, unsteady splits between subjects and objects, and deception. This "other" world is not about what unwittingly enters into scientific knowledge production but rather about what else emerges in the relations between scientists and investigative technologies, bodies and machines. It is about how, for example, scientists seem to disappear from the processes of knowledge production while maintaining that abstract appearance of "the scientist," of being nowhere or nobody in particular while being apparently everywhere and somebody. It is to ask, for example, what renders an electronic switchboard a neutral instrument of scientific practices and at the same time grants its system of color-coded signal lights the capacity of a subjecthood similar to an experimental subject seated at its console? And, it is to question what else transpires in these constructive spaces of scientific work such that scientists or experimenters are made to appear thing-like while things such as recording devices, bogus pipelines, and flashing signal lights become life-like, inspirited with phantasmic powers of objectivity as subjectivity *par excellence* (Lukacs, 1971; Taussig, 1980)?[1]

Phantoms are figures of transmigration and metamorphoses. One form of phantomizations is the shifting scene of resignifying in objective terms relations between scientists and apparatuses. Other forms emerge from the proliferation of machinic connections wherein scientific discourse mobilizes particular kinds of exchanges of skills between bodies and machines such that scientific selves become dislocated from their own bodies and relocated in investigative technologies. On the surface, these ghostly doubles appear as nothing more than extra pairs of eyes, ears, and hands. What they conceal, however, are the coacting tensions connecting phantasmic interiors with surface points of bodies and technologies (Macauley and Gordo-Lopez, 1995; Stone, 1995; Taussig, 1980). Reshaping one another, scientists and their ghostly doubles are generated by conflicts and struggles in dualities of objectivity versus subjectivity, truth versus fiction, good versus evil. Along with the ghostly doubles enabling splits between objectivity and subjectivity are the less-than-honorable ones – phantoms who are at once shadowy figures harboring the "dark" secret of science's technologies of deception and apparitional figures enabling scientific psychology's staging of the real (e.g., Star, 1991; Zizek, 1991). Taking their form as confederates, stooges, accomplices, paid participants, cyranoids, bogus pipelines, false feedback, cover stories, suggestions, illusions and the like, they are the laboratory phantasmagoria set in motion to manipulate, create, and stage cultural, social, and psychological life.[2] The various understandings of phantoms and phantomizations are thus interarticulated with those about the ghosts that haunt scientists and science – the senses as artful and the artfulness of scientific practices (Stafford, 1994). Confining phantoms either to the drama of scientific psychology's morality play or to a narrative of the failures of the project of scientific psychology would be to overlook phantoms' transformation of scientists, apparatuses, and the narrative of science.[3]

Bumping up against the Enlightenment project of scientific knowledge as transhistorical, transgeographical, and perspectiveless *and* quickened by historical struggles and negotiations around doubt, controversy, and skepticism troubling the subject of Enlightenment science, phantoms open science onto the terrain of subjectivism, fears, and desires (secret and known). To inquire into the transversals of spirits animating relations between humans and nonhumans, bodies and machines in the production of scientific knowledge is to raise the specter of divine truth, to query those ways in which the imaginary and the rational coextend and dwell in one another (Haraway, 1991a; Taussig, 1980). And to raise this specter is to evoke the Cartesian dread of "waking from a self-deceptive dream world, the fear of having 'all of a sudden fallen into very deep water' where 'I can neither make certain of setting my feet on the bottom, nor can I swim and so support myself on the surface,' and the anxiety of imagining that I may be nothing more than a plaything of an all-powerful evil demon" (Bernstein, 1983: 17).

Materializing out of concerns of particular historical moments (e.g., Finucane, 1984), phantoms make manifest the observing scientist's anxieties, fears, and desires around maintaining the split between objectivity and subjectivity, of shedding the body whose urges and desires threaten to disfigure reason, and of attaining the position of a subjectless or transcendent (immortal) knower (Bordo, 1993a; Keller, 1992). Paradoxically, desires for a disembodied rationality are also bound up with those for unity and wholeness, for a perfectible bodily form. In this way, phantoms are animated by the swings between a Cartesian desire for control and a Platonic one for perfectibility, between desire as a lack (of secure foundations, of inadequacies or flaws in "man's" being) and as an excess (of lusts and yearnings, or the undisciplined body), and between corporeality (mortality) and incorporeality (immortality) (Figueroa-Sarriera, 1995; Grosz, 1995). Studying phantoms' traffic with humans and nonhumans is thus, as Lilias Papagay, a fictional character in A.S. Byatt's *Angels and Insects* says of spirits and specters, "[one] way to know, to observe, to love the living, not as they were politely over teacups, but in their secret selves, their deepest desires and fears" (1992: 196–7).

So, enlivened by the opposing forces in the subject of knowledge, phantoms, on occasion, absorb the subjective excesses; they are the ghostly doubles of the subject of knowledge, "embodying" what has been channeled out of the subject of knowledge (wants and excesses) and into another entity (human or nonhuman). In this, phantoms are the points of contact between one and the "other" worlds of science, wherein, as Zizek says of "the empty surface on which phantasmagorical monsters appear," "phantom" becomes *the subject of the Enlightenment, that is to say, it is the mode in which the subject of the Enlightenment acquires its impossible positive existence"* (1991: 64). On other occasions, phantoms are those apparitional practices used to generate different kinds of imagined subjects, and to refigure machinic desire and technobodies. Phantoms are thus neither singularly good nor evil, an entity nor a practice, an integral nor fragmented subject nor object of knowledge, but rather translated beings bearing across the worlds of science, technology, and culture.[4]

In one and another transmigration, phantom materializations lead us into a study of the intertwined yet relatively unexamined histories of technology, investigative practices, and technologies of deception, and so into science's historical struggles with meanings of life and death, of the dreams of techno-salvation and the fears of techno-destruction, and of the hopes of attaining divine truth and the fear of meaninglessness (see Quinby, 1994). As such, phantoms denaturalize the "nature" of scientific relations and investigative practices, revealing all manner of scientific actors and actants to be hybrids formed out of new and unanticipated combinations of humans and non-humans, science and culture, politics and popular media (Haraway, 1992; Latour, 1993, 1994). Insofar as "phantom" forges political alliances, it is with those "other" kinds of figurations – monsters, vampires, cyborgs – whose socio- and psychodramas are summoned to mark our passing from the modern to the postmodern world, and to break faith with the unitary, rational subject (e.g., Copjec, 1994; Halberstam, 1995; Haraway, 1991b, 1992). As Donna Haraway says: "By the late twentieth century, our time, a mythic time, we are all chimeras, theorized and fabricated hybrids of machine and organism" (1991b: 150).

The "promises" of phantoms are thus not to be found in some effort to redeem technologies of deception or other assorted investigative technologies of experimentation.[5] Nor are they to be discerned as yet another route to debunk experimentation in psychology. Nothing could be farther from my interest in them. Besides, phantoms are much too canny to be caught in that modernist snare. They direct us instead to the "gaps left within us by the secrets [of science]" (Abraham and Torok, 1994: 175). Phantoms are an entry point to the "other" world of science, that history of open yet shrouded knowledges, lost events, infidelities to master discourses, instabilities of mind–body and other dualisms, pleasures and desires. Phantoms worry science's relation to itself as scientific: they, as Judith Halberstam and Ira Livingston's posthuman bodies, "engage posthuman narratives that have all but replaced previous masternarratives about humanity, its bodies, its subjects, its pains, and its pleasures" (1995: 4). As phantoms flit and strut, slip and glide across scientific psychology's staging of the "real," they gesture towards a rethinking of the production of knowledge, bodies, subjects, and subjectivity. This rethinking proceeds by way of the networked relations of science, culture, and technology in the histories of investigative technologies, technologies of deception, objectivity, and corporeality.

Cross Talk: Bodies and Machines

Our late-twentieth-century preoccupation with body parts and passing states of knowledge, truth, identity, self, and subjectivity is less about (re)instating a different origin story, categorical boundaries, or an "anything goes" position than it is about looking closely at the double work of modern belief. For social studies of science, this means examining how, as Bruno Latour puts it, ". . . *the modern Constitution allows the expanded proliferation of the hybrids whose existence, whose very possibility, it denies*" (1993: 34). Accordingly, science's social relations and investigative practices are technologies of translation, transformation, and purification of the very hybrids they bring into being, a process whereby hybrids are "naturalized" into distinct entities of routine scientific investigative instruments, scientists, and objects of study (de Certeau, 1984; Foucault, 1977; Galison, 1988; Haraway, 1992; Latour, 1993). What disappears from view are all those phantoms of the laboratory that run the invisible lines of interference in what I call the cross talk, or cross embodying practices, of bodies and machines. Allowing the clandestine spirit of this larger network of practices, discourses, instruments, delegations, and passings to "come out of hiding" (Latour, 1993: 139) means bringing into view this theater of invisible sensibilities.

As a preliminary example of the processes of translation and transformation, consider social psychologists' specter of divine detection, the bogus pipeline. Originating from "fantasies about discovering a direct pipeline to the soul (or some nearby location)," the bogus pipeline was imagined to bypass a number of problems bedeviling scientific psychology's efforts to lay bare the hidden interiors of subjective life (Jones and Sigall, 1971: 349). These problems included everything from demand characteristics, experimenter effects, evaluation apprehension, and subjects' thoughtlessness through to those of making inferences from behavior and to all that plagued rating scales. The power of the bogus pipeline, however, does not reside in the marvels of any one piece of equipment, for the bogus pipeline *qua* machine does not exist. Composed instead of a constellation of laboratory phantasmagoria (confederates appearing via videotape or in person, cover stories, gauges, and instruments), the bogus pipeline could appear as any one of a number of kinds of instruments or apparatuses, as, for example, a steering wheel from which subjects were hooked up to various meters, electrodes, and other machinic gizmos. Its dual phantasmic powers of objectifying investigative practices and of being omniscient turned on the phantasm of "*operat[ing] like lie detection devices in facilitating scrupulously truthful reporting*" (1971: 362; original emphasis; see Bunn, 1996).[6] Within the phantasmic space between scientists' fantasies and subjects' beliefs from culture about the "mystique and infallibility of lie detection" (Jones and Sigall, 1971: 353), the bogus pipeline was called into being. Once part of the scientific scene of laboratory experimentation, however, the bogus pipeline became further enhanced. It came to be that body–machine relation having the power to materialize the scientist as objective observer, technologies of deception as neutral tools of experimentation, subjects as the tricksters or deceivers, and fake meters as the marking device of inner (hidden) truths. The question here is not what or where are phantoms of the laboratory, for they seem to be the generative force, but rather where is science in this vast assemblage of technology and culture, bodies and machines. Is science simply the inscriptive or authorizing device? And, insofar as phantoms are conceived of as a productive force, from what interplay of machinic and spectral desires are they generated? What happens in these transformations such that machines become the coveted forces of inspiration and humans the heavy drag on scientific psychology?

Such couplings of machinic and spectral desires run through psychology's now century-long romance with apparatuses. This technological affair is about the cross talk of bodies and machines in psychology's struggle with demarcating the boundaries between the apparent and the real, subjectivity and objectivity. Phantoms of the laboratory offer one narrative account of this affair, a story evidenced through the conjunctions of histories of technologies of deception, investigative technologies, and objectivity in the discipline's larger project of a scientific psychology.

Lost Events, Infidelities, and Other Passings

Comparable to the emergence of laboratory techniques, relations, and arrangements from education, medicine, and industry in addition to prevailing knowledge interests of specific historical moments (Danziger, 1990; Morawski, 1988), the case can arguably be made that phantoms of the laboratory add a "lost" model to those previously identified as the founding shape-makers of scientific psychology, and more specifically social psychology. Treating phantoms of the laboratory as a lost model is not about staking a claim on some newly discovered territory but rather a symbolic vehicle through which can be organized what are typically regarded as distinct and disparate lines of research (cf. Halberstam, 1995; Zizek, 1991). Turn-of-the-century knowledge within and without the discipline on illusions, mesmerism, hypnosis, suggestion, "prestige suggestion," influence, imitation, and persuasion in conjunction with those forces driving the construction of a psychology grounded in positivist science structured some of the possibilities for phantoms to emerge, albeit in less than straightforward or synchronous ways.[7] One line is found in the subdiscipline of the psychology of deception, wherein investigators sought to turn studies of spiritualism or psychic phenomena into research on how people could be "duped into belief in the supernatural by their own natural, psychological limitations" (Coon, 1992: 149). Yet this line was itself dependent on others for its armature, supplied mainly by psychologists' "knowledge of hypnosis and suggestion, expectation, illusion, perception, and attention" (1992: 149). Just as techniques used by early mesmerists and hypnotists supplied ways to use suggestion for experimental manipulations (see Sidis, 1898), so magicians and tricksters furnished additional techniques for Jastrow's, Dessoir's, Binet's, and Triplett's fashionings of the psychology of deception (Coon, 1992; Hyman, 1989; Murphy et al., 1937). Whether sleights-of-advice or sleights-of-hand, these techniques of illusion succeeded by the misdirection of attention (Hyman, 1989). Social psychology too was said to have its beginnings in the experimental study of suggestion, and its "close counterpart," imitation (Murphy et al., 1937).[8] To these may be added lines of practice from late-nineteenth-century sociologists who donned disguises to enter the everyday world of tramps and miners (Elworthy, 1995), early-twentieth-century dramatic stagings of crimes in classrooms for subsequent tests of witnesses' accounts or jury deliberations (e.g., Dashiell, 1933, 1935; Marston, 1924 cited in Murchison, 1935), as well as elaborate role-playing by subjects of liars or truth-tellers to other subjects enacting the roles of jurors (e.g., Burtt, 1920), and early studies of suggestibility and gullibility in children and adults (Diserens and Vaughn, 1931; Murchison, 1935; Town, 1921; Young, 1931).

Yet another avenue of deception comes from psychology's interest in deceit: that is, in our human propensity to lie, cheat, draw upon "indirect methods" to "get around the other fellow," or to secure a desired end (Hartshorne and May, 1928: 19). What rarely enters into any of these considerations of the psychology of deception, however, is the discipline's incorporation of deception into its apparatuses of experimentation.[9] If noted at all, scientific deception is discussed as a concern with fraud (e.g., falsifying data, plagiarism), hoaxes, or with scientists being fooled by "fraudulent psychics" (e.g., Coon, 1992; Hyman, 1989), or by less-than-faithful subjects (i.e., subjects who deviate from the experimental script, either by resisting, catching on to the ruse, or by overperforming the role of the "good" subject). Put forward as separate and distinct lines of research, psychology's discourse ghosts the commerce of investigative practices amongst areas such as deception, illusion, and suggestion.

This commerce is less elusive once we disencumber ourselves of the need for some linear causal development of one to another form of suggestion or deception. In a way similar to that in which practices of suggestion and conjuring aid and abet one another's development elsewhere, so their interchange is imaginable in psychology's ensuing practices of trickery and stratagems to maneuver perceptions, induce attitudinal "sets," evoke behaviors and emotions, and manipulate attributes of social groups. However inadvertent, from early use on, these techniques went beyond their initial design, revealing various unintended, experimental influences stemming from the experimenter's instructions, the nature or "prestige" of the "suggester" (sex, physical characteristics; see Murphy et al., 1937; Town, 1921).[10] The dilemma was that the very techniques used to demonstrate the role of suggestion in everyday life were those self-same practices that exposed test situations and the scientific laboratory as social situations riddled with cues and suggestions (Murphy et al., 1937), even at the level of the experimenter's *mere* presence as a "social object" (Dashiell, 1935: 1104; Rosenzweig, 1933). Furthermore, the increasing use of techniques of deception brought about other experimental necessities, such as the practice of "initiat[ing] the subject into the 'fellowship of research' by pledging him to secrecy" (Rosenzweig, 1933: 349).

Efforts to counteract these forces of opposition to scientific neutrality helped to spur on the mechanization of experimental procedures. Mechanical devices, such as the victrola, were thought both to remove effects of the experimenter's presence and to standardize instructions by repeatedly delivering "uniform," "flawless" suggestions, and "working without the strong personal element" (Young, 1931). Similarly, a behaviorist-styled mechanical hypnotizer, fashioned out of the ordinary devices of a bell and a light that emanated warmth as it passed (presumably steadily and tirelessly) "back and forth over a subject from head to foot," became the instrumental hallmarks of neutrality, standardized practices, and unflagging workers. The recorder, bell, and lamp perform not simply as stand-ins for the experimenter's voice, hands, or arms because they carry within them the coupling of the machinic and spectral. That is, mechanization had to be hinged conceptually to scientific objectivity and objectivity to standardization (see Coon, 1993; Porter, 1995). Lost in the translation are the machinic desires of scientists, those ways in which scientists through their relations with machines resignify science as the managed work process and bodies as productive, tireless, and, moreover, emptied of desire, will, or moral capacity (see Banta, 1993). Enabling both the absent presence of the experimenter and the remaking of body–machine relations as perfectible scientific workers, mechanization was embodied with phantasmic powers.

Such an interplay of machinic and spectral desires stirred up the imagination of scientists. Nowhere does this become more evident than in the technologies of deception where phantoms of the laboratory proliferate in kind and function. Created out of bits and pieces of culture, science, technology, and popular media, phantom materializations are all about the play of spectral desires in the interchanges amongst discourse, apparatuses, and scientists. Recall Triplett, Binet, Dessoir, and Jastrow's turn-of-the-century conjurer model that drew on the ingenuity and know-how of magicians and tricksters to expose the fraudulent practices of trance mediums and to demonstrate the limits of the senses. Dashiell's apparitional practices were based more on the theater of the "real," where, for example, an "assistant" would appear to accidentally knock over some "complicated apparatus" (1935: 1135). Sherif's (1935, 1937) apparitional practices included textual devices of embedding "prestige suggestions" in passages and "cooperating" subjects to study social influence. These forms relied on combinations of inventiveness, skills, and instruments, on incidental fusions unanticipated by science. What science accomplishes is the translation of these marvels of the imaginative into incarnations of the rational.

To appreciate the full play of phantoms in their etheric doublings of objectivity discarnate and subjectivity incarnate, consider the following. Schachter (1950) rehearsed paid participants to role play standardized versions of "deviate," "mode," and "slider" subject positions; Festinger et al. (1956) had "participant observers" enter a social movement that prophesied the end of the world;[11] Asch (1958) trained confederates to create the appearance of a "majority effect," "true" or "compromise" partners. As a variation of Sherif's paradigm, Bray (1950) used a black "confederate" to represent "Negro" and a "white confederate" to pass as Gentile or Jew; in a variation of Asch's, Crutchfield (1955) automated the use of confederates through an electronic switchboard of light signals to simulate group judgments. Phantoms slipped into measuring instruments provoked self-doubts around gender or sexual identities (see Kelman, 1967; Jones and Sigall, 1971), while, elsewhere, "naive" subjects were secretly made accomplices by having them give "false" instructions about the experiment to the next "uninformed" subjects (Festinger and Carlsmith, 1959). Manipulations of race stereotypes through either stereotyped dialects voiced by unseen telephone callers or by confederates' skin color were introduced to measure their influence on white Americans' willingness to help "black" or "white" "victims" (Gaertner and Dovidio, 1986). The combination of cover stories, a medical accomplice giving accurate or inaccurate information along with drug injections, and elaborate scripts enacted by stooges induced particular emotional states (Schachter and Singer, 1962). Other instances of phantoms of the laboratory are: the personifications by Milgram's (1963) "victim," or "learner," "trained confederates" or "accomplices," and a "simulated shock generator" in an obedience study; Korte's (1971) "confederate" and "phantom" bystanders; Pilisuk's (1984) automated "stooge" strategies in simulated arms negotiations; videotaped interactions between male and female "confederates" enacting heterosexual attraction scripts (Hendrick, 1976, cited in Abbey, 1982); " 'smoke,' copied from the famous Camel cigarette sign in Times Square" filtering slowly into a laboratory to create an emergency situation (Latane and Darley, 1970); tape-recorded voices of "figment" subjects experiencing "fake" seizures (Darley and Latane, 1968); and Milgram's "cyranoids shadow[ing] the speech of their 'sources,' who, like Frank Morgan in 'The Wizard of Oz,' remain poised in another room eagerly spewing their words into a microphone and listening attentively to the proceedings so that they can feed their lines to the cyranoid on cue" (1992: 337).

In each instance, whether human or some combination of human and nonhuman, phantoms of the laboratory are apparitions invested with a mundane subjectivity *and* with a scientific one. Phantoms make seeable not only how scientific discourse constructs the boundaries between subjectivity and objectivity, but also how scientific discourse trades guise and disguise off one another to bring these very entities into being. For example, at the same time that Schachter reports the training and management of "paid participants" as "constant" factors rotated across experimental conditions, he writes that they are "like the subjects," and, moreover, "[t]hey were normal, pleasant boys with nothing that seemed immediately appealing or objectionable about them" (1950: 17). Transformed here is the outward appearance of the everyday and usual into the inward semblance of standardized and routine extensions of investigative technologies. The same kind of combination albeit in cyborg form is found in Milgram's description of the "cyranoid," whose "personality" was a "synthetic creation of the experimental procedure . . . hav[ing] no existence apart from the hybridization which the experiment created" (1992: 340). Phantoms channel historically specific manners of gender or race relations, as, for example the chivalry-type scenarios of "a lady in distress" in the late 1960s (Latane and Rodin, 1969; subsequently referred to as the "fallen woman," Latane and Darley, 1970), politics of race attributes and relations, historical atrocities, such as those of Nazi Germany translated into "obedience" of "learners" in a teaching situation, or "cold war" international relations and arms negotiations. Moreover, these human–nonhuman combinations of bells, electric light switches, recorders, and computer programs are devices transferred from the worlds of work and everyday pleasures to science. But the arrival, mix, or kind of materialization of phantoms in any one experimental scene is not derivable from scientific logic. Rather, scientific logic enters to transform and translate phantoms into investigative technologies – science manufactures the very phantoms it then articulates as component parts of scientific practice.

Gathering within them issues of public and private life specific to different historical moments (e.g., gender, race, social-historical atrocities) and an ever-growing set of scientific concerns (e.g., epistemological doubts, nagging problems around subject boredom, experimental demand characteristics, and "artifacts" of laboratory situations), phantoms have been proliferating in experimental psychology for roughly a century now, with few indications of their decline (e.g., Gross and Fleming, 1982). Folded back into these networks as well are the meanings traced through the terms of confederate, stooge, paid participant, and the like. As these terms hail from social, moral, religious, military, and political institutions and life, science's absorption of these terms reveals yet another angle on its internal drama of conflicts, struggles, and anxieties. The term confederate, for example, incorporates in its meaning the joint yet evidently opposing natures of being united with good (covenant with God, with Science) and with evil (with crime), while layered additionally by a history of political alliances that includes the threat of secession (southern states).[12] "Stooge" harkens back most likely to "student," as found in their frequent employ as stage assistants, helping hands of a conjurer. Added to this is its definition of being an instrument operated by someone else, as well as its association with institutions of surveillance, incarceration, or policing (e.g., first-time criminal offenders, military). And, "accomplice" carries within it the moral connotations of a "guilty" partner, whereas "participant" calls up the participant observer who "appears" to belong to the group under observation. On the one hand, the vestiges of these vast networks of manual art and labor, organizations, and hierarchical structures of governing subjects live on in phantom materializations. On the other hand, the unfaithfulness posed to positivist aims of ideological and value-free science by phantoms' relations with moral, religious, political, military, and criminal life is abjured by the language of experimentation. Contrarieties are thereby contained, rendered spiritless in what appears through their repeated use and installment into experimentation as nothing more than devices of experimental control, manipulation, and standardized procedures.

Uprooting these buried meanings and retracing the lost events and infidelities through the symbolic vehicle of "phantom" gathers together the doublings, contrarieties and apparitional practices to redirect our attention towards the "other" drama staged in scientific productions. This drama of phantoms of the laboratory is based on psychology's historical struggle with its scientific identity and status. Played out in local laboratory settings and within the subject of knowledge, it is a drama about the struggle for existence, and so about subjectivities and bodies. Where this becomes most pronounced perhaps is in psychology's efforts to reconcile scientific ethics and scientific deception. Often given through the metaphors of life and death, phantoms emerge in this debate as the sentries of the scientific light and the profligate souls of the darker side, the good double to be retained and the evil twin to be exiled from the house of science. Locating the split of good and evil as residing elsewhere – that is, as neither in the scientist nor the institution of science – enables the narrative of the scientist as the lone cultural hero who wrests the imagined force of scientific good from corrupting influences and with it the institution of science, and scientific betterment.

From Suggestion to Suspicion: Secrecy, Trust and Distrust

> If [the world we know] appears as a "marvelous motley, profound and totally meaningful," this is because it began and continues its secret existence through a "host of errors and phantasms." (Foucault, 1977: 155)

Whether phantoms as ghostly doubles of scientists, apparitional practices, or phantomizations turning simple devices into aristocrats of objectivity, phantoms spirited onto the scene some troubles of their own – secrecy, worries over detection and the loss of public trust, suspicions of psychological experimentation, and multiplying surveillance devices and measures. By the mid-twentieth century, the tensions of epistemological doubt were twinned with heightened ethical concerns issuing from the Nuremberg Trials, setting in further motion a gamut of surveillance and counter-surveillance investigative technologies (see Porter, 1992). Additionally, social psychology's laboratory worlds were caught in the swell of America's larger preoccupation with cold-war politics and a McCarthy-induced cultural form of paranoia bringing identities under new kinds of scrutiny. Fears around communism, atomic power, sex, and women out of control connected symbolically in this national impulse toward containment (see May, 1988). By any stretch of an appreciation of science as cultural practices, it becomes conceivable that a "culture of containment" might hold science in its grip as well. Such an impress might be felt, for example, in social psychology's increasing tendency to regard artifacts, seeming to mushroom at every experimental turn, as "threats" to its validity, its scientific status (Suls and Rosnow, 1988). Such forces might also be palpable in the expansion of ethic debates to encompass not only those worries of the 1950s about the reputation of the discipline, its laboratories and scientists (e.g., Berg, 1954; Krout, 1954; MacKinney, 1954; Sinick, 1954; Vinacke, 1954), but also those questions breaking by the 1960s of social psychologists' trading-off of content, creativity, and effort for "flamboyancy" or "style," of scientific imagination out of control (e.g., Kelman, 1967; Ring, 1967; Rubin, 1983).

Of course, neither the issue of threats of artifacts or of showy demonstration were new to science. What makes them so interesting at this moment is how they were punctuated anew. Debate and argument moved from procedural considerations to the grounds of knowledge production, from ethical concerns to ones about the repercussions of deception for psychology's "objects" of study, from the matter of concealing the true purpose of experiments to anxiety about deception-type studies concealing the "meaninglessness" of social psychology, and from fears about ethical restrictions cutting off the "lifeblood" of social psychological experimentation to its contrast of deception stifling human freedom by transforming "man [*sic*] into an object to be manipulated at will" and "threaten[ing] values most of us cherish" (Kelman, 1967: 5). Concerned that social psychology would wither on the scientific vine without its life force of technologies of deception, some psychologists predicted that whole lines of research would likewise be "nipped," and with this declared an end to their experimental careers (see Hunt, 1982). The vision differed for others, however, who saw the demise of social psychology as tied to the "zany manipulations" and "trickery" of "clever experimentation" that would ensure the "history of social psychology . . . be written in terms not of interlocking communities, but of ghost towns" (Ring, 1967: 120; see also Kelman, 1967; Rubin, 1983).

Wrought through the metaphors of life and death, sense and nonsense, these debates endowed phantom materializations with all manner of fears, anxieties, hopes, and dreams. Regardless of early discussion of such laboratory phantasmagoria transforming the very subjects psychology sought to study and possibly creating a "special class, in possession of secret knowledge" (Kelman, 1967: 8), the contradictory claims of open science and the open secret transpiring in relations amongst scientists, phantoms, and subjects were more often than not generative of new technologies of deception and measures of detection and suspiciousness (Kelman, 1967; Rubin, 1983; also see, Gross and Fleming, 1982; Sharpe et al., 1992).[13] And, while fears that the chicanery of laboratory experimentation might "die, like bloodletting" (Milgram, cited in Rubin, 1983), the artful ghosts in psychology's experimental machinery have unwaveringly enlivened and inspirited social psychological laboratory life. Invoked as what gives life to experimental science and as what science gives life to, phantoms contain the secrets of life and death, the potential for creativity and violent destruction, the desires for scientific security and the fears of scientific vulnerability.

Paradoxical as scientific psychology's proposition of "planned deception reveal[ing] truth" may be (Schaffer, 1992: 357), phantoms appear to be pivotal and incidental to scientific work and debate, to be sanctioned and forbidden, and to be spoken of endlessly and, much as Foucault said of sex, "exploit[ed] as *the* secret" (1978: 35; original emphasis). Even Oliansky's (1991) bold confession as a doubting confederate does not transgress the discursive bounds set by science. No matter that he experienced his confederate days as a "battle of nerves" over whether subjects were on to the artifice or not, or that this device served little in the way of experimental control, rigor, or standardization.[14] In the end, the ghostly paradigm of positivism lives on. By staying within the confines of established scientific debate, skeptics' and advocates' discourses mutually serve a productive repression. They doubly contain phantoms first by restricting their artifice to refinements in investigative technologies and second by restraining their troubling appearances to scientific ethics. It is the lost events, infidelities, and other passings of phantoms' place in experimental social psychology that are the more telling of the productive interplay of "truth" and "lies," of the conditions that readied the way for phantoms to enter, of the creation of "matrices of transformation" that bring new and odd combinations of human and nonhuman phantoms into being, and of the deployments of duplicity to misdirect attention from the open secret of scientists' desires and fears to the momentary and fleeting one of phantoms (see Foucault, 1978: 99). To play on Foucault's recognition of how in the history of sexuality "*scientia sexualis* . . . functioned, at least to a certain extent, as an *ars erotica*" (1978: 70–1), the ingenuity of phantoms and the semblance of positivism function as the pleasure of secret imaginings and the pleasure of controlling the secret – an *ars artifactula*.

"Perceptual Skepticism" and "Ingenious Pastimes"[15]

As Barbara Stafford (1994) details the history of "artful science" in the seventeenth and eighteenth centuries, the increasing visualization of knowledge was caught up in the tensions between "perceptual skepticism" and "ingenious pastimes." Artful artifice of conjurings, apparitions, magicians, illusionists, "body tricks," the "collusion of a confederate," animated automata, operators, and other spectacles of phantasmagoria had to be demarcated from experimental science (rational recreations) and from Enlightenment science's preoccupation with observation disembodied of contaminating influences. But herein, says Stafford, was the rub: "both the epistemological and the practical 'problem of experimentation' was that it relied on the play of fingers and the intervention of lensed instruments. The vexed question of how to transform the deft creator and perceiver of marvelous effects into an impartial *observer* of textualizable facts was thus of paramount importance to the scientific actors themselves" (1994: 140; original emphasis).

Holdovers from this tension between digitality and opticism are found in nineteenth-century science's changes in the meaning of objectivity. "Detachment," "disinterestedness," "indifference," and "remoteness" featured this objective scientific observer as one whose presence was marked by an absence – a phantasm of objectivity.[16] This seemingly contradictory position of observation – "aperspectival," as Daston (1992) deems it – also became equated with the "absence of any visible sign of manufacture," "facilitated by the development of measuring and distancing apparatuses" (Stafford, 1994: 103). All told, constructions of objectivity, as a "view from nowhere" (Nagel, 1986) or procedurally as "hands off" (Megill, 1991), particularize the subject (knower) as depersonalized, aperspectival, disinterested, removed and nonintervening. Such an epistemological groundwork readied the way for "silent" instruments to enter, as, for example, the "subjectless camera obscura," or, to extend Stafford's history of instruments to psychology's laboratory, the Crutchfield apparatus, bogus pipeline, or cyranoid (also see Keller, 1992). As technologies built from the intertwined yet not necessarily commensurate aims of distancing, standardization, experimental control, and the making of captivating spectacles, phantoms have long held a key place in such negotiations around digitality and ocularity, showy demonstration and scientific respectability. This divide was readily apparent in researchers' arguments about the ethics of technologies of deception where phantoms symbolized either showy demonstration or experimental "ingenuity" (e.g., Aaronson and Carlsmith, 1968; Festinger and Katz, 1953). Recognition of the more dynamic functions of phantoms in establishing scientific identity as disembodied rationality were thus bypassed.

From centuries ago, disembodiment, as Schaffer claims, was "one solution to the crisis of authority over the experimental body" (1992: 362). Apparatuses helped to make evident a "disembodiment of the scientist" and an "embodiment of skill" within the supposed "neutral" and "sincere" scientific instrument (Schaffer, 1992; Stafford, 1994). The shift that Schaffer finds in the "staged" science of the mid-eighteenth century from "the rituals of public performance towards the figure of the disembodied scientific genius" thus bears on phantoms of the laboratory as well (1992: 330). Human and non-human phantoms become manifest in particular ways, either by imbuing objects with the subjecthood of scientific actors or by translating subjects into scientific apparatuses. Through these processes victrola recordings, for example, were remade as the paragons of scientific administration, delivering "objectively uniform suggestions," and confederates were converted into a "variable manipulated across experimental conditions," objects or subjects of fascination or the horror of the threat attending pain or potential violence (Aaronson and Carlsmith, 1968; Bray, 1950; Crutchfield, 1955; Milgram, 1992; Schachter, 1950; Sherif, 1937). Bells, automated light signals, intercom systems, mechanized recordings, fake equipment, one-way mirrors coupled or decoupled from a host of phantom subjects enabled divisions of labor, distancing effects, standardization, the absent presence of scientific authority, and the management of scientific identity. They were also time-saving devices to "[mis]direct attention to the topic of study," (a claim advanced by Allen Funt of the television show *Candid Camera*, see Webb et al., 1966) and labor-saving ones, and so served provident ends.

Materializing through the eyes and hands of science, human and non-human phantom subjects are converted into "powerful techniques for the control and manipulation of variables" and the production of a "standard situation" that will evoke "powerful effects" (e.g., Festinger and Katz, 1953). Automation or mechanization more fully completes the transformation as with this a "powerful new research technique" both "simulates genuine" phenomena yet "preserves the essential requirements of objective observation" (Crutchfield, 1955: 198). Intercom systems, for example, disarticulated voice and presence by transmitting scripted recorded communications and exchanges (e.g., Korte, 1971). Computers decoupled unintended from intended effects by "blindly" assigning subjects to conditions, delivering preprogrammed responses, and coordinating the artifice of phantom appearances (e.g., Ellemers et al., 1993; Smith et al., 1994). Here the exchanges of competencies between scientists and phantoms become invested with steadiness of hand and eye, rational composure, and a finely tuned recording and observational instrument. Scientists' phantasmic solutions to obstacles of objective observation are turned into the crux of rational science itself.

In a curious twist of events, scientists' varied accomplishments of being absently present result in a scientist's voice, authority, and interventions being phantomized everywhere. Yet what, in the end, are we to make of these dislocations and relocations, these cross-corporeal moves of embodiment and disembodiment? Are they simply the vehicles through which the scientist achieves "passionless distance" as the "greatest virtue" such that "[w]hether he be a male or female, . . . this discursively constituted, structurally gendered distance legitimates his professional privilege, . . . the power to testify about the right to life and death" (Haraway, 1992: 312)? How do scientific desires for cloudless vision and phantasmal flights link up with the cross talk of bodies and machines in the remaking of scientific identity?

Technobodies: Transfiguring Mind–Body Relations

> The Enlightenment paved the way for synthetic realism, disembodied information, animated automata, created environments, and clairvoyant visualization devices. Its chief thinkers . . . pondered long and hard about the quality of magnified or diminished artificial life. They reflected on the rise of virtual imagery, simulated events, and an entire apparitional aesthetics of almost. . . . With refined lenses, they penetrated the inner sanctum of the material and immaterial realm in order to regain contact with the primal powers of body and mind. (Stafford, 1991: 465)

It was for Descartes, as for others, the body as trickster or deceiver of the soul, full of lusts, needs and desires as it was, that would, in the end, surely pose reason's demise (Bordo, 1993a). Using the example of the phantom limb, Descartes, in *The Meditations*, illustrated "the deception to which the inner senses are prone, just as he used arguments from illusion to illustrate the deception of the outer senses" (Grosz, 1994: 63). With phantom body impulses holding a possible sway over inner senses and phantasmagoria over outer ones, "phantom" registers the disquiet from yet another set of tensions around science's epistemological investments in visual culture, objective observables, and pure (uncontaminated) cognitions (e.g., Bukatman, 1995; Jordanova, 1995; Stafford, 1991, 1994). That a visibly absent limb could present its own kind of disruption to the presence of mind over body was, in a roundabout sort of way, instructive on the larger issue of the unruliness of bodily senses. Phantom body parts made visible the invisible unruliness or illogic of body sensations, and it is through this logic that the manifold functions of phantoms of the laboratory converge on science's epistemological rehearsals of the mind–body problem.

Enabled in part by mechanistic renditions of "man," and, in part, from at least as far back as the eighteenth century, by a host of practices put into the service of building the perfect artificial person, body phantoms' mediational work between one and the other world was readied by a "double consciousness" of human limitations and apparent machine limitlessness (e.g., Seltzer, 1992; Stafford, 1994; Wilson, 1995).[17] Symbolically, body phantoms in one and another materialization indicate at once a nostalgia for the body's completion and a lament for its inevitable lacks or incompleteness. For many, this dialectic infuses the "logic of prostheses" of the body–machine complex. Drawing on the case of the amputee, Grosz elucidates this logic as one of "two contradictory realities [being avowed] simultaneously: the reality of a living limb and the reality of its destruction" (1994: 72).[18] For Freud, bodily extensions, through tools and instruments, circle back to "man's" grapplings with "biological defects" and the limits of "'his' facticity," and forward, propelling "man" to become a "prosthetic god" (Freud, 1961: 38–9; Grosz, 1994: 79). Along similar lines, Wilson (1995) argues that the logic of prostheses twins a dream of a "godlike phallicity" with a reminder of body failings, of how the body slips – each bodily enhancement bearing the sign of its diminishment. For Keller, the "allure of mechanical surrogacy" is part of what fuels the pursuit to realize the Cartesian legacy of disembodied rationality (1992: 150); for Seltzer, body–machine discourses and practices make visible how "cultural forms become involved in social questions," including "the redrawing of the uncertain and shifting line between the natural and the technological in machine culture," and along with this the (re)making of "agency and of individual and collective and national identity in that culture" (1992: 4). These sorts of negotiations are about the cross talk of bodies and machines, and so about the coupling of machinic and spectral desires in that larger American cultural narrative of "bodies and persons" as things that *can* be made.

Insofar as phantoms are called out by a "kind of extension of the rest of the subject's psychical life" (Grosz, 1994: 73), and inasmuch as this psychical extension cuts back and forth between fears of bodily limitations and dreams of bodily enhancements, then those zones more heavily invested in body–machine interchanges are telling of what a social group is most anxious to preserve, make, or re-make (cf. Connerton, 1989). Phantoms can thus be seen as arising from "apparatuses of bodily production" (Haraway, 1994), revealing what science entrusts to "bodily automatisms" (Bourdieu, 1977), what it writes into and psychically invests in bodily practices along with what it writes out of and psychically divests from science's bodily practices. In these interchanges, the body and bodily instruments become intertwined through projections of bodily sensations and experiences onto the world and introjections of the "world and its vicissitudes into the body of the subject-to-be" (Grosz, 1994: 74). Along the transits of body–machine assemblages, inner realities (sensations) are mobilized and transformed into external ones, making them amenable to observation, manipulation, and control (Pinch, 1988), as, for example, in the techno-reconfigurations of seeing, touching, and speaking by means of mechanical devices, automations, electronic switchboards, and computerizations. Observation and memory are externalized, transformed into a track laid down, data banks, and the like. Fake or nonoperative pieces of equipment (bogus pipeline, shock machines, complicated-looking electric devices) strategically positioned in an experimental laboratory are psychically invested for how they might make manifest everything from threats of violence through to the desire for a "pipeline to the soul." Late-twentieth-century phantoms, such as the cyranoid, recombine thinking minds and speaking bodies for a new kind of hybrid subject. The exchanges of competencies, skills, and attributes inform us about the kind of materialization in effect, about the kind of body that counts – about shifting intelligibilities fitting "man" to technoscience and science to "technoman."

There are thus two kinds of intensifications going on in these body–machine coordinations – the making visible of certain functions, and the denial, disavowal, or repudiation of other ones, the externalization and enhancement of certain functions and the "ghosting" of others. As these phantom materializations proliferate, there is accomplished an increasing fragmentation of the divisions of mental and manual scientific labors of objectivity, dispersing them across countless body–machine configurations. Meanings of distance, detachment and so on are made to square with dispersion, such that the dislocations and relocations of skills between scientists and apparatuses are to signal distanced – objective – practices. Standardization of actors and actants are formed by bringing actions and practices in line with notions of repeatability and replication. Objectivity thus comes out as a hybrid empowered by translations of activities, actions, and practices and by remaking scientific subjectivity as ordered and rational from within. This remaking of scientific subjectivity, of bodies and minds, relies on the dissolution of social relationships into "relationships between mere things" (Taussig, 1980: 31). Just as "the real innovation of Taylorization becomes visible . . . in the incorporation of the representation work process *as* the work process itself" (Seltzer, 1992: 159; original emphasis), so it might be argued that the real ingenuity of phantoms' traffic with living bodies and machines rests with incorporations of representations of objectivity *as* the scientifically managed work process. The logic of standardization and the logic of prostheses thus crosscut one another in the continuous fashioning of scientific subjectivity (Seltzer, 1992). Bodies, body parts, social relations and practices are thereby transformed into the sign of science (cf. Balsamo, 1995), concealing the ultimate irony that technologies of distancing are the technologies of alliances, of contact, of becoming.

For science, phantoms have been a stabilizing node in an otherwise hidden social, cultural, technological, and scientific network of body–machine relations, discourses, and practices (cf. Latour, 1993; Pickering, 1995). Once revealed, these interfaces are shown to be where human agency changes form to bring forth a masculine subjectivity that coheres in mind *and* body (see Stone, 1993). Body–machine coordinations are not simply about the male body disappearing into the wizardry of automata, machines, computers, or virtual reality to achieve a final kind of autonomous and transcendent subject ("mind without body"). Nor would they seem to point solely to the panic (disappearing) male body (Kroker et al., 1989), repressed body, the disciplined body, or the standardized body (Balsamo, 1995). Rather, the transit between bodies and machines, while indicating the uncertainty and indeterminacy of either entity, are wound through and through with the dream to transcend the particularized male body and the haunting fear that this same body may not in the end count. Machinic phantasmagoria become improvements upon their human counterparts, and humans upon nonhumans, each prompting the other along in the scientific drama based in part on the spectral desires for limitlessness and in part on the cultural aesthetic of the self-made man (Hacking, 1986; Rotundo, 1993).[19] For these reasons, phantoms threaten less around ethics of scientific practice than they do around their "uncanny power" to reveal the other worlds of scientific production – ". . . its otherworldly form, its supernatural shape, wears the traces of its construction" (Halberstam, 1995: 106). From their otherworldly place, phantoms reveal how the lines drawn between objectivity and subjectivity, between mind and body, and between human and nonhuman fade, blur, and pass into one another, making visible anxieties around the uncertainty of human bodies in a technologically oriented future (Panchasi, 1995).

In these criss-crossings of the crisis of knowledge and the crisis of identity, the crisis of reason and the crisis of masculinity, phantoms open onto the terrain of objective science the subjective motors of desire and pleasure (e.g., Grosz, 1993; Kimmel, 1996). With this crisis bringing under renewed scrutiny masculinity and the male body, body–machine coordinations can be seen to shore up interchanges of power and performance (e.g., Bordo, 1993b). Traces of early-twentieth-century reworkings of masculinity in which strong bodies were taken to be synonymous with strong character (e.g., Hall's "super man," see Bederman, 1995), along with mid-century's emphasis on scientific management and instrumental attributes, haunt late-twentieth-century's body-sculptured muscled-men, armored cyborgs of popular culture, and sleek high-powered computer-like minded men. Out of this historical complex of bodies and machines, scientific identifications of observers as aperspectival, distanced, or detached are exposed as "phantasmatic efforts of alignment, loyalty, ambiguous and cross-corporeal cohabitation . . . they are the sedimentation of the 'we' in the constitution of any 'I' " (Butler, 1993: 105). Such "amalgams of old and new," of the we in the "I," yield up the masculinization of the subject of knowledge as an enterprise of assembly–disassembly zones sustained by the interplay of the machinic and spectral (Hayles, 1995).

This combination of old and new is visibly evident in two recent issues of the *APA Monitor*. In one, Rodin's *The Thinker* is adorned with a mortar

Figure 9.1 *Psychology's depiction of Rodin's* The Thinker. *(Illustration by John Michael Yanson.)*

board while balloons surrounding this male sculpture convey the "rational" form of scientific thought – critical steps modeled after a Popperian version of falsification (Murray, 1995). In the other, a front-page photo shows a man in shirt and tie wearing a "head-mounted display" with his hands "disappearing" into the white illumination of a computer monitor as he is said to be "diving into virtual reality" (Azar, 1996).[20] In this late-twentieth-century imaging of the interplay of perceptual skepticism and ingenious pastimes, the male thinker is grounded in positivism whereas the male in virtual reality becomes "active" in new worlds of "control" and "interaction" with the "research tool" of (his) "dreams" holding out the promise of transcending psychology's historical "inability to control natural settings"

Figure 9.2 *Psychologists dive into virtual reality (Illustration by John Michael Yanson.)*

(Azar, 1996: 1, 25). Phantom mediators in virtual worlds reconstruct eye-to-hand coordinations and the male body as solid, yet fluid, active, and in control of a new kind of virtual world. Echoing earlier dreams thought to be realized through automation and then computerization, phantoms pass from early human-like materializations to subsequent automated and computerized ones and, of late, into the laboratory world of virtual people. Still encircling laboratory phantoms is the double discourse of life and death, the natural and the artificial, the scientifically managed work process and the pleasures of the senses.

Shifting the Apparitional Scene

"Phantoms" shift the apparitional scene from traditional accounts of technologies of deception and associated ethics debate to the other productions staged in scientific psychology. As summoned here, phantoms bring into focus an expanse of body–machine coordinations and a full complement of pleasures and dangers through which bodies and subjects are not only made but also resignified in particular ways. Called out within the cross talk of bodies and machines are transfigurations of identity, scientific authority, objectivity, subjectivity, and bodies (Stone, 1995). A host of different actors and actants issue from changing technologies and conditions in cultural, industrial, and scientific life, and with these cross-corporeal assemblages of bodies and machines the links between masculinity and scientific authority, identity, and the body are transformed time and again (Bederman, 1995). Inspiriting these transformations are the politics of desire and knowledge interests, connecting the seemingly isolated moments of changing technologies and scientific practices with the longer history of the masculinization of knowledge production.

Thus, while phantoms gesture towards what might be considered a postmodern subject and subjectivity, they also trouble its terms of multiplicity, fluidity, shape-shifting, and hybridity. They do so by raising the specter of the gendered politics of desire and the imaginary that bring bodies and technologies into contact with one another such that multiplicity, fluidity, and so on are seen to harbor their own forms of standardization (Haraway, 1996). Phantoms do not rest easy with formulations suggesting that technology changes us, our bodies, minds, and consciousness or that we change technology, for bodies and technologies cross-index one another within knowledge/power relations of gender, race, class, and sexuality. Not all technobodies count in the same way. For these reasons, phantoms bump up against not only the neutral/rational subject of Enlightenment science but also recent social studies of science critiques that objectify and reify concepts such as social relations of practice or reflexivity. Phantoms haunt these formulations with questions about the kinds of subjects, subjectivities, or reflexive relations made visible by networks of bodies, machines, science, and culture and about those that are ghosted from these transitways.

But these otherwordly figures of transmigration point as well to the conjunctions of immaterial and material worlds, to the imaginary as a nearby resident to the rational, and to the doubling of enterprising recreation and disciplining labor in science. These conjunctions and doublings suggest places for feminists to intervene in the remaking of subjects and subjectivity in psychology as much as they invite us to unleash our own imaginations and desires as movement, practices, skills, and actions for a different scientific (techno)body politic.

Acknowledgments

Special thanks to Claudette Columbus, Susan Henking, Lee Quinby, and John Shotter for their always engaging discussion and constructive comments on phantoms and phantomizations. I would also like to thank reference librarians Joseph Chmura and Daniel Mulvey.

Notes

1 I am indebted to Claudette Columbus for pointing out parallels between my own and Taussig's work.

2 My first sighting of the term phantom in studies using deception was in Charles Korte's (1971) "Effects of individual responsibility and group communication on help-giving in an emergency." My interest in these kinds of phantoms of the laboratory arose during my research into investigative technologies in the history of small group research.

3 Morality play introduces an additional interesting angle on phantoms in the laboratory, for in social psychology's oft-discussed tendency to stage social life, phantoms enter into an enactment in which vices and virtues "appear as real people" (*OED*).

4 I am borrowing here from Salman Rushdie's tracing of the Latin roots of "translation" in "bearing across," which he draws on to characterize migrant writers such as himself as "translated men." "[P]eople belonging to such cultures of hybridity have had to renounce the dream or ambition of rediscovering any kind of 'lost' cultural purity, or ethnic absolutism. They are irrevocably translated" (cited in Mercer, 1994: 27–8). Also see Robert Lifton's (1993) use of Rushdie's notion of "translated" selves in his development of the postmodern self as protean.

5 Donna Haraway conceives of the "promises of monsters" as the "possibility for changing maps of the world, for building new collectives out of what is not quite a plethora of human and nonhuman actors" (1992: 327).

6 In an exquisite cultural history of the lie detector, Bunn shows how this instrument was brought to life through science, police, Hollywood and fiction. Inventors Keeler and Marston, for example, were the creators as well of comic book characters Dick Tracy and Wonder Woman, respectively.

7 For pointing me towards the areas of hypnosis and suggestion, and specifically to certain researchers, such as Bekhterev, Binet, Dashiell, and Sidis, I am indebted to Franz Samelson, Lloyd Strickland, and Kurt Danziger.

8 Applied variously in different subdisciplines, suggestion, as so many other concepts in psychology, underwent a number of conceptual refashionings. Bekhterev (1908) wrote that "suggestion" came from "everyday life," was specified subsequently through medical circles as hypnotic suggestion and thence broadened by others to "one of the ways of exerting influence of one person over another even under conditions of ordinary life" (Strickland, forthcoming: 4).

9 With respect to recent works, the focus of deception is on questions surrounding human nature, adaptiveness, and detection of deception (see *Journal of Nonverbal Behavior*, Fall and Winter, 1988). Also see Loyal Rue's (1994) *By the Grace of Guile*.

10 Murphy et al. report that "prestige" was recognized as an important factor of experimenters and of suggestibility as early as the late nineteenth century by researchers such as Vitali, Binet, and Binet's student, Giroud. Binet and Giroud demonstrated this in studies of progressive line length.

11 Alison Lurie's (1967) *Imaginary Friends* provides a fictional treatment of this research, astutely portraying how role-playing blurs fiction and reality.

12 For definitions presented here, see *OED*, 1989.

13 This proliferation included remaking subjects' suspiciousness into a practical strategy of "stooge detection" (see Neff, 1978). Little, however, was made of the more frequent use of women subjects in studies of deception (Gross and Fleming, 1982).

14 For a contrasting view, see Hunt, 1982.

15 Barbara Stafford argues that "in the wake of the perceptual skepticism cast by Hume and others . . . a broad gamut of extraordinary, marvelous, and crafty things were condemned" (1994: 3).

16 See Taussig (1980) for an additional perspective on phantom objectivity; also see Lukacs on phantom objectivity as "an autonomy that seems so strictly rational and all-embracing as to conceal every trace of its fundamental [human] nature" (1971: 83).

17 Stafford illustrates this search through the work of Jacques de Vaucanson's eighteenth-century cybernetic constructions "going so far as to upholster the right arm and hand . . . with real skin" (1994: 193).

18 That the study of phantom limbs seems to take implicitly the male body as its norm is evidenced by the notable silence on whether women's missing body parts, such as female organs, register phantom sensations. Grosz asks if this silence indicates that female organs are "already codified paradoxically as 'missing' organs" (1994: 71).

19 It is tempting to argue that crises of masculinity parallel crises of reason in science. Early-, mid-, and late-twentieth-century cultural "crises" in masculinity may provide some understanding of remasculinizations of the scientist and science, and are surely worth further study.

20 Virtual reality is described as a tool for research, entertainment, and military training.

References

Aaronson, E. and Carlsmith, J. (1968) "Experimentation in social psychology," in G. Lindzey and E. Aaronson (eds), *The Handbook of Social Psychology*, (2nd edn). Reading, MA: Addison-Wesley. pp. 1–79.

Abbey, A. (1982) "Sex differences in attributions for friendly behavior: do males misperceive females' friendliness?" *Journal of Personality and Social Psychology*, 42: 830–8.

Abraham, N. and Torok, M. (1994) *The Shell and the Kernel: Renewals of Psychoanalysis*. Chicago: University of Chicago Press.

Asch, S. (1958) "Effects of group pressure upon the modification and distortion of judgments," in E. Maccoby, T. Newcomb, and E. Hartley (eds), *Readings in Social Psychology*. New York: Holt, Rinehart and Winston.

Azar, B. (1996) "Diving into virtual reality," *The APA Monitor*, 27: 1, 24–6.

Balsamo, A. (1995) "Forms of technological embodiment: reading the body in contemporary culture," *Body & Society*, 1: 215–38.

Banta, M. (1993) *Taylorized Lives: Narrative Productions in the Age of Taylor, Veblen, and Ford*. Chicago: University of Chicago Press.

Bederman, G. (1995) *Manliness and Civilization: A Cultural History of Gender and Race in the United States, 1880–1917*. Chicago: University of Chicago Press.

Berg, I. (1954) "The use of human subjects in psychological research," *American Psychologist*, 9: 108–11.

Bernstein, R.J. (1983) *Beyond Objectivism and Relativism: Science, Hermeneutics, and Praxis.* Philadelphia: University of Pennsylvania Press.

Bordo, S. (1993a) *Unbearable Weight: Feminism, Western Culture, and the Body.* Berkeley, CA: University of California Press.

Bordo, S. (1993b) "Reading the male body," *Michigan Quarterly Review*, 32: 696–737.

Bourdieu, P. (1977) *Outline of a Theory of Practice.* Cambridge: Cambridge University Press.

Bray, D.W. (1950) "The prediction of behavior from two attitude scales," *Journal of Abnormal and Social Psychology*, 45: 64–84.

Bukatman, S. (1995) "The artificial infinite: on special effects and the sublime," in L. Cooke and P. Wollen (eds), *Visual Display: Culture Beyond Appearances.* Seattle, WA: Bay Press. pp. 255–89.

Bunn, G. (1996) "Constructing the suspect," *Borderlines*, 40: 5–9.

Burtt, H.E. (1920) "Sex differences in the effect of discussion," *Journal of Experimental Psychology*, 3: 390–5.

Butler, J. (1993) *Bodies that Matter: On the Discursive Limits of "Sex."* New York: Routledge.

Byatt, A.S. (1992) *Angels and Insects.* New York: Random House.

Connerton, P. (1989) *How Societies Remember.* New York: Cambridge University Press.

Coon, D. (1992) "Testing the limits of sense and science: American experimental psychologists combat spiritualism, 1880–1920," *American Psychologist*, 47: 143–51.

Coon, D. (1993) "Standardizing the subject: experimental psychologists, introspection, and the quest for a technoscientific ideal," *Technology and Culture*, 34: 757–83.

Copjec, J. (1994) *Read my Desire: Lacan against the Historicists.* Cambridge, MA: MIT Press.

Crutchfield, R.S. (1955) "Conformity and character," *American Psychologist*, 10: 191–8.

Danziger, K. (1990) *Constructing the Subject: Historical Origins of Psychological Research.* Cambridge: Cambridge University Press.

Darley, J. and Latane, B. (1968) "Bystander intervention in emergencies: diffusion of responsibility," *Journal of Personality and Social Psychology*, 8: 377–83.

Dashiell, J.F. (1933) "Experiments in the sifting of testimony," *Psychological Bulletin*, 30: 720.

Dashiell, J.F. (1935) "Experimental studies of the influence of social situations on the behavior of individual human adults," in C. Murchison (ed.), *A Handbook of Social Psychology.* Worcester, MA: Clark University Press. pp. 1097–149.

Daston, L. (1992) "Objectivity and the escape from perspective," *Social Studies of Science*, 22: 597– 618.

de Certeau, M. (1984) *The Practice of Everyday Life.* Berkeley, CA: University of California Press.

Diserens, C.M. and Vaughn, J. (1931) "The experimental psychology of motivation," *Psychological Bulletin*, 28: 15–65.

Ellemers, N., Wilke, H., van Knippenberg, A. (1993) "Effects of the legitimacy of low group or individual status on individual and collective status-enhancing strategies," *Journal of Personality and Social Psychology*, 64: 766–78.

Elworthy, S. (1995) "Tramps: narratives of research and the popularization of social science in late-nineteenth-century America." Paper presented at the Twenty-Sixth Annual Meeting of Cheiron, Brunswick, Maine.

Festinger, L. and Carlsmith, J. (1959) "Cognitive consequences of forced compliance," *Journal of Abnormal and Social Psychology*, 58: 203–10.

Festinger, L. and Katz, D. (eds) (1953) *Research Methods in the Behavioral Sciences.* New York: Dryden Press.

Festinger, L., Riecken, H.W., and Schachter, S. (1956) *When Prophecy Fails.* Minneapolis, MN: University of Minnesota Press.

Figueroa-Sarriera, H.J. (1995) "Children of the mind with disposable bodies: metaphors of self in a text on artificial intelligence and robotics," in C.H. Gray (ed.), *The Cyborg Handbook.* New York: Routledge. pp. 127–35.

Finucane, R.C. (1984) *Appearances of the Dead: A Cultural History of Ghosts.* Buffalo, NY: Prometheus Books.

Foucault, M. (1977) *Discipline and Punish: The Birth of the Prison.* New York: Vintage Books.

Foucault, M. (1978) *The History of Sexuality* (vol. 1). New York: Vintage Books.

Freud, S. (1961) *Civilization and its Discontents* (trans. and ed. J. Strachey). New York: W.W. Norton.

Gaertner, S. and Dovidio, J. (1986) "The aversive form of racism," in J. Dovidio and S. Gaertner (eds), *Prejudice, Discrimination, and Racism*. Orlando, FL: Academic Press.

Galison, P. (1988) "History, philosophy, and the central metaphor," *Science in Context*, 2: 197–212.

Gross, A.E. and Fleming, I. (1982) "Twenty years of deception in social psychology," *Personality and Social Psychology Bulletin*, 8: 402–8.

Grosz, E. (1993) "Bodies and knowledges: feminism and the crisis of reason," in L. Alcoff and E. Potter (eds), *Feminist Epistemologies*. New York: Routledge. pp. 187–215.

Grosz, E. (1994) *Volatile Bodies: Toward a Corporeal Feminism*. Bloomington, IN: Indiana University Press.

Grosz, E. (1995) *Space, Time and Perversion: Essays on the Politics of Bodies*. New York: Routledge.

Hacking, I. (1986) "Making up people," in T.C. Heller, M. Sosna, and D.E. Wellberg with A.I. Davidson, A. Swidler, and I. Watt, *Reconstructing Individualism: Autonomy, Individuality and the Self in Western Thought*. Stanford, CA: Stanford University Press. pp. 222–36.

Halberstam, J. (1995) *Skin Shows: Gothic Horror and the Technology of Monsters*. Durham, NC: Duke University Press.

Halberstam, J. and Livingston, I. (1995) *Posthuman Bodies*. Bloomington, IN: Indiana University Press.

Haraway, D.J. (1991a) "Situated knowledges: the science question in feminism and the privilege of partial perspective," in D.J. Haraway, *Simians, Cyborgs, and Women: The Reinvention of Nature*. New York: Routledge. pp. 183–202.

Haraway, D.J. (1991b) "A cyborg manifesto: science, technology, and socialist-feminism in the late twentieth century," in D.J. Haraway, *Simians, Cyborgs, and Women: the Reinvention of Nature*. New York: Routledge. pp. 149–81.

Haraway, D.J. (1992) "The promises of monsters: a regenerative politics for inappropriate/d others," in L. Grossberg, C. Nelson, and P.A. Treichler (eds), *Cultural Studies*. New York: Routledge. pp. 295–337.

Haraway, D.J. (1994) "A game of cat's cradle: science studies, feminist theory, cultural studies," *Configurations*, 1: 59–71.

Haraway, D.J. (1996) "Modest witness: feminist diffractions in science studies," in P. Galison and D.J. Stump (eds), *The Disunity of Science: Boundaries, Contexts, and Power*. Stanford, CA: Stanford University Press. pp. 428–41.

Hartshorne, H. and May, M. (1928) *Studies in Deceit* (vol. I). New York: Macmillan.

Hayles, N.K. (1995) "The life cycle of cyborgs: writing the posthuman," in C.H. Gray (ed.), *The Cyborg Handbook*. New York: Routledge. pp. 321–35.

Hunt, M. (1982) "Research through deception," *New York Times Magazine*, 12 September: 66–7, 139–43.

Hyman, R. (1989) "The psychology of deception," *Annual Review of Psychology*, 40: 133–54.

Jones, E.E. and Sigall, H. (1971) "The bogus pipeline: a new paradigm for measuring affect and attitude," *Psychological Bulletin*, 76: 349–64.

Jordanova, L. (1995) "Medicine and genres of display," in L. Cooke and P. Wollen (eds), *Visual Display: Culture beyond Appearances*. Seattle, WA: Bay Press. pp. 202–17.

Keller, E.F. (1992) "The paradox of scientific subjectivity," *Annals of Scholarship*, 9: 135–53.

Kelman, H.C. (1967) "Human use of human subjects: the problem of deception in social psychological experiments," *Psychological Bulletin*, 67: 1–11.

Kimmel, M. (1996) *Manhood in America: A Cultural History*. New York: Free Press.

Korte, C. (1971) "Effects of individual responsibility and group communication on help-giving in an emergency," *Human Relations*, 24: 149–59.

Kroker, A., Kroker, M., and Cook, D. (1989) *Panic Encyclopedia: The Definitive Guide to the Postmodern Scene*. Montreal: New World Perspectives.

Krout, M. (1954) "Comments on 'The use of human subjects in psychological research',"

American Psychologist, 9: 589.

Latane, B. and Rodin, J. (1969) "A lady in distress: inhibiting effects of friends and strangers on bystander intervention," *Journal of Experimental Social Psychology*, 5: 189–202.

Latane, B. and Darley, J. (1970) "Social determinants of bystander intervention in emergencies," in J. Macaulay and L. Berkowitz (eds), *Altruism and Helping Behavior*. New York: Academic Press.

Latour, B. (1993) *We Have Never Been Modern*. Cambridge, MA: Harvard University Press.

Latour, B. (1994) "Pragmatogonies: a mythical account of how humans and nonhumans swap properties," *American Behavioral Scientist*, 37: 791–808.

Lifton, R.J. (1993) *The Protean Self: Human Resilience in an Age of Fragmentation*. New York: Basic Books.

Lukacs, G. (1971) *History and Class Consciousness* (trans. Rodney Livingstone). London: Merlin Press.

Lurie, A. (1967) *Imaginary Friends*. New York: Avon Books.

Macauley, W.R. and Gordo-Lopez, A. (1995) "From cognitive psychologies to mythologies: advancing cyborg textualities for a narrative of resistance," in C.H. Gray (ed.), *The Cyborg Handbook*. New York: Routledge. pp. 433–44.

MacKinney, A.C. (1954) "Deceiving experimental subjects," *American Psychologist*, 10: 133.

May, E.T. (1988) *Homeward Bound: American Families in the Cold War Era*. New York: Basic Books.

Megill, A. (1991) "Introduction: four senses of objectivity," *Annals of Scholarship*, 8: 301–19.

Mercer, K. (1994) *Welcome to the Jungle: New Positions in Black Cultural Studies*. New York: Routledge.

Milgram, S. (1963) "Behavioral study of obedience," *Journal of Abnormal and Social Psychology*, 67: 371–8.

Milgram, S. (1992) "Cyranoids," in *The Individual in a Social World: Essays and Experiments* (2nd edn). New York: McGraw-Hill.

Morawski, J. (ed.) (1988) *The Rise of Experimentation in American Psychology*. New Haven, CT: Yale University Press.

Murchison, C. (ed.) (1935) *A Handbook of Social Psychology*. Worcester, MA: Clark University Press.

Murphy, G., Murphy, L.B. and Newcomb, T.M. (1937) *Experimental Social Psychology: An Interpretation of Research upon the Socialization of Individual* (revised edn). New York: Harper and Brothers.

Murray, B. (1995) "What it takes to think like a psychologist," *The APA Monitor*, 26: 38.

Nagel, T. (1986) *The View from Nowhere*. Oxford: Oxford University Press.

Neff, J. (1978) "Experimental research as practical action: stooge detection and bias," *Symbolic Interaction*, 1: 61–73.

Oliansky, A. (1991) "A confederate's perspective on deception," *Ethics and Behavior*, 1 (4): 253–8.

Panchasi, R. (1995) "Reconstructions: prosthetics and the rehabilitation of the male body in World War I France," *differences*, 7: 109–40.

Pickering, A. (1995) *The Mangle of Practice: Time, Agency, and Science*. Chicago: University of Chicago Press.

Pilisuk, M. (1984) "Experimenting with the arms race," *Journal of Conflict Resolution*, 28: 296–315.

Pinch, T.J. (1988) "The externalization of observation: an example from modern physics," in I. Hronszky, M. Feher, and B. Dajka (eds), *Scientific Knowledge Socialized*. Dordrecht: Kluwer Academic Publishers. pp. 225–43.

Porter, T. (1992) "Objectivity as standardization: the rhetoric of impersonality in measurement, statistics, and cost-benefit analysis," *Annals of Scholarship*, 9: 19–59.

Porter, T. (1995) *Trust in Numbers: The Pursuit of Objectivity in Science and Public Life*. Princeton, NJ: Princeton University Press.

Quinby, L. (1994) *Anti-apocalypse: Exercises in Genealogical Criticism*. Minneapolis, MN: University of Minnesota Press.

Ring, K. (1967) "Experimental social psychology: some sober questions about some frivolous values," *Journal of Experimental Social Psychology*, 3: 113–23.

Rosenzwieg, S. (1933) "The experimental situation as a psychological problem," *Psychological Review*, 40: 337–54.

Rotundo, E.A. (1993) *Amerian Manhood: Transformations in Masculinity from the Revolution to the Modern Era*. New York: Basic Books.

Rubin, Z. (1983) "Taking deception for granted," *Psychology Today*, 17: 74–5.

Rue, L. (1994) *By the Grace of Guile*. Oxford: Oxford University Press.

Schachter, S. (1950) "Deviation, rejection, and communication," PhD thesis, University of Michigan (University Microfilms, No. 1712).

Schachter, S. and Singer, J. (1962) "Cognitive, social, and physiological determinants of emotional state," *Psychological Review*, 69: 379–99.

Schaffer, S. (1992) "Self evidence," *Critical Inquiry*, 18: 327–62.

Seltzer, M. (1992) *Bodies and Machines*. New York: Routledge.

Sharpe, D., Adair, J.G., and Roese, N.J. (1992) "Twenty years of deception research: a decline in subjects' trust?" *Personality and Social Psychology Bulletin*, 18: 585–90.

Sherif, M. (1935) "An experimental study of stereotypes," *Journal of Abnormal and Social Psychology*, 29: 371–5.

Sherif, M. (1937) "An experimental approach to the study of attitudes," *Sociometry*, 1: 90–8.

Sidis, B. (1898) *The Psychology of Suggestion*. New York: D. Appleton.

Sinick, D. (1954) "Comments on 'The use of human subjects in psychological research'," *American Psychologist*, 9: 589.

Smith, H., Spears, R., and Oyen, M. (1994) " 'People like us': the influence of personal deprivation and group membership salience on justice evaluations," *Journal of Experimental Social Psychology*, 30: 277–99.

Stafford, B. (1991) *Body Criticism: Imaging the Unseen in Enlightenment Art and Medicine*. Cambridge, MA: MIT Press.

Stafford, B. (1994) *Artful Science: Enlightenment Entertainment and the Eclipse of Visual Education*. Cambridge, MA: MIT Press.

Star, S.L. (1991) "Power, technologies and the phenomenology of conventions: on being allergic to onions," in J. Law (ed.), *A Sociology of Monsters: Essays on Power, Technology and Domination*. New York: Routledge. pp. 26–56.

Stone, A.R. (1993) "What vampires know: transsubjection and transgender in cyberspace." Paper presented at "In Control: Mensch–Interface–Machine," Kunstlerhaus, Graz, Austria, May.

Stone, A.R. (1995) *The War of Desire and Technology at the Close of the Mechanical Age*. Cambridge, MA: MIT Press.

Strickland, L. (ed.) (forthcoming) *Suggestion and its Role in Social Life by V.M. Bekhterev (1908)*, trans. T. Dobreva-Martinova. New Brunswick, NJ: Transaction.

Suls, J. and Rosnow, R. (1988) "Concerns about artifacts in psychological experiments," in J. Morawski (ed.), *The Rise of Experimentation in Psychology*. New Haven, CT: Yale University Press. pp. 163–87.

Taussig, M. (1980) *The Devil and Commodity Fetishism in South America*. Chapel Hill: University of North Carolina Press.

Town, C. (1921) "Suggestion," *Psychological Bulletin*, 18: 366–75.

Vinacke, W.E. (1954) "Deceiving experimental subjects," *American Psychologist*, 9: 155.

Webb, E., Campbell, D., Schwartz, R., and Sechrest, L. (1966) *Unobtrusive Measures: Nonreactive Research in the Social Sciences*. Chicago: Rand McNally.

Wilson, R.W. (1995) "Cyber(body)parts: prosthetic consciousness," *Body & Society*, 1: 239–60.

Young, P.C. (1931) "A general review of the literature on hypnotism and suggestion," *Psychological Bulletin*, 28: 367–91.

Zizek, S. (1991) "Grimaces of the real, or when the phallus appears," *October*, 58: 44–68.

10

The Return of Phantom Subjects?

Jill Morawski

Traveling in tandem, this essay and Betty Bayer's study of phantoms that directly precedes it, examine what appear to be distinct qualities ascribed to the observer and the subject. The experimenter/observer is conventionally (and even epistemologically) exempted from a host of common assumptions otherwise made about humans. In contrast, the subject/participant is routinely vested with characteristics that are acknowledged, both implicitly and explicitly, as being made (constructed) or found (natural). While exploring the connectedness of these two types of experimental actors, I want to take the analysis one step further to confront some worrisome problems in constructionist theories.

The most obvious connection between these two predominant but dubitable types of experimental entities – the experimenter and the subject/participant – is the splitting of subjectivity entailed in presuming them. In her chapter, Bayer excavates related splits, notably those occurring with the character of the experimental confederate who is at once the knower and the ignorant, the visible and the invisible, the rational and the not entirely so. In its binary configuration, that "phantom" reconfirms the original splitting of the knowing, agentic observer and the naive, passive subject. Starting with such evidence of multiple splittings, we need to ascertain how they are sustained. More to the point of this essay, we need to comprehend how and why modern psychology configures and upholds certain notions of subjectivity and certain subjectivities.

These main research characters, the experimenter and the subject so called, have been the topic of various social constructionist analyses of experimentation. However revealing of the structure of investigative practices, such studies are largely incomplete for they often rely on antiquated notions of subjectivity and stop short of (or circumvent) producing any viable reconceptualizations. Most constructionist accounts in psychology fail to posit an alternative conception of the observer and his or her acts of objectivity, articulate the (social) relations of research encounters, and/or consider the reflexive or looping effects of research and theorizing. A psychological science beyond positivism and naive empiricism, I will propose, requires workable solutions to these unfinished tasks. In addressing these projects, I draw upon recent endeavors in science studies as instructive models for reimagining the subjectivities of observers and participants alike.

Undoing Subjectivities

In a recent novel about academic life, *Moo*, Jane Smiley (1995) describes deconstruction as the pastime intellectuals took up when Marxism declined. Deconstruction stands, at least for some people outside the labyrinth of academe, as a weapon purportedly being readied for use in the next assault on culture. Although distinct from deconstruction, social construction in psychology shares the appearance and sometimes the reality of serving primarily as criticism, albeit an internal criticism of intellectual thought. To make such a comparison is not to assert that constructionism has furnished only critique for it also has introduced new visions. For instance, dismantling central psychological constructs, whether they be child abuse, cognition, aggression, the family, or statistical reasoning, at once demonstrates the insolvency or unreality of these constructs and also points to other phenomena or effects at work. Nor is making such a comparison with deconstruction meant to condemn constructionist theory as errant or unusable but, rather, to suggest its current partiality: beyond its function as critique (in itself not a fault), constructionism is incomplete. It is wanting, first, of a self-acknowledged contemplation of its epistemic place and, second, of a workable notion of subjectivity.

In their seemingly earnest regard for subjectivity, constructionists are in good company. Conventional psychology has been reminded repeatedly of its impoverished image of the subject. Just as constructionists have unpacked the faults of dominant paradigms, so humanist psychologists have written cogently of the elision of values and moral agency in mainstream psychology's confection of the subject, and critical theorists have recorded psychology's failure to consider the subject and subjectivity in terms of institutional structures, power, and ideology. These problems of subjectivity are not unique to psychology. In diverse disciplinary niches, from history to feminist studies, scholars are acknowledging their own failures to theorize subjectivity adequately. In his synoptic appraisal of cultural studies, Richard Johnson wrote:

> Above all, *there is no account of what I would call the subjective aspects of struggle*, no account of how there is a moment in subjective flux when social subjects (individual or collective) produce accounts of how they are conscious political agents, that is, constitute themselves politically. To ask for such a theory is not to deny the major structuralist or poststructuralist insights: subjects are contradictory, in process, fragmented, produced. But human beings and social movements also strive to produce some coherence and continuity, and through this, exercise some control over feeling, conditions and destinies. (1986: 69)

Such ambitions to reconceptualize subjectivity sometimes are driven by the desire for theory correctness. Sometimes, however, they are motivated by necessity. As bell hooks warned, "should we not be suspicious of postmodern critiques of the 'subject' when they surfaced at a historical moment when many subjugated people feel themselves coming to power for the first time" (1990: 28)? Our critiques of essentialism "should not be made synonymous with a dismissal of the struggle of oppressed and exploited peoples to make ourselves subjects;" we need to "find ways to construct self and identify that are oppositional and liberatory" (1990: 28–9).

Even granting that constructionism is not special in its abeyance of the subject and subjectivity, it nevertheless is important to ascertain how constructionism falls short in this regard. Within psychology, versions of constructionism at present constitute the only viable and articulated alternative to essentialist or naive positivist conceptions of human kinds. Constructionists certainly have not ignored the subject of the subject; as noted, they have produced some of the most revealing expositions of psychology's reigning models of subjectivity. As it happens, these expositions also illustrate some limitations of constructionists' renditions of subjectivity. Taken together, constructionist studies of the beings in psychological research deftly disassemble the mythic, canonical histories of psychology which merely record abstracted ideas and crystallized discoveries. From these revisionist studies, for instance, we now know some of the ways in which subject identities were created within experimental settings to fit aggregate statistical models and the practical needs of bureaucratic, commercialized society (Danziger, 1990). The psychology of subjects was crafted through elaborate experimental tactics, including substitutions of human by non-human subjects (Morawski, 1988), coercion and silencing of subjects' reports (Gillespie, 1988), and fashioning research practices, like debriefing, to strengthen the authority of voice in the experiment (Harris, 1988). Investigations such as these make some connections between experimental practices and the resultant psychology of subjective experience; most notable, they reveal how research techniques construct psychological subjectivity. Such historical reappraisals also include analyses of written discourse which show how the actors, analysts, and subjects alike are represented and produced in and through texts. They reveal, for instance, how the rhetoric of expertise endows the experimenter–author with power, rationality, and masculinity (Lopes, 1991; Morawski and Steele, 1991). Discourse studies detail how the psychologist can move between author, observer, and "plain old guy" while the subjects are, indeed, subject to the imposition of (culturally specific) identities (Billig, 1990; Lamb, 1991; Stringer, 1990). Studies of publication rules uncover a lingering behavioral rhetoric which, through the elimination of first person accounting and the insistence of technical, operational descriptions, sometimes yields texts without mental processes or actors. Through scientific rhetoric "[t]he individual author is replaced by his method; the individual subject is replaced by the statistical patterns of behavior that are reported" (Brown, 1992: 58).

These and related studies constitute a literature from which is emerging a clearer sense of how the specific practices of experimentation, from subject selection to the final explanatory claims derived from the data, function to sustain methodological canons as well as to describe and inscribe subjectivity. Other investigations, too numerous to enumerate here, further examine the invention of subjectivity by analysing particular psychological theories or constructs; they explore psychological concepts in their entirety. Such analyses have unpacked the prescriptive language, philosophical presuppositions, political motivations, and methodological devices constituting scientific studies of battering (Lamb, 1991), field dependence (Haaken, 1988), the self (Cushman, 1990), sexuality (Fine, 1988; Tiefer, 1994), infancy (Bradley, 1989), and so on. The present focus is on the studies of experimental practices. They are sufficient to identify three troubling shortcomings in constructionist appraisals of subjectivities and subjects, be they the subject status of observers or the observed.

First, constructionist accounts (like the experimental studies they analyse and replace) ignore or discount the expanse of subjective experiences; they do not represent the full dynamics of subjectivities. Absent from these analytic interrogations are the fractionalizings, phantomizings, and holy and unholy alliances that transpire in research events. Yet, the multiplicity of the confederate's subjectivity (as documented in Bayer's chapter) indicates how subjectivities need not be, and probably are not, singular or monochromatic. Likewise absent from most constructionist inquiries is the mobilizing of agency, resistance, subversion, resentment, or rebellion. These complexities and other apparently bothersome qualities of experimental actors hardly receive attention, despite the fact that many aspects of experimental routines have been established precisely as guards against such unwelcome features of agency on the part of experimenters and subjects alike. In fact, the techniques and texts of experiments literally document researchers' realizations that experimental situations are sites of potential rebellions and complicitous play, and that all participants hold such potentials – from experimenters and subjects to phantoms/confederates. Even experiments that assess the unfaithful actions of subjects are produced through a modicum of unfaithful acts of experimenters (and sometimes confederates). Set against these absences in constructionists' renditions of subjectivities is plentiful evidence of the mobility, fluidity, and resistance of subjectivity. In fact, in searching for subjects' own reports of experimentation (records of subjects' voices that were not mediated or translated by experimenters), I found *only* accounts by subjects who refused, resisted, or otherwise contended the experimental experience (Morawski, 1994). To some considerable degree, therefore, studies of the construction of subjects and subjectivities in experiments have read what *transpires at the surface* more or less as what *is* reality. Even as committed nominalists, constructionists apparently work like empiricists: they take what is immediately seen and named as what exists and ignore possibilities of deeper meanings, symbolism, and the indeterminacy of actions.

A second shortcoming of constructionist studies involves the analysts themselves. Few constructionists position themselves in any but one relation to their subject matter. Most display the well-rehearsed strategy of a detached, distant, and occasionally visionary observer – the figurehead of the experimenter. As such, most constructionist studies, like the positivist productions they are interrogating, are playgrounds of masquerade wherein abstracted writings are produced by elusive, cloaked, or even phantom beings. The analyst roams everywhere around the experimental sites being excavated and yet is nowhere to be seen. Rarely do analysts contemplate even their tactical or theoretical positions, never mind their own subject statuses. Steve Woolgar (1988) has introduced the term "ontological gerrymandering" to refer to the investigative practices whereby analysts attempt to exonerate themselves from the assertions of relativism which they are making about the entities or ideas they are examining. One ready tactic for distinguishing the analyst from those others is to differentiate "between deconstructor and deconstructed" whereby "the former presents the argument as if s/he was immune from the structures applied to the target of the argument" (1988: 99).

These two problems in constructionist work are implicated in a third shortcoming. Through the theoretical flattening of subjectivities and the exoneration of analysts' own subject senses, most studies recurrently whisper or otherwise express longings for wholeness, unity, and stability in all participants, including the (temporally removed) analysts. The decision not to see beyond singular conceptions of subjectivity, conceptions that fundamentally accord with those held by positivist experimentalists, perpetuates, perhaps inadvertently, the dream of autonomous actors. Even when role playing their experimental parts, these actors appear to function as reasoning, (mostly) rational beings. Experimental psychology has been built upon this very conception of subjectivity, this ideal of the rational and autonomous self; it is a taken-for-granted ideal. As Ben Bradley has written of developmental psychology, "Neither the infant nor the psychologist needs to struggle with ambiguity or to develop its own unique meaning. The meaning is simply *there*, 'written on the rocks' " (1994: 89). Constructionists have unpacked some of the social enactments that are required to realize certain methodologies, data, or theories, but they leave untouched this taken-for-granted natural or "found" subjectivity, written on the rocks so to speak.

To highlight these three shortcomings is not to claim that the constructionist project fails us, but rather that as currently articulated and implemented, it is unfinished. Its incompleteness is understandable. After all, constructionism in psychology stands as a recent and audacious move to renounce several long-revered traditions: empiricism, realism, positivism. If we acknowledge the impressionable vestiges of our intellectual background and, perhaps, even its lingering seductiveness, then the aforementioned shortcoming of constructionism can be comprehended in broader terms. This intellectual background consists of multiple commitments. In an exploration of the current state of feminist theory, Kathy Ferguson (1993) named some underlying metatheoretical commitments that have guided feminist thought and constructionism as well. Ferguson contrasted a "genealogical metatheory" serving to interrogate and interrupt what are taken as natural categories and an "interpretive metatheory" aiming to privilege subjective experience as a source of insight. In feminist theory, it is the play of these contending metatheories or, rather, the analysts's relative allegiance to one and the other, that gives form and meaning to her analysis. Yet, tensions produced by these different metatheories also can result in contradictions and inconsistencies.

Constructionists, then, can be seen as working not only *against* a deeply entrenched worldview but also *within* a field of metatheoretical tensions. Why would we not, in our analyses, clasp onto the comforts of a tradition that soothes and smoothes over anxieties of self as well as self–other relations? The splittings of subject positions and the isolated, privileged stance of the observer are comforting social customs; they are also tools of persuasion. This mode of operating guards our own vulnerabilities just as it empowers us as intellectual workers. It likewise enables a protective cognitive paranoia with its projections of undesirable attributes onto others, whether those others be the subjects of experiments or the subjects of our critical appraisals of experiments. Adopting the prevailing conceptions of subject positions and subjectivities comforts us by providing methodological neatness and moral order.

A Return to Our Problems

The continued dependence on classic notions of subjectivity is not solely about psychic comforts but also, to some extent, arises from our yearning to embrace genealogical and interpretive metatheories alike. Many of us have a desire to claim simultaneously the indeterminacy and intermediacy of subjectivities *and* subjectivities that are as moral and as personal as the political can become. Instead of sliding back and forth between these aspirations, or seeking solace by retaining the dominant conception of the subject, it is worth considering how both might be retained: how subjectivities might be found just as they are made. This move, however, ultimately requires abandonment of the older splittings of subjects and an acknowledgment that the observer is not removed or isolated, but that she must stand somewhere – in the world.

Desires for workable conceptions of subjectivities and a place for the observer may not, in fact, be had by all investigators who work within a constructionist framework. Not all constructionists share a commitment that is as ambitious as an aspiration to forge a better science – a distinctly moral, political, and personal science at that. Rouse (1996) has described what is possibly a parallel condition in science studies: while some progressive science studies scholars perceive their project as disinterested analysis, aiming for nonpolitical examinations of the totality of scientific practice, other scholars, notably but not solely those who are feminist in orientation, see their work as a moral and political project that ultimately aims to realize a better science. Although the lines demarcating these two groups might be fuzzier than Rouse suggests, we need to consider the possibility that constructionists also differ among one another in their objectives. The existence of such differences would help explain why some researchers are bothered, while others are not, about matters of subjectivity, research relations, the observers' stance, and the reflexive dynamics of social processes. For those of us who see these matters as problems requiring attention, our cousins in science studies are helpful allies: their conceptual explorations of new forms of scientific practices offer constructive guidance.

Toward an Observing Objectivity

For twentieth-century psychology, the signature quality of the objective observer has been defined as absence: the absence of biases or subjectivity. Subjectivity is defined as a set of regrettable but alterable attributes, beliefs, values, or interests that leak from the untrained or poorly trained observer into the investigative process. Objective observers are cleansed of these properties: they are transported from commitments and space, abstractly standing nowhere. Championed originally in experimental inquiry, this ideal observer sometimes reappears as the author of constructionist analyses.

Studies in the history, philosophy, and sociology of science have demonstrated how this objectivity (as ascribed to the ideal observer) is neither a philosophical absolute nor an abstract ideal. Rather, it is invoked and practiced as a means of managing the subjectivity of observers. As Daston and Galison found in their examination of nineteenth-century notions of objectivity, "It is an ethos of restraint, both external restraints of method and quantification and internal restraints of self-denial and self-criticism. Otherwise put, objectivity is a morality of prohibitions rather than exhortations, but no less a morality for that" (1992: 122).

Other scholars have similarly identified scientific conceptions of objectivity with the internal governance, or politics, of science, on the one hand, and with morality, on the other hand. Considerable research has shown how objectivity is an accomplishment of routine investigative practices. It is not that some abstract concept of objectivity is deployed in scientific work, but rather that scientific practices function to manufacture and operationalize it. Ideals of value-neutrality or objectivity thus are a form of power that is "exercised less visibly, less consciously, and not on but through the dominant institutional structures, priorities, practices, and languages of the sciences" (Harding, 1992: 567).

Objectivity relays not just power but also morality. Scientific practices (and the representations of the world produced through them), depend, in Woolgar's words, on "a moral order" of representation (1988: 109). Although the role of the observer is assumed to be neutral and detached, in actuality the self or agent who observes is crucial to this moral order – he or she is a "disregarded agent of representation" (1988: 109). Recognizing moral agency in science does not necessarily have the same implications as detecting scientists' personal biases; the search for scientists' biases generally proceeds with the assumption that such conditions, once detected, can be removed, thus ultimately enabling the realization of objective science. By contrast, heeding the presence of moral agency disturbs the very premises of scientific work. Some science studies scholars are now calling for acknowledgment of an overarching agency – moral agency – of observers, including science studies investigators themselves (Fuller, 1988; Gooding, 1992; Rouse, 1992). Rouse has suggested that researchers in the cultural studies of science find "normative issues inevitably at stake in both science and cultural studies of science, but see them as arising both locally and reflexively. One cannot but be politically and epistemologically engaged" (1992: 20).

If observers cannot but be politically involved, and if objectivity is power and morality, then what is to be done next? The question, of course, makes sense only to those analysts who take the study of science to include the project of improving science. This project has gone by various names including "successor" science (Harding, 1986), a "rehabilitation of the scientists' sense of agency" (Fuller, 1988: 423), or a genuine "cultural studies of science" (Rouse, 1992). What I have been intimating is that these aims should have a more certain place within the constructionist agenda.

Feminist science studies has moved to answer this question, particularly in regard to rethinking and redoing objectivity. In this vein, Haraway has described "situated knowledges" which begin with the premise that "[t]here is no unmediated photograph or camera obscura in scientific accounts of bodies and machines; there are only highly specific visual possibilities, each with a wonderfully detailed, active, partial way of organizing the world" (1988: 583). Rather than reclaim an identity of analysts, Haraway has proposed a "critical positioning" that takes the observer's stance as mutable, partial, moral, and political. Feminist embodiment, then, is not about a new identity; it "is not about fixed location in a refined body, female or otherwise, but about modes in fields, inflections in orientations, and responsibility for difference in material-semiotic fields of meanings" (1988: 588). Sandra Harding (1991) has called for "traitorous identities," selves built through solidarity with oppressed others who enact "strong reflectivity," a researchers' continual gazing back on his/her cultural situation, recognizing all the while how the object of inquiry also gazes back.

These reconfigurings of the objective observer bear some resemblance to the practices of confederacy and phantomizing described in Bayer's chapter in that both sorts of entities defy classic subject–object divisions. Yet these newer conceptions also explicate a remaking of the politics and morality of objective observers. Rather than obscuring the power and morality of objective practices, they call for the redistribution of power and elucidation of moral ambitions. In these models of scientific action, the objective observer stands somewhere, and that place is in a specific, identifiable relation to the objects of inquiry – the so-called subjects.

Research Relations

The proposals for remaking objective practices acknowledge that the object also is active, whether that activity is seen as agency, reactivity, or resistance. In other words, conceptions of objectivity as political, moral, and situated knowledges usually involve radical reformulations of the world to be known as well as the knowing subject. As Jane Flax warned, "if we do our work well, 'reality' will appear even more unstable, complex, and disorderly than it does now" (1990: 183). In advocating observers' need to engage reflexively in analysing their own cultural situations, Harding (1991) called for awareness of how the object of inquiry gazes back. Haraway (1988, 1994) too has argued that instead of being taken as an inert or passive thingness, objects in the world be perceived as active agents. The purpose of taking these objects as agentic or active is not to anthropomorphize them but to become cognizant of their generative capacities in scientific production and realize that their possibilities, as well as their limitations, actually materialize in research interactions.

Many constructionists have described how the subject (object in the world) is made in and through research enterprises. Little work has emphasized the active, productive features of these subjects. As noted earlier, constructionists (including myself) who do suggest active subjects often have leaned on humanist notions of autonomous actors. Feminist revisions of science are not greatly helpful in this regard, for their primary focus usually is on nonhuman objects in the natural world, not on humans participating in complex interactions. Largely missing from both programs are acting subjects and their participation in research.

Investigation of subject qualities and the relations of research can begin with a clearer sense of what is missing from most critical inquiries as well as from the scientific studies themselves. The case of premenstrual syndrome (PMS) illustrates what goes unnoticed, but it is by no means an exceptional case. PMS, some constructionists have proposed, is an invention, one that makes and delineates the experiences of women during their reproductive years (ages 12–50). It has been demonstrated that the concept of PMS is a recent one, appearing in the research literature only in the 1930s and gaining visibility only after the 1960s. Also acknowledged are the negative and damaging dimensions of PMS: defined as a mental health deficiency, PMS alters women's emotional and functional states mostly in detrimental ways. Despite these critiques and despite the fact that empirical evidence of the existence of PMS is wanting, even after hundreds of studies have been conducted, many researchers continue to subscribe to the syndrome. They, along with many clinicians and ordinary people, believe that PMS exists and that it warrants serious attention. PMS, it would seem, is a manufactured psychological condition, produced through sexist values and even some good intentions of researchers, including feminists, who seek to understand women's nature better. Ordinary beings and researchers alike apparently assimilate these manufactured psychological ideas and states. Although this example flattens somewhat the constructionist explanation and blurs the different positions about what is invented and what is not, it nevertheless illustrates the working assumption of passive (although reasonable) actors who are the recipients of the designation PMS. What critical and constructionist analyses omit are the dynamic psychological processes that lead to the acceptance and internalization of psychological classifications like PMS. Likewise elided is any consideration of subjects or subjectivities whose qualities extend beyond a passive acceptance and reasoned assimilation of scientifically produced knowledge. Subjects are recipients of classifications; they are simply the material of invention.

This case, along with our previous discussions, points to several problems in explicating research relations and the involved subjects who are the objects of that research. The idea that the psychological is made is not all that many constructionists rely upon: they also depend upon certain questionable givens about subjectivity. Proceeding with the basic assumption that we can know what is going on socially and intrapsychically merely by analysing the psychology produced in the research literature is unwise. In its very form, research already represents a construal of the (passive) subject. By taking such a partial view, even the committed, critical constructionist risks slipping into the misconception that they are rescuing the subject. bell hooks has warned about such rescues of the "other," the purportedly disadvantaged or disenfranchised:

> This "we" is that "us" in the margins, that "we" who inhabit marginal space that is not a site of domination but a place of resistance. Enter that space. Often this speech about the "Other" annihilates, erases: "No need to hear your voice. Only tell me about your pain. I want to know your story. And then I will tell it back to you in a new way. Tell it back to you in such a way that it has become mine, my own. Re-writing you, I write myself anew. I am still author, authority. I am still the colonizer, the speaking subject, and you are not at the center of my talk." (1990: 151–2)

Related to these problems in analysing the subject is another: the tendency to overlook how the psychological processes in scientific manufacturing of the subject are themselves complex, multidynamic, and sometimes contradictory. Conventional PMS researchers regularly and earnestly labor with the complications of research relations, ever adjusting their research methodology, for instance, to guard against subject compliance, duplicity, complicity, and sometimes even resistance. In fact, the entire history of psychology's methodology can be read as an ongoing chronicle of facing the horrors of complex research relations and subjectivities. Despite these heroic research efforts, critical interrogations of the scientific making of phenomena such as PMS rarely attend to them.

If resolution of these problems is added to the project of creating new conceptions of objectivity, then an additional issue arises. If we embrace the commitment to better science, specifically to a science that knows itself better, then it is logical to expect that we also be committed to enhancing the lives of our subjects. The enhancement of subjects' lives entails creating more veridical representations of them but extends further to making them more aware of their experiences, actions, and interpretations. Thus, explanations of PMS must proceed beyond demonstrating that psychological constructs are imposed on women's lives: explanatory accounts also should show how these impositions transpire and how women do and can accept, rebel, or even condemn them.

In the standard form in which it is utilized, constructionist theory cannot take these steps. Wavering between genealogical and interpretive metatheories, most constructionists have sought the safety – the distance, abstraction, and political security – of the former while minimizing the latter. A solution, I suggest, rests first with accepting both metatheories. This solution requires embracing dualities. It also necessitates an envisioning of the full dynamics of scientific life, one that incorporates not just the reflective feedback of individual actors but their connection to cultural processes as well.

Dualities and Feedbacks

Up to this point I have entertained ways to move beyond the inadequate conceptions of the observer/analyst, to remove the vestiges of positivist ideas of objectivity. I also have argued for making related changes in our conceptions of subjects and research relations. These suggestions for inquiry intimate what now needs to be made explicit: the genealogical orientation invariably risks a slippage into antiquated conceptions of science and personhood. The interpretive agenda thus needs to be brought back to the foreground. The interpretive project is woven into my suggestions. Its threads loop through the very notions of a political and moral life of analysts. It also winds through the assertions that subjects of our analyses sometimes balk, push, or at least gaze back, and even when they comply it is often with lament. Grounding this project is the commitment to enhancing self-understanding in both science and personhood. Constructionist inquiry often evades these features of interpretive metatheories because they appear to violate the pledge to nominalism, to representing (objects in) the world as invented and not discovered. However, underriding my analysis is a conviction that it is possible to have it both ways. One can follow both genealogical and interpretive traditions, comprehend human nature as both made and found, and accept the indeterminacy as well as the experienced knowing of the world and self.

This arch conviction depends upon a willingness to imagine that we can retain two kinds of subjects, one capable of positioning, vigilance, and reflexive monitoring and the other one susceptible to the effects of the winds of time and serious whimsies of the sciences which describe and inscribe it. One approach and, I think, the only feasible one, is to enter in the space between these two big conceptions of subjects, deferring neither to the absolutism of realism nor the epistemological relativism of social constructionism. Following Ian Hacking's proposal, we might adopt a "dynamic nominalism" claiming "not that there was a kind of person who came increasingly to be recognized by bureaucrats or by students of human nature, but rather that a kind of person came into being at the same time as the kind itself was being invented" (1986: 228). Accordingly, the actuality of persons and their psychological states need not be questioned, but the matter of origins becomes more complex. The analyst is not prior to or privileged over the analysed persons; both have bounded possibilities for personhood that are circumscribed by social and material conditions. And both sorts of persons can seize their possibilities such that sometimes "our classifications and our classes conspire to emerge hand in hand, each egging the other on" (1986: 228).

As stated here, Hacking's proposal is a rather general one. However, his recent history of multiple personality elaborates on the basic thesis (Hacking, 1995). Multiple personality is neither a determinate or fixed mental condition, nor is it a categorization laid upon and in the heads of certain people. Rather, multiple personality, like other human kinds, is the result of a looping effect:

> A new or modified mode of classification may systematically affect the people who are so classified, or the people themselves may rebel against the knowers, the classifiers, the science that classified them. Such interactions may lead to changes in the people who are classified, and hence in what is known about them. . . . Inventing or molding a new kind, a new classification, of people or of behavior may create new ways to be a person, new choices to make, for good or evil. (1995: 239)

There is indeterminacy in such feedbacks. Classifications entail the retroactive redescription and re-experiencing of actions, such that the "action-paced sense of what people did may be invested with different meanings at different times" (1995: 248). In turn, "if these are genuinely new descriptions, descriptions not available or perhaps nonexistent at the time of the episodes remembered, then something is experienced now, in memory, that in a certain sense did not exist before" (1995: 249).

Also elaborated through the case of multiple personality is the place of agency and morality: choice and self-knowledge are both attributes and virtues of humans. Persons make decisions about the constitution of their selves, and in seeing themselves as constituted. With these characteristics lie possibilities for understanding the world in interpretive as well as genealogical terms, for having our constructionist cake and making and eating it too. Workable spaces actually exist between interpretation and genealogy and between nominalism and realism. Extended contemplation, rather than dismissal, of such dualisms resembles science studies projects that acknowledge both constructionist and realist features of scientific inquiry. Playing with, rather than refuting, these doubles may be just a starting point for yet unforseeable theoretical perspectives, but currently it enables generative and inclusive play.

We can learn from the lives of phantoms (alias confederates, accomplices) that places in between not are only real but productive. However, unlike the experimentalists who engineered phantoms and confederates, we can comprehend places in between as generative; we can discern how phantoms are not just architected, technical specters, they are human kinds. In such reconfigurations, the deceit of phantoms, like the self-deceit of constructionists and realists alike, can be transformed through self-consciousness. Faithfulness to some extent then can be restored. Instead of fashioning theories and practices that make or sustain illusions, we can more self-consciously proceed in the creation of realities, remaining ever mindful of the differences as well as connections between performance and knowledge, experience, and expression.

Coda

In this chapter I have asked much of the reader. To go patiently through a list of bald criticisms of constructionist practices. To use a phantom, a ghost, as a prototype for reimagining not only the actors of psychological research but also the kinds of theories we contrive. To shift back and forth between ostensibly disparate disciplinary works. To celebrate dualities and to do so against strong intellectual impulses to rid theory of any detectable binaries. These demands serve primarily to stretch our theoretical bodies and, more specifically, to show the connections between notions of objectivity, subjectivities, research relations, and larger reflexive processes (feedbacks).

What I have described, however, is also about refashioning specific practices in constructionist inquiry. Carried through sometimes broad sweeps of theorizing are realizable proposals for that refashioning. The suggestions begin and end with a reconsideration of subjectivities, everyone's subject statuses. A list of such realizable ambitions includes the following:

1 Our analyses are not and should not be about unified subjects. That myth need no longer constrain our examination of subjectivity.
2 Everyone participates. The practices of inquiry are collaborative and include participation *against* as well as *within* the research agenda.
3 Research practices are constituted through (and constitutive of) a moral order in which the analyst is an unequivocal member.
4 Reflexivity, as acts of self-consciousness, is routine. Such acts are constitutive of finding and making our human kinds.
5 Subjectivity is about movement – positioning and being positioned. Phantoms, allies, and confederates show how the researchers, as well as the subjects, move. Mobility is inevitable and can be desirable.
6 Subjectivity is about being controlled and being in control, about knowing and being unknown, and about not knowing and being known. The ironies of subject positions deserve appreciation. The open secret structures of social constructionist inquiry need to be probed.

As a brave beginning, our interrogations need to explore the specifics of the analysts' psychological dynamics: our own projections, strategies for self-empowerment, and complicity in repressing as well as maintaining relations of power.

References

Billig, M. (1990) "Rhetoric of social psychology," in I. Parker and J. Shotter (eds), *Deconstructing Social Psychology*. London: Routledge. pp. 47–60.

Bradley, B.S. (1989) *Visions of Infancy*. London: Polity Press.

Bradley, B.S. (1994) "Darwin's intertextual baby: Erasmus Darwin as precursor in child psychology," *Human Development*, 37: 86–102.

Brown, R.H. (1992) "Poetics, politics and professionalism in the rise of American Psychology," *History of the Human Sciences*, 5: 47–61.

Cushman, P. (1990) "Why the self is empty: toward a historically situated psychology," *American Psychologist*, 45: 599–611.

Danziger, K. (1990) *Constructing the Subject: Historical Origins of Psychological Research*. New York: Cambridge University Press.

Daston, L. and Galison, P. (1992) "The image of objectivity," *Representations*, 40: 81–128.

Ferguson, K.E. (1993) *The Man Question: Visions of Subjectivity in Feminist Theory*. Berkeley, CA: University of California Press.

Fine, M. (1988) "Sexuality schooling, and adolescent females: the missing discourse of desire," *Harvard Educational Review*, 58: 29–53.

Flax, J. (1990) *Thinking Fragments: Psychoanalysis, Feminism, and Postmodernism in the Contemporary West*. Berkeley, CA: University of California Press.

Fuller, S. (1988) *Social Epistemology*. Bloomington, IN: University of Indiana Press.

Gillespie, R. (1988) "The Hawthorne experiments and the politics of experimentation," in J. Morawski (ed.), *The Rise of Experimentation in American Psychology*. New Haven, CT: Yale University Press. pp. 114–37.

Gooding, G. (1992) "Putting agency back into experiment," in A. Pickering (ed.), *Science as Practice and Culture*. Chicago: University of Chicago Press. pp. 65–112.

Haaken, J. (1988) "Field dependence research: a historical analysis of psychological construct," *Signs*, 13: 311–30.

Hacking, I. (1986) "Making up people," in T.C. Heller, M. Sosna, and D. Wellbery (eds), *Reconstructing Individualism: Autonomy, Individuality, and the Self in Western Thought*. Stanford, CA: Stanford University Press. pp. 222–36.

Hacking, I. (1995) *Rewriting the Soul: Multiple Personality and the Sciences of Memory*. Princeton, NJ: Princeton University Press.

Haraway, D. (1988) "Situated knowledges: the science question in feminism and the privilege of partial perspective," *Feminist Studies*, 14 (3): 575–99.

Haraway, D. (1994) "A game of cat's cradle: science studies, feminist theory, cultural studies," *Configurations*, 1: 59–71.

Harding, S. (1986) *The Science Question in Feminism*. Ithaca, NY: Cornell University Press.

Harding, S. (1991) *Whose Science? Whose Knowledge? Thinking from Women's Lives*. Ithaca, NY: Cornell University Press.

Harding, S. (1992) "After neutrality: science, politics, and 'strong objectivity'," *Social Research*, 59: 567–87.

Harris, B. (1988) "Key words: a history of debriefing in social psychology," in J.G. Morawski (ed.), *The Rise of Experimentation in American Psychology*. New Haven, CT: Yale University Press. pp. 188–212.

hooks, b. (1990) *Yearning: Race, Gender, and Cultural Politics*. Boston: South End Press.

Johnson, R. (1986) "What is cultural studies anyway?" *Social Text*, 16: 38–80.

Lamb, S. (1991) "Acts without agents: an analysis of linguistic avoidance in journal articles on men who batter women," *American Journal of Orthopsychiatry*, 61 (2): 250–7.

Lopes, L.L. (1991) "The rhetoric of irrationality," *Theory & Psychology*, 1: 65–82.

Morawski, J.G. (1988) "Impossible experiments and practical constructions: the social bases of psychologists' work," in J.G. Morawski (ed.), *The Rise of Experimentation in American Psychology*. New Haven, CT: Yale University Press. pp. 72–93.

Morawski, J.G. (1994) *Practicing Feminisms, Reconstructing Psychology: Notes on a Liminal Science*. Ann Arbor, MI: University of Michigan Press.

Morawski, J.G. and Steele, R.S. (1991) "The one and the other: textual analysis of masculine power and feminist empowerment," *Theory & Psychology*, 1: 107–31.

Rouse, J. (1992) "What are cultural studies of scientific knowledge?" *Configurations*, 1: 1–22.

Rouse, J. (1996) "Feminism and the social construction of scientific knowledge," in L.H. Nelson and J. Nelson (eds), *Feminism, Science, and the Philosophy of Science*. London: Kluwer Academic Publishers. pp. 195–215.

Smiley, J. (1995) *Moo*. New York: Alfred A. Knopf.

Stringer, P. (1990) "Prefacing social psychology: a textbook example," in I. Parker and J. Shotter (eds), *Deconstructing Social Psychology*. London: Routledge. pp. 17–32.

Tiefer, L. (1994) *Sex is Not a Natural Act and Other Essays*. Boulder, CO: Westview Press.

Woolgar, S. (1988) *Science: The Very Idea*. New York: Tavistock.

Index